Miraculous Plenty

Irish Religious Folktales and Legends

Edited and Annotated by
Seán Ó Súilleabháin

Translated by William Caulfield

"Do ġoideas-sa agus d'fuaduiġeas gaċ éinní ár
féadas riaṁ. Má ḃuail éinne liom ba ġáḃtaraí ná mé
héin, níor ċuireas éinní riaṁ ċun aon lóin dom héin aċ é
taḃairt don té ba ḃoiċte a ḃuail riaṁ liom. Siné
seasaiṁ dom-sa. Agus níl éinní ar siúl agatsa aċ ag
bailiú gaċ éinní ós gaċ éinne a ḃuailfió leat; ní fearr
leat é ḃailiú ón duine saiḋḃir ná ón té is a ḃoiċte; ná,
b'féidir, an té ná béaḋ dóitin a ḃroicfeast aige nó ná
béaḋ neart a' léine a ċur ar a leanḃ ná ar a ḋrom féiniġ,
priocfair an t-airgead uaiḋ có mait is a priocfair ón
té go mbéaḋ sé spárta aige!"

Sin é mo scéal-sa, agus do ċuala ó ḋaoine críona ġur
scéal fíor ab eaḋ é.

102.   Leaġaḋ an Ċoinnleora

Ḃí dá ḃriteáir ann aon am aṁáin agus bí siad 'na
gcionn an-ṁait do n-a ċéile. Táinic an bás ar
duine aca agus ġeall sé don ḃriteáir eile go dtiocfaḋ
sé arais agus go n-innseocaḋ sé dó goidé d'éiriġ do
nó cé'n áit ar cuireaḋ é, oíce an tórraiṁ.

Ḃí an ḃriteáir ag feiteaṁ leis, agus b'fada leis go
dtigeaḋ an t-am go ḃfeiceaḋ sé é nó go ḃfuiġeaḋ sé
scéala ar bit uaiḋ. Ċuaiḋ sé amaċ, agus bí aige le dul
tar áit fliuċ salaċ a bí ann. Nuair a bí sé ag dul tar
an pluid, moṫuiġ sé mairgneaċ ḃeag astoiġ ann agus
laḃair sé.

"I n-ainm Dé," adeir sé, "an tú atá annsin?"

"Is mé," arsa seisean.

"Óċ! Óċ!" adeir sé. "Náċ fuar an áit atá agat!"

"Cuir anuas bárr do ṁéire go díreaċ," adeir sé, "go
ḃfeiciḋ tú."

Ḃí coinnleóir leis ina láiṁ, bí oíce deas socair suaiṁ-
neaċ ann, agus car cuir sé síos a láṁ aċ cuir sé síos an
coinnleóir. An méid a cuaiḋ síos ins an uisce den
ċoinnleóir, leaġ sé, agus car fan a ḋat den ċoinnleóir
aige aċ an méid a bí ina ḋorn, bí teas có mór sin.

"Cé fad curta mé?" arsa seisean.

"Ó," arsan ḃriteáir, "níl tú curta aċ ó indé anuas."

"Ó!" adeir sé. "Saoil mé go raib mé curta le
céad bliain!"

From *Scéalta Cráibhtheacha* 1952

103.   TURAS LOĊA ḊEIRG

Bhí bean ann am amháin agus bhí sí an-bhocht, agus smaointigh sí go rachadh sí faid le Loch Dearg, agus chuaidh. Chaith sí trí lá agus trí oidhche annsin, mar is gnáthach, ach nuair a bhí sí ag teacht arais smaointigh sí go bpillfeadh sí agus go ndéanfadh sí turas do cibé anam a ba mhó a bhí i bpian i bPurgadóir. Pill sí agus níor stad go ndearnaidh sí trí lá agus trí oidhche eile i Loch Dearg.

Ar a bhealach 'na' bhaile dhuite, cad é tchí sí ach caisleán an-deas, agus tig buachaill amach as agus d'iarr uirthe dhul isteach; ach dúirt sise nách rachadh, nó go raibh sí maith go leor air. Annsin bhain sé litir as a phóca agus thug dhuite í, agus d'iarr uirthe dhul suas 'un tighe agus tabhairt d'fhear an tighe é héin. Chuaidh sise suas agus bhuail ar an ndoras, agus táinig cailín aimsire amach agus dúirt an bean seo léithe a rá le fear an tighe teacht amach, go raibh gnaithe aici leis. Táinig seisean amach agus thug sí dho an litir, agus d'aithin sé ar an bhomaite gheárr gurab scríobhadh a mhic héin a bhí ann, a bhí curtha le tamall. 'Sé rud a bhí sa litir ná gur iarr an mac ar an tsean-fhear an bean bhocht seo a chongbháilt agus bean uasal a dhéanamh dhuite, nó gurab eisean an t-anam a ba mhó bhí i bpian i bPurgadóir, agus gur thug sí turas Locha Dearg le n-a anam nó go ndeachaidh sé 'na Flaitheas.

104.   AN FEAR NÁR ĊAOIN A ĊLANN

Bhí fear ann fadó agus bhí triúr mac aige. Cailleadh beirt aca nuair a bhí siad óg. Maith go leór, d'fhás an buachaill eile suas ina fhear breá mór, agus bhí an áit faoi héin ag obair ins an mbaile. Faoi dheire cailleadh a athair agus a mháthair, agus ní raibh duine ar bith aige ar deire ach é féin. Bhí sé uaigneach go leór ar feadh abhfad. Aon oidhche amháin chuaidh sé amach ag siúlóid agus níorbh fhada amuigh dhó nó gur casadh a mháthair dhó—bhí sí marbh le tamall an uair seo.

"Muise, Dia dhá réidhteach!" ar seisean léi. "Ar annso atá tusa, agus mise ag guí ar do shon gach lá ó d'fhág tú an saol seo?"

"Ó," ar sise, "b'fhearr dom an beirt eile mac a bhí agam ná an méid guí a rinne tú ariamh."

Contents

Foreword

Many people first encounter cultural expressions in a translated form. English, as spoken in Ireland, has often been the bridge between Irish and English and syntax, structure and vocabulary are intrinsically linked. Of its nature, folklore is an international comparative subject. Collectors and scholars depend a great deal on translated works as a means of gaining insight and furthering research.

It is essential to bear in mind that even texts in Irish are removed from the original storytelling context and might be regarded as an interpretation of the performance as documented by the collectors. Thus, translated tales have emerged from a multi-layered process. This does not undervalue the importance of disseminating traditional material in the original or in translated form.

Comhairle Bhéaloideas Éireann/The Folklore of Ireland Council is pleased to publish *Miraculous Plenty: Irish Religious Folktales and Legends,* a translation of *Scéalta Cráibhtheacha.* The aims and objectives of An Chomhairle are not dissimilar to those of *An Cumann le Béaloideas Éireann/The Folklore of Ireland Society* as each body works towards a deeper understanding and wider dissemination of Irish folklore. The National Folklore Collection, University College Dublin is dependent on both bodies and the three organisations work hand in hand.

It would certainly please Seán Ó Súilleabháin, former archivist with the Irish Folklore Commission, that his collection *Scéalta Cráibhtheacha* should appear in translation and reach a wider audience. His complete dedication to Irish folklore, including religious lore, has already benefited so many people and will now benefit a great many more.

William Caulfield accepted the challenge that Prof. Bo Almqvist proposed a number of years ago and produced the translation of all one hundred and thirty-five tales. A number of colleagues within Irish Folklore have made the publication a reality. These include Prof. Bo Almqvist whose introduction documents Seán Ó Súilleabháin's work as well as providing further understanding and interpretation of religious folktales and legends. Críostóir Mac Cárthaigh and Prof. Seosamh Watson has have given generously of their expertise and time. Dr Séamus Ó Murchú and Deirdre Uí Éanacháin also gave valuable assistance in preparing the work for publication.

The continued support of the Publications Committee of Comhairle Bhéaloideas Éireann is deeply appreciated.

Ríonach uí Ógáin
Editor
Folklore Studies
Lá Fhéile Míchíl 2011

Introduction

Two great scholars, two great books

Seán Ó Súilleabháin's *Scéalta Cráibhtheacha* ('Religious Tales') — which now appears here in English translation under the title *Miraculous Plenty: Irish Religious Folktales and Legends* — is one of the first two books in the Irish language I read from beginning to end; the other was Séamus Ó Duilearga's *Leabhar Sheáin Í Chonaill.* That was over half a century ago, and since then I have constantly returned to both books, both for professional purposes and for pure pleasure. As general editor of the series of folklore books published under the auspices of *Comhairle Bhéaloideas Éireann* (The Folklore of Ireland Council), I played a part in the publication of the third edition of *Leabhar Sheáin Í Chonaill* in 1981[1] as well as in the production of Máire Mac Neill's translation, *Seán Ó Conaill's Book,* which appeared simultaneously. It was much to my regret, however, that it was not possible at the time to reissue *Scéalta Cráibhtheacha* (which was first published in *Béaloideas, Iris an Chumainn le Béaloideas Éireann/The Journal of the Folklore of Ireland Society* 21, 1951–52, and also issued as a separate book in 1952) or provide for a translation of that work.

The Folklore of Ireland Society, which undertook the publication of the first edition of *Leabhar Sheáin Í Chonaill,* deserves great credit for having now shouldered the task of preparing for publication the present complete translation of *Scéalta Cráibhtheacha* in co-operation with Comhairle Bhéaloideas Éireann.[2] Since

---

1   The first edition was published in 1948.

2   Some of the stories in *Scéalta Cráibhtheacha* were translated earlier by Seán Ó Súilleabháin himself and included in his anthologies *Folktales of Ireland* (London, 1966) and *Legends from Ireland* (London, 1977). In the former work are included translations of tales nos. 27 b, 33 b, 46 and 135 (on pages 47–51, 144–149, 136–143 and 165, respectively); the latter work includes translations of tales nos. 3, 8, 10, 21, 39, 40, 51, 59, 62, 65, 73, 75, 77, 88, 89, 90, 92, 95, 97, 98, 100, 101, 104, 105, 112, 113, 116, 134, and 135 (see notes 160–162 and 164–166 in *Legends from Ireland*). Another translation of no. 75, also by Seán Ó Súilleabháin, is found in the article 'The Devil in Irish Folk Narrative' in F. Harkort, K. C. Peeters und R. Wildhaber, hrsg., *Volksüberlieferung, Festschrift für Kurt Ranke* (Göttingen, 1968), 280–281. A translation by Máire MacNeill of no. 80 is found in *Seán Ó Conaill's Book* (pages 322–323).

I greatly admire the book, and since I was privileged to know Seán over many years and profit much from his friendship and scholarly generosity, I am grateful for the opportunity to pen this introduction, in which an attempt will be made to outline the importance of the book from a national and international perspective.

Séamus Ó Duilearga, Honorary Director of the Irish Folklore Commission, and Seán Ó Súilleabháin, Archivist at that institution, had shared ideals and goals, though their background and temperament differed greatly. In a very similar manner, *Leabhar Sheáin Í Chonaill* and *Scéalta Cráibhtheacha* have many characteristics and qualities in common, while at the same time differing radically from each other. While the former collection, undertaken by an Antrim man, covers the repertoire of a single storyteller from Kerry, and includes stories on a wide range of topics – such as hero tales, international wonder tales, romantic tales, jokes and anecdotes, and folk legends about supernatural beings – the latter work features stories, selected by a Kerryman, drawn from several scores of storytellers from different parts of Ireland, but dealing with a limited topic: narratives relating to religious beliefs and phenomena as they were understood and interpreted by ordinary people in all areas of Gaelic Ireland. Within this restricted scope, however, the tales are wonderfully varied, in content as well as in the emotional reactions they produce. The work includes stories about Our Lord, the Blessed Virgin and saints and priests, others dealing with demons and devils; some holding up to our view pictures of the most sublime and touching piety, divine mercy and eternal bliss in heaven while others offer the most gross and frightening descriptions of revenge, retribution and torture in the ever-lasting fires of hell. In short, *Scéalta Cráibhtheacha* is a unique work of the greatest importance to anyone who wishes to acquire an understanding of the way country people in Ireland and, for that matter, elsewhere in pre-industrial Europe, thought and felt about moral and religious issues of central importance in their lives.

In stressing the uniqueness of *Scéalta Cráibhtheacha*, it is of course far from my intention to denigrate its forerunners. Just as *Leabhar Sheáin Í Chonaill* was to some extent triggered by Douglas Hyde's *Sgéalta Thomáis Ua Chathasaigh*[3] and *Ocht Sgéalta ó Choillte Mághach*,[4] Seán Ó Súilleabháin's work has affinities with that scholar's *Legends of Saints and Sinners*.[5] However, just as *Leabhar Sheáin*

---

3   *Irish Texts Society* 36 (Dublin, 1939).

4   Baile Átha Cliath, 1936.

5   Dublin, 1915.

Í Chonaill surpasses its models, *Scéalta Cráibhtheacha* is vastly superior to its forerunner, not only in its wider scope and greater variety – *Legends of Saints and Sinners* contains only about one third of the number of stories found in *Scéalta Cráibhtheacha* – but also by virtue of the logical arrangement of the material and the quality of the commentaries.

Seán Ó Súilleabháin's background

The reasons for Seán's success in bringing together and editing *Scéalta Cráibhtheacha,* and his professional achievements generally, are manifold. Seán was born in Tuosist, Co. Kerry in 1903.[6] In this 'wild, rough, old and venerable district' – to use the words with which he himself characterises it in his introduction to the poems of Diarmuid na Bolgaí[7] – Irish was widely spoken at the beginning of the twentieth century and good storytellers, comparable to Seán Ó Conaill, Peig Sayers and their likes in south and west Kerry, were remembered and even still to be heard. Seán never ceased to pay homage to his beloved home district, which he has also touchingly described in his article 'Tuaith Siosta na bhFionna-Bhrú nAolta'.[8] It is abundantly evident that Seán's interest in the traditional tales and songs of his native region was awakened in his early childhood and grew and developed during his formative years. Of great

---

6   For a general account of Seán's life and activities see Eoghan Ó Súilleabháin, 'Seán Ó Súilleabháin (1903–96), Múinteoir agus Cartlannaí Béaloidis', *Journal of the Kerry Archaeological and Historical Society* 27 (1994), 89–106. See also Patricia Lysaght, '"Don't Go Without a Beaver Hat', Seán Ó Súilleabháin in Sweden"', *Sinsear* 7 (1993), 49–59 and the same author's 'Seán Ó Súilleabháin (1903–1996) and the Irish Folklore Commission', *Western Folklore* 57:2–3 (137–151). Obituaries include Bo Almqvist, 'Seán Ó Súilleabháin (1903–1996)', *Béaloideas* 64–65 (1996–97), 366–369 and Séamas Ó Catháin, 'In Memoriam: Seán Ó Súilleabháin, 1903–1996', *Folklore* 108 (1997), 106. Furthermore, there is an unpublished MA-thesis in Irish from the Department of Irish, National University of Ireland, Galway, by Kenneth O'Donoghue, entitled *Seán Ó Súilleabháin, Ceannródaí Léann an Bhéaloidis* (presented in 2009), and a wealth of information is available in the National Folklore Collection, University College, Dublin, not least a series of video interviews with Seán undertaken by Séamas Ó Catháin in 1984. Various aspects of Seán's work in the Irish Folklore Commission are dealt with in Mícheál Briody, *The Irish Folklore Commission 1935–1970: History, ideology, methodology* (Helsinki 2007). Furthermore, valuable information concerning Seán's life and work can be gained from the series of video interviews conducted with Seán by Séamas Ó Catháin in 1984 (National Folklore Collection V0032–33). It is to be hoped that somebody will undertake fuller book-length treatment of Seán's life and work.

7   *Diarmuid na Bolgaighe agus a Chómhursain* (Baile Átha Cliath, 1937), vii.

8   *Journal of the Kerry Archaelogical and Historical Society* 2 (1969), 102–107.

importance in this context were his father and his circle of friends which included the gifted folklore collector Pádraig Ó Laoghaire.[9]

Seán Ó Súilleabháin as folklore collector

Having received his training in St Brendan's College in Killarney and de la Salle College in Waterford, Seán went to live for twelve years in the Decies, Co. Waterford, where he held teaching positions in various places. During this time he was also in direct contact with the rich and flourishing Irish folk tradition of the area. The similarities, as well as the differences, between the stories, customs and beliefs he now observed and those familiar to him from home heightened his interest in folklore even more. In consequence of this he also started to collect folklore from his home area – where his enthusiasm for oral traditions was shared by two of his brothers, both schoolteachers, who had remained closer to the parental home – and in adjacent areas of Co. Cork, as well as in Co. Waterford. Soon after the establishment of the Folklore of Ireland Society in 1927, Seán also made contacts with that body and got to know Séamus Ó Duilearga who had been appointed as editor of the Society's journal *Béaloideas*. It was in that forum that Seán published the first fruits of his collections and studies. Particular mention should be made of the miscellany of charms and folk prayers from Kerry which appeared in *Béaloideas* 3 (1933), under the title 'Cnuasacht orthaí agus paidreacha ó Chiarraighe', since they bear witness to an interest in folk religion which was to find expression on a grander scale in *Scéalta Cráibhtheacha*.[10] One does not as a rule think of Seán as a folklore collector. His other duties did not give him many opportunities for collecting. Nevertheless his early collecting activities, and his personal acquaintance with many storytellers later on in life, were of importance in developing that unfailing ability to recognise what is good and genuine, an ability rarely found except in those who have been actively involved in field collecting. It is evident, too, that he took pride in the material he collected himself, since he included two tales from his own recordings (6b and

---

9   Seán paid tribute to his memory in an article in *Béaloideas* 3 (1932), 409–412, in which he also provided valuable information on Ó Laoghaire's informants.

10 Other notable contributions of Seán's to *Béaloideas* are 'Seanchas na Tuaithe' (volume 4 [1933–4], 361390), a collection of tales and traditions from his native Tuosist, and 'Cnuasacht Déiseach' (volume 9 [1939], 38–46, a miscellany of lore collected in an old people's home in Waterford City). A collection of tales and traditions collected by Seán in Co. Waterford has been edited and published by Máirtín Verling under the title 'Béaloideas ó Bhaile an Bhuitléirigh' in *An Linn Bhuí, Iris Ghaeltacht na nDéise* 5 (2001), 127–138.

135), both from Béara, Co. Cork, in *Scéalta Cráibhtheacha*. Both of these tales are excellently told, the latter a veritable gem of philosophical wisdom that stands as a worthy tail-piece to the whole collection.

Among the storytellers Seán knew well were the Blasket Islanders Seán Ó Súilleabháin (Seán Mhicil) and Peig Sayers. The former who, as Peig Sayers' son, Mícheál Ó Gaoithín ('An File') told me, was an excellent storyteller but most reluctant to 'give' any of his tales to those who were not of the Ó Súilleabháin family, became particularly friendly with Seán for the reason that they shared both the same surname and family name. A fine story told by this Blasket man, 'The Saint and the Robber', is included in *Scéalta Cráibhtheacha* (no. 49).[11] Though it is uncertain whether Seán ever took down any stories from Peig,[12] it is certain that he heard her tell stories and that he keenly appreciated her artistry. He was one of the first to realize the special scholarly importance of the collections made from her by Robin Flower, Kenneth Jackson and others, and he translated a substantial number of Peig's tales into English. He also expressed friendship and admiration

---

11   This particular version, however, was not recorded by Seán but by Robin Flower, so Seán Ó Súilleabháin the Blasket man must have made some exceptions to his rule not to allow his stories to go outside the clan. I can also vouch that the peculiarity was not inherited by his children, since I was myself fortunate to have the opportunity to record a version of 'The Saint and the Robber' from his son Mícheál ('Dagha').

12   Seán knew Peig before he started to work for the Irish Folklore Commission. In 1933 he spent a month of his holidays camping on the Blasket with three of his friends. During that time he also got to know Tomás Ó Criomhthain (the author of the famed autobiography *An tOileánach*, which was translated into English under the title *The Islandman*), as well as Eon Ó Súilleabháin (who figures prominently in his grandson Muiris Ó Súilleabháin's book *Fiche Blian ag Fás* (*Twenty Years'A-Growing*). Peig, Seán himself stated in an article in *Inniu* (3 Aibreán, 1964 [reprinted in Breandán Ó Conaire, ed., *Tomás an Bhlascaoid* (Indreabhán, 1992, 166)]), was then at the height of her ability as storyteller ('*i mbláth a cumais chun eachtraíochta*). Again, according to Seán himself in his 1962 article, he often visited Tomás, Eon and Peig while he was on the island, 'talking to them and writing down legends and stories from them' (*ag caint leo agus bheith ag breacadh síos seanchais agus scéalta uathu*). In the event that Seán actually took down any stories from Peig – which it would seem most natural to suppose from his words – these stories appear to be lost. The only item from Seán's collections in the National Folklore Collection stated to be from Peig is a proverb – *Gach nudhacht i dtigh sé is mó gheibheann cion* ('Everything that is novel in a house gets most attention') – which is included in NFC 31: 179 and marked 'Peig Sayers, sa Bhlascaoid'. Whatever about the issue of Seán's early collecting from Peig in 1933, he was among those who made the last recordings from her (together with Kevin Danaher and An Seabhac [Pádraig Ó Siochfhradha]), in 1952 in St. Anne's Hospital in Dublin (cf. B. Almqvist and P. Ó Héalaí, *Labharfad Le Cách/I Will Speak to You All* (Baile Átha Cliath, 2009), 182–183). It should be noted, too, that it was Seán who organised the headstone on Peig's grave, and he delivered an oration when it was unveiled.

for Peig in many other ways.[13] It is easily understandable, therefore, that he should have chosen to include two of Peig's best tales in *Scéalta Cráibhtheacha* (nos. 120 and 131). He was also a close friend of Peig's son, Mícheál Ó Gaoithín who, like his mother, was a noted storyteller.[14]

Archivist in the Irish Folklore Commission
The most important watershed in Seán's life was without doubt his appointment as archivist to the Irish Folklore Commission on its establishment in 1935. It then became Seán's task not only to arrange and index the vast collections that were subsequently brought into the Commission's archives – thanks to the efforts of its full- and part-time collectors, or by questionnaires and other means – but also to read and evaluate that material and give advice and instructions to the collectors. In the process of this, he developed an overview of the material and an insight into the interests, strength and weaknesses of the respective collectors that is unmatched, and likely ever to remain so. From this knowledge he profited much in the selection of material for *Scéalta Cráibhtheacha*. Texts collected in the nineteenth century – at a time when folktales and legends were often unreliably recorded, in many cases even deliberately tampered with – have not been included. Instead, Seán drew almost exclusively from manuscripts in the custody of the Irish Folklore Commission.

Collectors represented
From the Commission's holdings of tales collected prior to its establishment in 1935 only a few have been found worthy of inclusion in *Scéalta Cráibhtheacha*. These exceptions are stories taken down by collectors noted for their accuracy and

---

13   The credit of being the first to translate a tale of Peig's goes to Kenneth Jackson. However, he translated only one short anecdote (printed in the journal *Folk-Lore* XLVIII [1937], 268). Seán translated a sizeable number of tales of various kinds from Peig (see *Folktales of Ireland* [London, 1966], 57–60, 192–204 and *The Folklore of Ireland* [London, 1974], 35–43, 70–74, 83–6, 109–112, 120–123 and 126–127).

14   This Mícheál Ó Gaoithín ('An File') is not to be confused with Mícheál Ó Guithín ('Bradhm'), also from Baile an Bhiocáire, Dún Chaoin, the teller of story no. 35(a). That two excellent storytellers by the same name should have lived less than a stone throw's distance from each other is indeed a fine illustration of the extent to which storytelling was alive in the Corca Dhuibhne Gaeltacht – and to some extent even after – the first half of the nineteenth century. The two storytellers in question also shared a number of tales. A good instance of this is offered by versions of 'The Devil's Son' recorded by me from 'An File' which show close similarities to the version told by 'Bradhm'.

faithfulness to the words as actually spoken by the tellers. In this category are the story from Séan Ó Conaill (no. 80), taken down by Séamus Ó Duilearga, and those recorded on Ediphone by Robin Flower (the tale from the Blasket Islander Seán Ó Súilleabháin and the two tales from Peig Sayers, referred to above). The great bulk of the stories, however, Seán selected from the collections of the full- and part-time collectors employed by the Commission from 1935 onwards, people who had been carefully instructed as to how collecting and transcription were to be carried out and who, in many instances, used Ediphone recording machines. Among these collectors several, whose very names themselves are a guarantee of excellence, figure prominently in the notes to the individual tales at the end of the book, e.g. Seán Ó hEochaidh (from Donegal), Liam Mac Coisdeala (from Mayo and Galway), Proinsias de Búrca (also from Galway), Colm Mac Gilleathain (Calum Maclean, the Scottish collector whose fame was to become greater in his homeland, but who for a while also collected in Co. Galway), Seosamh Ó Dálaigh and Seán Ó Dubhda (both from the Dingle Peninsula, Co. Kerry), Tadhg Ó Murchú (Iveragh, Kerry and south-west Cork). Waterford is also represented by a tale (no.114) taken down by Nioclás Breathnach, the most prominent collector of that county. From all this it is evident that Seán has sought to give all areas in Gaelic Ireland their fair share, and that he has achieved that goal.

Nevertheless such pre-eminent figures in the field of Irish folklore collecting as the above-mentioned have not contributed all the material in *Scéalta Cráibhtheacha*; many stories of great value have been harvested by less well-known collectors and even, in three instances (18, 19, 60 and 89), by anonymous collectors. All this is specified in the notes to the individual tales at the end of the book and need not be gone into in detail here. What does deserve mention, however, is that a not insignificant number of the tales chosen by Seán for inclusion were collected by women. This is particularly noteworthy in view of the fact that the full-time collectors, from whose collections there was so much material to choose from, were all men. However, *Scéalta Cráibhtheacha* contains three tales from Co. Cork collected by Áine Ní Chróinín (better known under her married name Anne O'Sullivan) who for a while was attached to the Irish Folklore Commission but changed direction and became an Old Irish scholar of note. Furthermore, the female collectors include three other Áines: Áine Nic an Liagha, the collector of two tales from Donegal, Áine Ní Chonaill and Áine Ní Ruadháin, who collected one tale each from Mayo, as well as Anna Ní Éigeartaigh, with one story from Donegal. Represented are also Bríd Ní Shúilleabháin and Máire Ní Ghácháin with one story each, from Co. Kerry and Co. Mayo respectively.

In one instance (no. 89) a tale collected by a school child has been included. Perhaps this was because no other version of the tale in question was known to Seán and because it dealt with St Martin in whom Seán took a special interest.[15] Be that as it may, it is evident that Seán's reliance on material taken down by professional collectors and his sure aesthetic sense in picking out the best and most representative material from the rest of the manuscript collections combined to create an anthology of unmatched quality.

Storytellers represented

Since the great collectors were eager to collect as many tales as possible from the best storytellers they knew, it is but natural that such star performers are represented by more than one story in Seán's anthology. Apart from Peig Sayers and Séan Ó Conaill, to whom we have already referred, Seán Crithin of Cill Maolchéadair might be mentioned from Co. Kerry, and they are joined by Diarmaid Mac Coitir from Cork, Éamonn de Búrca from Galway and Sorcha Bean Mhic Grianna from Donegal, to give just a few examples. It is not only in instances where a particular tale was absent from the repertoires of famous tellers that stories from little-known tellers have been included; the latter versions have also been preferred wherever they were especially pleasing from an aesthetic point of view or contained traits of particular interest.

As to the gender of the storytellers, between one fourth and one fifth of the stories in *Scéalta Cráibhtheacha* were told by women. This is a remarkably high percentage in view of the fact that the vast majority of the collectors were men. The lack of closer investigation into the proportions between male and female tellers of other genres of tales renders it difficult to state categorically that women had a special preference for religious tales. It would not surprise me, however, if this should turn out to be the case. What is certain – though Seán is unlikely to have wanted to prove or disprove anything in relation to the matter – is that the stories in *Scéalta Cráibhtheacha* indicate strongly that a high proportion of the bearers of religious tales were women, and there is much to indicate that women played a greater role in the preservation and telling of religious tales than they did in relation to other tale genres.

---

15   Evidenced, for instance, by his article 'The Feast of Saint Martin in Ireland' in W. Edston Richmond, ed., *Studies in Folklore in honor of distinguished service professor Stith Thompson* (Bloomington, 1957), 252–261.

Classification of material

Among the qualities that made Seán especially well equipped for his position as archivist was his orderly and logical mind. Prominent also was his ability to arrange and present his material in a clear and pedagogical way. These abilities were to some extent inborn but no doubt also developed during his career as a teacher. No particular system for the classification of religious tales was available to Seán when *Scéalta Cráibhtheacha* was conceived. The eleven sections into which he divides his material – Our Saviour and His Mother; Priests; The Devil; Imposition of Penances; Visits to the Other World; The Rebellious Angels; Saints; Return of the Dead from Purgatory; Piety; God Deals Justly; and Varia – do not constitute a watertight system, inasmuch as there are many tales that could be fitted in under more than one of the headings. Indeed Seán himself calls attention to this fact. Nevertheless it is a model that greatly facilitates the survey of the material and which will have to be seriously taken into account in further attempts at classification.

Scholarly commentary

Seán's ambitions went further, however, in that he also wanted to make the material in *Scéalta Cráibhtheacha* available to international researchers. This he achieved by means of English summaries and notes in which references are made to relevant literature, in foreign languages as well as in Irish and English and, above all, through listing the type- and motif-numbers relevant to the respective tales, the so-called 'AaTh' or 'AT' numbers, in Anti Aarne's and Stith Thompson's classic work *The Types of the Folktale,* and the motif assignations in the latter scholar's *Motif Index of Folk Literature.* An understanding of the importance of Irish folktales in an international context not only to those engaged in studies in comparative folklore but also to many other branches of learning, e.g. philology, history, the history of literature and the history of religion had been given to him by Séamus Ó Duilearga and by C. W. von Sydow, Reidar Th. Christiansen and other Scandinavian scholars, under whose guidance he studied, following in Ó Duilearga's footsteps. It was thus he acquired the tools of the trade that had enabled him to compile his magnificent *A Handbook of Irish Folklore*, modelled on a classification system worked out by Swedish scholars, published in 1942, eight years before *Scéalta Cráibhtheacha.* This later enabled him to shoulder – in co-operation with Reidar Th. Christiansen – the gigantic task of creating a national type catalogue of folktales (following the layout in Aarne's and Thompson's *The Types of the Folktale*), which was published under the title *The Types of the Irish Folktale*, appearing as No. 188 in the series FF Communications in 1962.

In sum, Seán was a professional folklorist, the second person in Ireland worthy of that title. It is his professionalism, which is apparent everywhere in his annotations to *Scéalta Cráibhtheacha*, that endows the collection with a special value.

Additions to the commentary

Though much of Seán's commentary in *Scéalta Cráibhtheacha* is of permanent value, it is natural that much of it now, almost sixty years after the publication of the work, is in need of revision and amplification. A full-scale attempt at bringing the notes up to date would be a major task and cannot be undertaken here. It may be useful, however, to call attention to some studies which have appeared since 1950, and which are of special importance to the study of religious tales in general or to the specific tales included in *Scéalta Cráibhtheacha*.

It should be noted in particular that references to Types and Motif-Index numbers in the original Irish work pertain to the 1928 edition of *The Types of the Folktale* and to the first (1932–36) edition of the *Motif–Index*. Both of these have since been superseded, the former initially by a second revision in 1961 and then by Hans-Jörg Uther's three-volume work *The Types of the International Folktales* (FF Communications 284–286, Helsinki 2004), the latter by a revised and enlarged edition that appeared in six volumes, published in Copenhagen 1955–58. References to type- and motif-numbers have been updated in this translation.

Furthermore, thanks to the references in *Types of the Irish Folktale,* it is now possible to gain access to all printed and manuscript versions in English and Irish of those tale types that are included in the Aarne–Thompson and Uther catalogues. In addition, Seán took the opportunity to comment more fully on some of the tales in *Scéalta Cráibhtheacha*, in the notes to stories he included in his anthology *Folktales of Ireland,*[16] and in the article he contributed to the *festschrift* for Frances Lee Utley.[17]

In his seminal work, *Studies in Irish and Scandinavian Folktales,* Reidar Th. Christiansen devoted a chapter (pages 188–213) to religious and legendary tales which, apart from general commentaries, contains material of special relevance to some of the particular tales included in *Scéalta Cráibhtheacha*. Of immense value to the study of the mediaeval background of the stories in *Scéalta Cráibhtheacha*

16　See footnote 1 above.

17　'Eitiological Stories in Ireland', *Mediaeval Literature and Folklore Studies,* eds. J. Mandel and B. Rosenberg (New Brunswick, New Jersey, 1970, 257–274). This article contains notes on stories 1, 2, 12, 73 and 135 in *Scéalta Cráibhtheacha*.

are Frederick C. Tubach's *Index Exemplorum* (FF Communications 204, Helsinki, 1969) and Dorothy Ann Bray's *A List of Motifs in the Lives of Early Irish Saints* (FF Communications 252, Helsinki 1992).

Two studies by Irish scholars, Martin McNamara's *The Apocrypha in the Irish Church* (Dublin, 1975) and Liam Ó Caithnia's *Apológa na bhFilí* (Baile Átha Cliath, 1984) should also be consulted. Thanks to the former work a number of the stories in *Scéalta Cráibhtheacha* can be traced back to mediaeval ecclesiastical sources, while the latter provides us with instances of *exempla* treated or included in Irish poems from the period 1200–1650. In Pádraig Ó Héalaí's doctoral thesis on folk legends about New Testament figures in Irish tradition, all collected variants in Irish are listed, as well as those in English, including those tales in the section Our Saviour and His Mother, below.[18] Of particular interest to students of religious legends are a number of other articles by Ó Héalaí, in particular 'Muire sa Bhéaloideas' (dealing with the popular image of the Holy Virgin),[19] 'Moral Values in Irish Religious Tales',[20] and 'An Fhéile i Scéalta Cráifeacha an Bhéaloidis' (on the theme of hospitality in religious tales).[21] Among Irish scholars following in Seán Ó Súilleabháin's footsteps, special mention should be made of Dáithí Ó hÓgáin, who devoted a chapter in his book *The Hero in Irish Folk History* to the heroic image of the saint,[22] and whose encyclopaedia of Irish folk tradition, *Myth, Legend & Romance* (London, 1990) and *The Lore of Ireland* (Cork 2006) contain many entries of great relevance to the study of *Scéalta Cráibhtheacha*, in particular those referring to the various saints dealt with in stories nos. 65–92.

Among studies on individual stories in *Scéalta Cráibhtheacha* the following are among those worthy of special attention:

1. *The Tree that Bent Down*: P. Ó Héalaí, 'An Crann a Chrom: Scéal Apacrafúil', *Léachtaí Cholm Cille* 14 (1983), 151–172.

---

18   'An Slánaitheoir ag Siúl ar an Talamh: Finscéalta i mBéaloideas na hÉireann faoi Shaolré Phearsana an Tiomna Nua – Innéacs Léiritheach mar aon le Réamhrá agus Staidéir.' 1–2, Ph.D. thesis, National University of Ireland, 1993, soon to appear under the title *An Slánaitheoir ag Siúl ar an Talamh. Innéacs scéalta faoi phearsana an Tiomna Nua i mbéaloideas na hÉireann maille le Réamhrá agus Staidéir*.

19   *An Sagart*, Earrach 1979, 9–18, *ibid.*, Samhradh, 25–27.

20   *Béaloideas* 42–44 (1974–76), 176–212.

21   *Léachtaí Cholm Cille* 30 (2000), 7–27 (this article has special bearing on stories nos. 14, 18, 93 and 130 in *Scéalta Cráibhtheacha*.

22   Dublin, 1985, 4–61.

2. *The Tinker and the Blacksmith*: P. Ó Héalaí, 'Tuirse na nGaibhne ar na Buachaillí Bó: Scéal Apacrafúil Dúchasach', *Béaloideas* 53 (1985), 87–129.

8. *Sight to the Blind*: C.A. Watkins, 'Modern Irish Variants of the Enchanted Pear Tree', *Southern Folklore Quarterly* 30 (1966), 202–213 and K. P. Wentersdorf, 'Chaucer's Merchant's Tale and its Irish Analogues', *Studies in Philology* 63 (1966), 604–629 and same author, 'The Enchanted Pear Tree Motif in Irish Folklore', *Folklore* 77 (1966), 21–30.[23]

11. *A Ship-full Drowned on Account of One Man*: Josef Szövérffy, *Irisches Erzählgut im Abendland, Studien zur vergleichenden Volkskunde und Mittelalterforschung* (Berlin, 1957), 119–20. P. Ó Héalaí, 'An Timpeallacht trí Shúile an Chreidimh, Feithidí agus an Slánaitheoir', *Téada Dúchais. Aistí in ómós don Ollamh Breandán Ó Madagáin*, eag. M. Ó Briain agus P. Ó Héalaí (Indreabhán, 2002), 317–319.

14. *As We Give, We Get*: Szövérffy, *op.cit.*, 120–121.

15. *The Cockroach, the Earwig and the Beetle*: P. Ó Héalaí, *op. cit.* ('An Timpeallacht trí Shúile an Chreidimh, Feithidí agus an Slánaitheoir'), 320–327.

18. *Miraculous Plenty; the Passion*: P. Ó Héalaí, '"Lean Ar Do Láimh": Seanscéal Idirnáisiúnta i mBéaloideas na hÉireann', Séamas Ó Catháin, ed., *Northern Lights, Following Folklore in North-Western Europe, Aistí in adhnó do Bo Almqvist/Essays in honour of Bo Almqvist* (Dublin, 2001), 279–291.

19. *The Thief on the Right Hand*: P. Ó Héalaí, 'An Gadaí Conáich', *Sinsear. The Folklore Journal* 4 (1982–83), 11–29.

21. *Conor of Ulster and the Passion*: Szövérffy, *op.cit.*, 48–86, cf. also same author, 'Heroic Tales, Medieval Legends and an Irish Story', *Zeitschrift für Celtische Philologie* 25 (1956), 183–210.

30. *The Priest and the Ghost*: Anne O'Connor, *Child Murderess and Dead Child Traditions* (FF Communiciations 249, Helsinki 1991, 90–96); same author, '"Petticoat Loose" Traditions in Ireland', *Béaloideas* 70 (2002), 51–82 and (Bern/Oxford, 2005).

35. *The Devil's Son*: In addition to Séamus Ó Duilearga's pioneering study to which Seán made reference, see now Jaqueline Ní Fhearghusa, 'The Devil's Son as Priest – Distribution, form and function of a story on the borderline

---

23 It might be mentioned as an example of Seán Ó Súilleabháin's exceptional services to fellow scholars that he provided English translations of all Irish versions of this particular tale to both Watkins and Wentersdorf.

between folktale and folk legend', *Béaloideas* 62–63 (1994–95), 89–108 and works referred to there.

53. *The Woman Who Went to Hell*: Jan-Öjvind Swahn, *The Tale of Cupid and Psyche (Aarne-Thompson 425 and 428)* (Lund, 1955), 329–33; Joe Radner, '"The Woman who Went to Hell": Coded values in Irish Folk Narrative', *Midwestern Folklore* 15:2 (1989), 41–51.

64. *The Stream of Orthúlán*: Anne O' Connor, *Child Murderess and Dead Child Traditions* (FF Communiciations 249, Helsinki 1991, 65–68.

65. *Saint Patrick and* Crom Dubh: Máire Mac Néill, *The Festival of Lughnasa*, Dublin 1982 (1st ed. 1962); Ó hÓgáin in *Cothú an Dúchais: Aistí in Omós don Athair Diarmuid Ó Laoghaire*, eag. M. Mac Conmara agus Éilís Ní Thiarnaigh, Baile Átha Cliath, 1997, 174–181.

71. *The Twelve Apostles*: Mac Néill, *op. cit.*, *Festival of Lughnasa*; Ó hÓgáin, *op. cit.* (*Cothú an Dúchais*), 169–171.

75. *The Woman in the Tavern*: Seán Ó Súilleabháin, 'The Devil in Irish Folk Narrative' (see above, footnote 1), 279–281.

76. *It's a Long Monday, Patrick*: Mac Néill, *op. cit.*, 399–400, 667–668; Ó hÓgáin, '"Moch Amach ar Maidin Dé Luain!" – Staidéar ar an seanchas faoi ollphiasta i locha na hÉireann', *Béaloideas* 51 (1983), 87–125.

79. *The Hole of the House of Liabán*: Mac Néill, *op. cit.*, 121.

89. *Saint Martin's Night*; 90. *Saint Martin and the Gambler*; and 91. *The Little Black Sheep*: cf. Seán Ó Súilleabháin's own article 'The Feast of Saint Martin in Ireland' in W. Edson Richmond, ed., *Studies in Folklore in Honor of Distinguished Service Professor Stith Thompson* (Bloomington, 1957), 252–261. See also Billy Mag Fhloinn, 'Martinmas Tradition in South County Clare: A Case Study', *Béaloideas* 75 (2007), 79–108.

95. *Between the Stirrup and the Ground*: Bengt af Klintberg, '"Betwixt the Stirrup and the Ground": Some Remarks on an English Epitaph and a Scandinavian Folk Legend', in Séamas Ó Catháin, *op. cit.* 1–8. This is an exciting study that takes us from St Augustine's Confessions via Camden's *Remains Concerning Britain* (first published in 1605) and Swedish, Danish and Norwegian folklore texts to Graham Greene's use of the motif in his novel *Brighton Rock*. See for this story also B. af Klintberg, *The Types of the Swedish Folk Legend* (FF Communications 300), Helsinki 2010, sub C 83, *Blessed between the stirrup and the ground*.

105. *The Straight Road*: Szövérffy, *op. cit.* (*Irisches Erzählgut im Abendland, Studien zur vergleichenden Volkskunde und Mittelalterforschung* (Berlin, 1957), 141–

151 and same author, 'A Medieval Story and its Irish Version', in W. Edson Richmond, *op. cit.*, 55–65.

Conclusion

Seán would no doubt have been pleased if he had known that so much scholarship has been inspired in recent years by his work on Irish religious tales and that so much of it has been carried out by scholars he knew and whose mentor in many cases he had been. Not least would it have delighted him that so much of this scholarship has appeared in the Irish language. But with his deep understanding of the essential international character of folklore and importance of folklore studies in a broad perspective, he would also have been pleased to see *Scéalta Cráibhtheacha* appear in translation. I am convinced that many students of religious tales and folk religion in numerous countries will be inspired to undertake further research on the many intriguing stories and beliefs contained within these pages. But one need not be a folklorist or a theologian to appreciate these stories. They have an intrinsic value in themselves, as gems of imagination and artistry. So those who feel so inclined would do well to simply enjoy them for their own sake and not to bother about the scholarship. It will not bite!

It was not long after Seán Ó Súilleabháin's death in 1996 that people in his native Tuosist started planning for the best way to keep his memory alive. It was decided to organise a yearly *Éigse* to take place in his home parish. At the first of these gatherings, in 1997, I was honoured by the invitation to give a lecture on the importance of Seán's achievement. In that lecture I pleaded for a translation of *Scéalta Cráibhtheacha*. The next year, when I once again gave a lecture at the *Éigse*, this time more specifically on *Scéalta Cráibhtheacha*, I had the pleasure of announcing that my seed had fallen on good ground, and that William Caulfield had begun the task of translating the book. Now that we have the translation in front of us in its final form, I trust my vanity will be forgiven if I take great pride in claiming to have been the godfather of this book. I am convinced that it will stand as a worthy monument over a great scholar and a good man, and I hope that it will give new readers as much pleasure as the original version has given me ever since I made my first acquaintance with it in a far away country long ago.

Bo Almqvist
Professor emeritus of Irish Folklore
University College Dublin

Translator's Note

It has been recognised for some time that a translation of Seán Ó Súilleabháin's important Irish-language collection of religious tales and legends *Scéalta Cráibhtheacha* (1952), was long overdue. This publication is intended to bring this rich store of narratives to the attention of a wider audience.

Irish spelling has undergone many changes since the original work was published and as a result *Scéalta Cráibhtheachna* would now appear as *Scéalta Cráifeacha* in the normalised spelling. It is hoped that this English translation will encourage interest in a new edition of the original text with standardised spelling.

It is obvious, however, that the publication *Miraculous Plenty* has much to offer scholars and general readers at home and abroad who are not able to read and enjoy them in the original Irish, and it is this need I have tried to fulfil. I have attempted to render the stories as I might have heard them told in English around my grandmother's hearth in south-east Mayo in the 1940s a place where Irish and English have sat side by side. The spoken English of the district seemed to suit this material. I hope that my translation will enable the reader to experience the story much as the original hearers did, as closely as possible, and to experience a sense of the art of the different storytellers as well as the content of the tales and legends.

I have included the terms that have transferred from Irish to English, such as 'yerra' from the Irish word *dhera* and 'musha' from the Irish words *muise* and *mhuise* meaning 'indeed'. Both words are still widely heard in English speech in Ireland and I have used them as a token reminder of how words are absorbed by one language from another.

William Caulfield

Seán Ó Súilleabháin's Preface

When Douglas Hyde published his *Religious Poems of Connaught*, more than fifty years ago, he showed people at home and abroad part of a rich heritage of religious poetry and prayer which had nurtured the hearts and spirits of most of the Irish people for many hundreds of years. People who had no knowledge of the folklore of the Gaeltacht districts were astounded when they read his collection on account of the vast difference between the material in it and the official prayers and hymns to which they were accustomed. When *Carmina Gadelica* was published in Scotland it produced a similar reaction.[24]

This book is a companion volume of those two, even though it consists of religious tales only and excludes prayers, poems and charms. The same Irish mentality informs all three books. The tales in this book were collected in the Gaeltacht areas of Ireland and most of the original narrators have gone to their eternal reward. May God grant them their just place in Heaven and may He likewise reward the diligent collectors who took down in writing all that is printed here!

Of course this is not the first time that religious tales from the Irish Gaeltacht have appeared in print. Many fine examples have been published from time to time in books and magazines, not to mention shorter examples cited in the lives of the saints. However, these were intermingled with other narrative forms and one would have to read them all to get an accurate impression of the subject matter of religious tales. This book, therefore, is an attempt to classify and present in one book those tales from the Gaeltacht as they were collected over recent years. I would not go so far as to say that these are the best of their kind in Irish folklore but I feel that those in search of such stories will find interesting examples of the genre in these pages and find new versions they had not previously encountered.

I have selected these tales from manuscripts assembled by the Irish Folklore Commission over the past seventeen years. A small number of manuscripts was inherited by the Commission from the Folklore of Ireland Society and the Irish

24　A. Carmichael i–v (Edinburgh, 1928–1941).

Folklore Institute, but most of the tales were collected and written down by the Commission's own collectors. For a variety of reasons only a small proportion of the huge collection has been catalogued to date, so I have confined my choices, for the most part, to the catalogued collection with the odd tale culled from a cursory glance through the remainder. Many more remain to be collected and I have no doubt that a more comprehensive collection could be assembled if these tales and those already collected were fully catalogued. However, Rome wasn't built in a day and all things come to him who waits!

Our forefathers have kept alive these and hundreds more tales, as yet uncollected, passing them down from generation to generation by the fireside, since the time they were first composed or imported from abroad. While it is obvious that most of them are of Irish origin we have no idea as to when or by whom even one of them was composed. Their form and underlying philosophy would indicate that they were composed or re-shaped in the Middle Ages. The international stories may have come here at any time in many different ways and some may even have been composed here. It's very hard to tell. What is certain is that those Irish people who invented stories had a thorough knowledge of the folktales of Europe, as they wove into the fabric of their works hundreds of motifs that were common in Europe at one time. They say that tales get legs and no sooner were new ones invented than they spread like wildfire throughout the country. Irish was the predominant language here in those days and people loved these tales and continued to pass them, together with all kinds of other stories, on down through the years regardless of war, peace or famine. It's hard to say how long a lease of life remains for them in the future daily life of the Gaeltacht, but I hope that the knowledge and love of them will live on in manuscript and print for a very long time.

At one time similar religious tales were widely known and loved in Europe and the Orient. Then, over time, they faded out there just as ours are currently doing. There have been strong spiritual and cultural links between Ireland and Western Europe for the best part of two thousand years, with a mutual borrowing and lending of spiritual support and comfort for most of that time. This has left obvious traces in some of these tales. Most people in Western Europe would have appreciated them as much as did most of our own people up to recent times since they had shared roots in faith and civilization. I have no doubt whatsoever that the Russian storytellers who provided the material for Afanasiev's wonderful collection of similar tales[25] a hundred years ago would have enjoyed these tales too if they heard them, as indeed would have very many other peoples in the East since they all shared the same cultural values.

Those who are familiar with Irish folklore will have little difficulty in understanding the underlying philosophy of these tales. Those who are blind to this aspect of our culture may find them strange and fail to fully understand or to enjoy them. In judging these tales it is important to remember that they were composed hundreds of years ago and that people's attitudes have changed in many ways since then. The old outlook had its own strengths and weaknesses, and allowances should be made accordingly. These tales give us an insight into a way of life and civilization that has changed drastically, if it has not vanished altogether. If the reader likes what he sees there is much to be learned and pleasure to be derived from them.

It should be stressed that these tales were composed and told, not merely for pleasure, but also for purposes of instruction. Most of them carry a moral, and it should not be difficult for anyone who follows the tale to learn the lesson involved. The language is straightforward with no half-truths or hidden meanings. Some things may strike theologians as odd or improper but these, in particular, should understand that any unorthodoxy, such as there might be, is not contrived. The composers of the tales were not learned scholars or theologians but ordinary mortals who preferred to tell a good story from their own perspectives, adding a large dash of colourful imagination here and there. They combined religious truths with folk belief when it suited their purposes, without distinguishing between the two. For example, take the tale of the devil's son becoming a priest. It will surprise many people that any Christian would invent such a tale or that ordinary pious people, who were known to love and respect their clergy, would even listen to it, not to mention passing it on for hundreds of years. But we must remember that the public have always loved to put a veneer of truth on fictitious tales, however outlandish or unpalatable they might be. They were unable to visualise abstract concepts such as good and evil except in the context of fictitious characters that were seen to portray those characteristics. The 'Son of the Devil' was merely a conventional character in the same way as the 'Son of the King of Ireland' or the man who lived long ago was. All were fictitious characters that existed only in the context of the tale.

---

25 *Narodnuiya Russkiya Legendui* (Moscow, 1859).

Another aspect of these tales is the many similarities with the tales of the lives of the saints in Irish literature. There is a strong thread of good sense and vivid imagination at work here. There is, however, a limit to the number of imaginary motifs as the same ones crop up again and again – for example the object that is thrown into the sea and is later found in the stomach of a fish. Some of these tales are a veritable cornucopia of motifs, many of which are not germane to the plot. This is how the tales evolved, constantly changing in minor details while maintaining their essential form at the same time. It is one of the great wonders of the old tales that they remained so faithful to the original intention despite being changed and adapted to suit the different occasions and circumstances. The fact that they survived for so long, while remaining true to their origins, is a tribute to the art of the travelling storytellers. They could put the right spin on a tale without overstepping the bounds with detail changes. Really good storytellers were few and far between and the many inferior versions available illustrate that.

These tales should be judged on simplicity and naturalness, not forgetting the conviction with which they were told. They are yet another testimony to the strength and tenacity of the faith in the hearts of the tellers. It was accepted that this faith was central to daily life and was there to be practised. The next world was never far from their minds. When they spoke of Our Saviour or His Mother, they spoke of them as two of their own, with whom the faithful had conversations and dealings on a daily basis. It was not out of a lack of respect towards them that they told stories about them but out of a deep love and feeling for them. This was a human response and should be viewed as such. This same natural approach was a regular feature of storytelling in the Middle Ages and is easily observable in the many stories told about Saint Francis.

The Irish have long been noted for their devotion to their religion. Those who have kept the Irish language as their spoken tongue to the present day deserve special credit. They have passed down to us the old prayers, religious poems and tales for hundreds of years despite their sufferings and the lack of official church teaching due to the severity of the Penal Laws. Those prayers, poems and tales were their comfort and inspiration and, by the grace of God, helped them to keep the Faith alive. If the reader bears those facts in mind he will be less inclined to find any fault with the tales and derive all the more benefit and enjoyment from them.

I would like to make the following points clear about the tales I have selected. I have grouped, under a given title, the tales that shared a common theme (e.g. Priests, the Devil, Saints, etc). Of course, one could not stick strictly to this plan as some tales might be arranged under any of two or three headings. What I have done in those cases was to place each under the main heading or section involved. Yet again, there were cases where different versions of the same tale were so unalike that I decided to include two or three of them, one after the other, particularly if each was collected in different provinces. In that way the reader can see for himself how a tale gradually changed in the telling from place to place.

Nowhere else in Western Europe in our own times could a set of religious tales be recorded from tradition like that assembled by the collectors of the Irish Folklore Commission. It was God's will – *moladh go deo Leis!* – that we should have had the opportunity to reap this rich harvest over the past twenty-five years. I hope that the work will benefit our people in the years ahead.

Our Saviour and His Mother

'Glory be to Him who redeemed us by His suffering.'

The tales in this section deal with the earthly life of Our Saviour and His Mother. Some were borrowed from other countries but the majority were composed and passed on here. As with every other tale in Irish folklore, we have no idea as to the identity of the authors.

These are apocryphal tales. That is to say, they are attempts by our ancestors to put flesh on the bare bones of the Gospels. There is very little account of the daily lives of Our Saviour and His Mother in the sacred scriptures. Ordinary laymen in Christian countries, particularly during the Middle Ages, noted this lack in the Gospels and began to fill in the gaps based on their faith and their experience of the world. The result had a warm human flavour. The Hindus, Persians, Jews, Greeks, Romans, Slavs and Teutons all created such unofficial tales and the Irish followed the tradition. In those days it was quite common to use these tales to account for natural phenomena that people did not understand and examples of this can be found in this collection.

There is a palpable humanity and sincerity about these tales even where the truth is a bit stretched. The Christ portrayed here is very often not the Christ of the Gospels. We here in Ireland would find it incredible that Our Saviour would leave His Mother alone with a corpse in a wake-house to teach her not to comment on people's defects. Neither would we accept that Our Saviour would countenance the drowning of a ship full of people just because one sinner among them deserved such a death. But then we should not expect present-day logical standards from people who lived ages ago; we ourselves are not perfect. If we remember the origin of these tales and the deficiency of the Gospels that prompted them, it will add to the enjoyment and benefit we can derive from them.

1. The Tree that Bent Down

(a) When the world was first created it was ordained in Heaven that the Son of God would come on earth in Ireland, to convert the people and give them good example. It was also ordained that Máire would be the name of the mother.

Accordingly, any woman who bore the name of Máire was warned that she should behave properly and well. Some women tried to do so but were unable. But Our Mother kept the faith and believed in the Son of God and in His Father. On the feast of Our Lady, near Saint Patrick's Day, she was going to the well with a pail to bring home some water. She bent down to fill the pail and a voice spoke to her from the water and said that she would become the mother of the King of Graces, if she were willing. She answered the voice and said that she would have a hundred thousand welcomes for anything coming from the Father but that the voice should promise her in English, in Irish and in Latin that if anybody wore the Garment of Righteousness and behaved well in this life she would be able to rank his soul with the angels. The voice departed and returned and told Máire Bhreathnach that her wish would be granted. Then she was married to Saint Joseph. One day as they were walking through the garden of Paradise she said to Saint Joseph:

'Would you ever pick some of the fruit from that tree for me?'

'Wouldn't you ask the father of your child,' said Saint Joseph, 'it's him you should be asking.'

The Holy Child spoke from her womb:

'Bend down, O tree, that my mother may get whatever fruit she wishes!'

The tree bent down and she got all the fruit she wanted from it. Saint Joseph knew at once that he had done wrong.

'Go in, Máire,' said he, 'and lie down on your bed,
Till I go to Jerusalem to repent of my sins.'
'I won't go in,' said Mary, 'and I won't lie on my bed,
The King of Graces has forgiven you for any sins you may have committed.'

(b) Saint Joseph and Our Lady were out walking one day, long ago. As they were nearing a town they saw a fine house with a lovely garden. Our Lady was very much taken by the apples on the trees. She asked Saint Joseph to reach up and get her some of the apples from the trees. He told her he wouldn't, but to ask the father of her child to get them, as she had more right to make demands on him. The Infant Jesus spoke up from His Mother's womb and said to the tree:

'Bend down, O tree, so that my mother may get what she craves.'

And the tree bent down so that she was able to get what she wanted.

'Go in, Máire,' said Saint Joseph, 'so that I may go to Jerusalem to repent of my sin:
Go in and lie on your bed!

I will go to Jerusalem
To repent of my sin.'
Our Lady said:
'I won't go in,
And I won't lie on my bed!
The God of Graces has forgiven you
What sins you have committed.'

They walked on and arrived at the town and went into the first house they met there. They asked for lodgings for the night and the man of the house said that he had no lodgings for the likes of them. So they left and walked on. Now there was a young girl in that house who was born without any hands and it seemed that she would have liked them to have been put up for the night. As they walked on, the girl was watching them and they went into a stable where there were cattle and an ass. She walked down to the side of the stable where the ass was and, after they were inside for a while, the girl went to the door. Our Lady called out to her to put her shoulder to the door and press it in. She replied that she couldn't open the door since she had no hands. However, she put her shoulder to the door and it opened for her. And there was the Infant Jesus crawling across the floor, and Our Lady told the girl to bend down and bring the Child to her. When she bent down to pick up the Child to bring Him to His Mother, the finest pair of hands you ever saw grew on her and she lifted the Child. The girl was overjoyed. When she had left the Child with Our Lady she went off home and her people couldn't make out how or why she suddenly got such a fine pair of hands. And they all came out to meet her and couldn't do enough for her. You see, they didn't recognise her at first, until they saw what He had done for her.

2. The Tinker and the Blacksmith

Once upon a time, the Mother of God was out walking with her Son. It was a pitch-black night and there was very heavy rain. Not only was it pouring rain but there was a strong wind blowing away the shawl that was round herself and Our Saviour. He was only an infant at that time. The pair of them were so wet that anybody would have pity on them. She was trudging on, the poor creature, until she came to a hovel by the side of the road. She heard a noise inside as if someone was beating tin with a hammer. It wasn't quite night and the door wasn't closed. She stood at the door and said 'God bless all here'. There was a tinker inside making basins so she asked him, in the name of God, to make a pin for her that would keep the shawl secure around herself and the child. The tinker was most uncivil and ordered her away saying that he had more to do than to be making pins for everybody that passed the road. So she went off sadly.

She walked on till she came to a forge. There was a blacksmith inside blowing the bellows. The fire was over to one side. The Blessed Virgin said 'God bless the work' and asked him, in the name of God, to make her a pin that would secure the shawl around herself and the Child.

'I will, and welcome, my good woman,' said the blacksmith, 'why wouldn't I? Come in out of the rain and dry off yourself and the Child while I'm doing it. It's a bad night for anybody to be out.'

The blacksmith wasn't surly like the tinker. He put more coal on the fire, worked the bellows, and set out a stool for her and told her to warm and dry herself and the Child. Before long he had made the pin for her and with his own hands secured the shawl around them when they were ready to go.

The Blessed Virgin gave him her blessing and asked God that he might never want for work. And that's the reason why blacksmiths are always lucky and that tinkers are always wandering the world because surliness is not a good thing.

3. Seven Loves of a Mother for her Son

Saint Joseph and the Virgin Mary were walking in a glen one day and the Blessed Virgin heard a terrible noise approaching. The Infant Jesus was with them at the time.

'Watch out, Son,' said the Virgin Mary, 'listen to the noise approaching in the glen.'

'Don't worry, Mother,' said the Son of God, 'My Father Himself will save us.'

'Oh, You are my seven loves, Son!' said she.

'Oh, Mother,' said He, 'it's a poor legacy you're leaving to the women of the world that each will have seven times as much love for her son as he will have for her!'

They say that that's why a mother has seven loves for her son.

4. Rewarding the Women

The Virgin Mary was out walking another day and carrying her Infant on her back and she had to cross a big marsh on the side of a mountain. She met a pair of well-dressed girls on the marsh. One of them had great pity for the poor woman who was worn out from carrying her Child and thought she ought to carry it for her for a while.

'My poor woman,' said she, 'give me the child and I'll carry it for you over the marsh. I know this place better than you do and I know a little path through it. I'll be able to manage better than you.'

The other girl looked at her and made a face at her:

'Well,' said she, 'aren't you the foolish girl ruining your lovely dress carrying a poor woman's child?'

'Oh, the poor woman is a pity,' she replied.

She put the child on her back and off with her through the bog. She found the little path that she followed for about two miles without even soiling her feet. When they were safely across, her path lay in a different direction. Never knowing that the poor woman was the Virgin Mary, she handed her the Child and said, 'God protect you now, I'm going this way.'

When the girls were out of their hearing, the Virgin Mary said to her only Son:

'Now, my Child, what reward would you wish for that girl who carried you so far? I'd have found it very hard work even on my own. I didn't know the path and we'd have been in trouble.'

'Well, Mother dear, I'd wish her to have her head bent always and plenty of work to do to get her safely through life.'

'Oh my Son,' said she, 'and what would you wish for the other girl who wouldn't soil her fine dress for you?'

'To hold her head high always,' said He, 'on top of the world always, plenty to eat and drink and lots of pleasure.'

'Well, if that's the case,' said she, 'I pity the poor girl that carried You across the marsh.'

'Oh Mother,' said He, 'isn't it a short time we'll be in this world. She'll have happiness and joy yet, not like the other girl.'

5. Our Lady and Saint Brigid

(a) When Our Lady was expecting Our Saviour there was a pattern with dancing at the crossroads. She wasn't able to pass through the crowd. Saint Brigid was with her and Saint Brigid told Our Lady to wait a while. She saw a harrow in a field. She took out all the teeth in it and replaced each one with a candle. She lit the candles and then pulled the harrow with a rope through the crowd. The crowd followed Saint Brigid in one direction and then Our Lady and Our Saviour went in the other direction.

Then Our Lady told Saint Brigid that she was very grateful to her; only for her she wouldn't have been able to get through the crowd.

'And you shall have your reward!' said she, 'I'll put your feast-day before mine!'

And that's the reason why Saint Brigid's day is before that of Our Lady.

(b) The Virgin Mary and Saint Brigid were travelling together. Saint Brigid was travelling with her for some time. One Sunday the Virgin Mary didn't want to go to the chapel as she didn't want to be seen. Saint Brigid told her that she would make a cross that she would wear on her head, and everybody would be so busy looking at it that they would take no notice of her; they'd all be so busy looking at the cross that they'd have no time to look at her. So they went to Mass in the chapel and Saint Brigid did as she promised.

That was the first cross that was ever made. They are being made here ever since. The Virgin Mary then gave her own feast day to Saint Brigid in gratitude for saving her embarrassment in public. So she gave Saint Brigid the first day and took the following day for herself.

6. Eating Cold Flesh

(a) The Son of God and His Mother were travelling the world, preaching to people and urging them to show charity to one another. He was begging alms like a poor man. The day was nearly spent and they were coming towards a town. They met a man who had two deformed feet.

'Musha, my Son,' said His mother to the Son of God, 'didn't you give that poor creature a very crooked pair of legs?'

He said nothing and they kept walking until they came to a house. There was a light in the house.

'Mother,' said He, 'you go into that house; you'll get a night's lodgings there and I'll go on to the next house and we'll meet again in the morning.'

His Mother went into the house He showed her. Inside there was a corpse laid out, a candle lighting and a tobacco pipe on the table. She didn't see a single soul till morning. She passed the night as best she could. When she met her son, the Son of God, in the morning and said:

'Musha, Son, wasn't that a queer house you sent me to last night?'

'Why was that, Mother,' said He, 'what did you find?'

'There was a corpse laid out, a candle lighting and a tobacco pipe. '

'Did you take any bite out of the corpse?' said He.

'I did not,' said she, 'and why should I?'

'Would you not find it easier to take a bite out of the corpse,' said He, 'than out of the poor creature you found fault with last night?'

'True enough,' said she, 'but I didn't think it was any harm. I hope,' said she, 'that you'll forgive me if I've done wrong.'

'You have already been forgiven,' said He, 'by the God of Graces insofar as you have sinned.'

(b) The Son of God and His Mother were going their way together one day, and in the evening they met a man who had a physical blemish. And His Mother called to the Son of God to look at the man with the blemish. He pretended not to hear her and she called to Him a second time.

'Come here,' she said, 'and look at this odd-looking fellow.'

He pretended not to hear her but continued on His way. They travelled on and night was starting to fall.

'You'd better find a roof for us for the night as it's going to be a bad night,' she said.

He made no reply to her. It seems that He didn't like what she had said earlier. Then he saw a light in a wood and He said to her:

'You go over to that light and you'll find a little house there and stay there till morning. You'll get shelter for the night there.'

'Where will we meet in the morning?' she asked.

'I'll meet you here, at the entrance to the house,' He said.

So she went in as far as the house and the door was closed. She opened the door but there was nobody inside. She turned to leave but the night had got pitch black so she couldn't leave. It was much brighter when she entered than when she turned to leave. She wasn't long inside until a man came in carrying a sheep. He saluted the stranger and put down the sheep and killed it. He quickly put it in a pot and set it to boil. When it was cooked he went down into the room and brought up a cradle with two worn-out old hags in it. He gave them some of the soup and some of the meat with his two bare hands, as much as they could eat. When they had eaten their fill he took the two of them and brought them back down to the end of the house. Then he came back up and gave a plate of the meat to the stranger, the Mother of God, but she didn't touch it as she was disgusted. She could hardly wait for daybreak, but when it came she went out to the place they had agreed to meet. Her Son was standing there waiting for her.

'Oh!' said she, 'that was a funny place you sent me last night, a hovel without shelter or food or drink!'

'Did you get anything to eat?' said He.

'I did,' said she, 'cold meat that wasn't half boiled.'

'Well,' said He, 'it's a long time since yesterday evening when you were eating cold flesh! You were eating it then alright but you got enough of it last night!'

Ever since that time we have an old saying based on what the Son of God said. When anybody is backbiting or criticising his neighbour, he is 'eating cold flesh'.

7. The Son of God and the Man with the Oats

Long ago, the Son of God was walking around with His Mother. On the way they came upon a man shelling oats. He went up to the man and asked him for a grain of oats. The man refused Him and said he wouldn't give Him any.

'If I wet my finger,' said He, 'will you give me what sticks to it?'

'I will,' said he.

He wet his finger and put it into the heap and nine grains stuck to it. He went to the miller and asked him would he grind the nine grains for Him. The miller said that it was impossible to do that. He said to try, and that it might be possible. He pressed the miller so hard that he eventually gave in and set the mill turning and didn't he get nine bags of meal out of the nine grains of oats! And when he went back to the first man he was very sorry that he had refused Him. He realised that he was dealing with a saintly man but he didn't know that it was the Son of God.

8. Sight to the Blind

Long ago, when Our Saviour and His Mother were going around, He was beginning to work His miracles. They were walking along, walking the road, when they met a blind man sitting beside the road. When they had passed him His Mother remarked that the man was blind.

'He is, indeed,' said He, 'and if he is, there is his wife above in the wood there with another man. But,' said He, 'I'll give him back his sight so that he can see her.'

'Oh, well,' said His Mother, 'if you're going to do that find some excuse for the poor woman.'

As soon as He said the word the blind man stood up and was looking all round him; and he looked up at the wood and saw his wife. She realised at once that he had seen her and came down to him immediately. When she arrived:

'You were inside in the wood with that man,' he said.

'If I wasn't there,' said she, 'you wouldn't have got your sight back!'

And that's the reason why women can always find an excuse, right down to the present day.

9. The Loaves and Fishes

When Our Saviour was in Jerusalem he gave a dinner to five thousand people with five loaves of bread and two fishes. He had the two haddock in His hands, and from that day to this, they carry the mark of His thumb on them. There was a man in the crowd who thought that the food and drink might be scarce enough. God said to him:

'There'll be plenty and to spare of food and drink,' said He, 'but you won't be eating any of it.'

He asked the crowd to stone the man so they bent down to pick up stones to throw at him.

'Let any man,' said He, 'that has never sinned, cast a stone!'

Well, there wasn't a man in the crowd that could cast a stone. They had all sinned at one time or another. But the man died anyhow, so he wasn't at the dinner. And they all ate and drank their fill and there were seven baskets full of remains left over!

10. The Jews and the Pig

One day, when the Son of God and His Mother were walking together they met three Jews on the road and when they saw Him coming, one said to another:

'Here comes the Son of God and His Mother, and let's see can He perform a miracle.'

There was a big barrel at the side of the road. They put one of the Jews under the vessel and the other two waited by the roadside until He came up to them. They started talking and after a while one of the Jews asked the Son of God what they had under the barrel. He said that it was a pig. The two burst out laughing. After a while they lifted up the barrel and out ran a young pig. When they saw that, the pair never said a word. They knew only too well that He was God and that He had miraculous powers. They said they'd be converted and they'd believe anything He taught them from that day on. That was alright, but no Jew ever ate any pork from that day to this for fear it would be from the pig that was under the barrel!

11. A Ship-Full Drowned on Account of One Man

I often heard the old saying that a ship-full is drowned on account of one man and you'd think that that was a great injustice! Now this is a tale about that very thing.

Our Saviour and the apostles were walking by the shore and making their way on a terrible day, with a strong northwesterly wind and heavy, squally showers. Eventually they came to a harbour where there were a lot of vessels sheltering. They saw a ship making ready to sail. Now some of the apostles were very interested in boats and fishing but there came a sudden, very heavy squall and Our Saviour said:

'We'd better take shelter.'

So they did, and in a very short time – the rain eased off – Saint Peter looked out to see the ship but there wasn't sign or sight of it. He asked Our Saviour where did the ship go that was heading out as they took shelter, because it couldn't have gone out of sight wherever it went.

'Oh, she couldn't be gone,' said He, 'and she hasn't gone. She has sunk and all that were on her are at the bottom of the sea.'

'Oh, now,' said Saint Peter, 'surely You could have found some way of saving them!'

'There was nothing I could do,' He said, 'it had to sink on account of one single man. Did you never hear the saying that a whole ship-full of people should drown on account of one man?'

'I often heard it, and if I did, I still think it's completely wrong to drown a whole ship-full of people on account of one man!'

'Well, it's done now, anyhow,' said He.

They moved on and came to a meadow where they found a hive of bees. Our Saviour asked Saint Peter to go and bring Him a fistful of the bees as He needed them. Saint Peter went and roused them and put his hand in and took a fistful of them and it wasn't long before one of the bees stung him. She stung him so badly that he got confused and tightened his fist and killed every bee in it and made a mess of the lot. He came to Our Saviour, and handed them to Him.

'Well, what good are these to me?' He said, 'Aren't they all dead? Why didn't you bring them to me alive?'

'I couldn't,' said he, 'because one of them stung me and stung me very badly and got me so confused that I had to kill the lot.'

'Well,' said He, 'why didn't you just kill the one that stung you and then bring the rest of them to Me? Sure, the others didn't do you any harm?'

'I don't know about that,' said he, 'but I got in such a passion that I killed the lot in one go.'

'There you are,' said Our Saviour, 'not so long ago you were finding fault with God for drowning a whole ship-full on account of one man. It was exactly the same with you when you couldn't bring me the bees alive.'

'I couldn't help it!' said he.

12. Greed in the Church

(a) On account of a hard heart, but a good heart, Saint Colmcille had plenty of food and drink but couldn't bear to give any of it to the poor who came begging. The poor complained about him and Our Saviour told them to tell Colmcille to hang a small bag inside his door and, as the poor came looking for alms, all they'd have to do was put their hands in the bag and each would find in it the amount that was due to him. This was done and one day a shaky, lame, old man came by and put his hand in the bag and found a penny. A fine, strong, strapping, young man came after him and put his hand in the bag and found a shilling. Next day, Colmcille went out to his garden to water the flowers; and a man called to the house and asked for alms from the housekeeper. The girl was baking bread. She said that she had orders from her master not to give alms to anyone.

'Well, give a bit of the dough to a poor man who's hungry and your master won't miss it,' said he.

The girl gave him a bit of dough and he moved over to the fire and laid the dough at the back of the fire. After a while, Colmcille looked up and saw, growing out of his chimney, a tree that was forty feet high in full bloom and with leaves as big as plates! He ran into the house and asked the girl if anybody had been in the house since he left it. The girl said that a man had called a short time ago and asked for alms and that she had given him a bit of dough. He asked her was the man long gone. She said he wasn't. He asked whether the man had gone east or west. She said he had gone west. Colmcille ran along the road, as fast as his legs could carry him, until he saw the man ahead of him on the road. He threw himself on his knees and begged his forgiveness. He knew that the man was Our Saviour.

'Since you have plenty yourself why don't you give alms to the poor?' said Our Saviour.

'While You gave me plenty, You didn't give me a generous heart that would part with as much as the eye could see,' said Colmcille.

'There was an old man there yesterday', said Colmcille, 'he put his hand in the bag and all he got was a penny. Then a fine, strong, strapping lad put his hand in the bag and he got a shilling. What was the reason for that?' said Colmcille.

'That fine strong strapping lad had a good heart and didn't keep the shilling longer than it took him to reach the first public house on his way,' said Our Saviour.

'And the raggedy, lame, old man is now lying dead down there by the shore of that lake there and his clothes are lined with money,' said He. 'Now, go down there and take all those clothes and throw them out in the lake as far as you are able!'

Colmcille went down and, while he was taking off the clothes, out fell a gold coin worth four pounds. Colmcille coveted the coin so he slipped it into his pocket. He rejoined Our Saviour on the road.

'Was he there?' said Our Saviour.

'He was,' said Colmcille.

'Did you throw the clothes out into the lake?' said Our Saviour.

'I did,' said Colmcille

'Did you throw everything that was in the clothes out into the lake?' asked Our Saviour.

'Well,' said Colmcille, 'a four-pound gold coin fell out of the clothes and I put it in my pocket.'

'Oh! you've left an affliction on the Church forever,' said Our Saviour.

That's why priests are all so fond of money!

(b) In Saint Paul's time, they used to say that he was very mean, that he would begrudge giving anything to the poor or sharing anything. He had a servant-girl. One day, the Virgin Mary and her blessed Only Son called by. The girl was making oaten cakes. The Virgin Mary asked for alms.

'Arrah, I'd be terrified to give you anything,' said she, 'but here's a fistful of dough and you can make a bun of it and bake it in another house.'

The Virgin Mary took it and threw it in the fire. A tree, the likes of which nobody ever saw before, grew up the chimney at once. They say that it nearly touched the sky. Paul was out in the garden and said he:

'What is this marvel?'

He ran in.

'What's going on here?' he said to the girl.

'Arrah, musha, it was a poor woman that came in,' she said, 'and asked me for a bit of the dough I was kneading. Since I had no other alms to give her, I gave her a fistful of dough. She threw it in the fire and that grew out of it.'

'Oh! I'm sure that was the Virgin Mary! There isn't another person could do that. Did you see which way she went?'

'She went down that lane,' said she.

He went off after her and spoke to her and she answered him:

'Indeed,' said she, 'you lack for nothing. You have plenty to give.'

'Oh! I've plenty to give,' said he, 'but you didn't give me a big enough heart.'

'Oh!' said she, 'go to the doctors and get them to take away that layer of fat around your heart and you'll have a heart as big as anyone.'

He went to the doctor and told him the tale. He was given sleeping drops and put to sleep. He was opened up and they removed a big strip of the lining that was around his heart and he became one of the best men that ever lived.

His heart opened up.

(c) When Our Saviour was in this world, Saint Peter was the one most often in his company. Himself and Saint Peter were going the road one day and a fine, strong, strapping, young man came up to them and asked for alms from Our Saviour.

Our Saviour put His hand in His pocket and handed him a shilling. Later on in the day, a shaky, poorly-dressed, old man came up to them and he, too, asked for alms. Our Saviour put His hand in His pocket and gave the man a penny. Saint Peter marvelled at this.

'Musha, Lord,' said he, 'why did you give only a penny to that poor old man and yet you gave a shilling to that young man we met a while back?'

'Wait a while,' said Our Saviour, 'maybe the penny will last longer with the old man than the shilling with the young man.'

That evening they were walking along and what did they see but an old man lying dead on the side of the road, and who was it but the old man Our Saviour had given the penny to that morning!

'Oh! now, Lord,' said Saint Peter, 'look at this poor man dead on the side of the road! Maybe he died of the hunger. And if you had given him the shilling this morning,' said he, 'he might still be alive instead of lying here dead by the roadside.'

'Peter,' said Our Saviour, 'search his clothing and see would you find money or anything.'

Saint Peter started searching and what did he find but a bag of money!

'Now, what did I tell you?' said Our Saviour.

'Take that bag now,' said Our Saviour to Saint Peter, 'and throw every penny in it out into that lake!'

Saint Peter took the bag of money and went down to the lake. He started to throw the money into the lake but it broke his heart to part with it so he put some of it into his pocket. When he returned:

'Did you throw it out into the lake, Peter?' said Our Saviour.

'I did,' said Peter.

'Indeed you didn't,' said Our Saviour, 'you kept some of it. Alas,' said He, 'that is what will leave the greed for money in every single person who will follow you in my service!'

13. The Son of God and the Man with Five Pounds

There was a man, long ago, and a long time ago it was. If I had been there then, I wouldn't be here now. I'd have a new tale or an old tale or, maybe, I mightn't have any tale at all! This man had five pounds and he had no way of hiding it. So he gave it to the Son of God to mind for him. Off he went and came across a man who was about to build a house. He asked the man what he was doing and the man said that he was going to build a house.

'And how,' said he, 'can you build a house, and you without a penny?'

'Ah, sure, won't God provide the money,' said the man about to build the house.

The man who had asked God to mind his money began to wonder and said to himself:

'Maybe,' said he, 'He'll give my five pounds to him! I'd better go after my five pounds.'

He went back to the Son of God again and the Son of God asked him what he wanted.

'I want my five pounds back.'

'Oh, I'll give you back your five pounds,' said the Son of God. 'Go into that room,' said He, 'and take your five pounds: but take only your five pounds.'

The man went in and the room was piled high with money. He stuck his two hands into the piles of money and tried to take away the full of his two fists. But not a penny more than his own five pounds could he grasp though he tried till he was exhausted. He took the five pounds and returned to Our Saviour.

'Did you get your five pounds?' said the Son of God to him.

'I did,' said he, 'but tell me, O Son of God, what do you want all that money for?'

'Well,' said the Son of God, 'I have it for the man who told you I'd give him money for people like him, but I haven't a penny for you except your five pounds!'

14. As We Give, We Get

The Virgin Mary and Our Saviour were going along one day and they met a poor woman.

'Mother,' said He, 'give that poor woman a penny.'

The Virgin Mary gave the poor woman a penny. They moved on a short distance and met a man who was begging alms.

'Mother,' said He, 'give that poor man a shilling.'

The Virgin Mary gave the man a shilling. When they had gone a little further:

'Well,' my Son, 'said she, 'aren't you the strange one, giving a shilling to a drunkard who'll only go down to the public house and spend it, and yet you'd only give a penny to the poor woman who might mind it!'

'Oh, Mother,' said He, 'the penny will last her a lot, lot longer than the shilling will last him. The shilling won't last long with him!'

It's exactly the same with us: as we give, we get, and that is how God told it to the Virgin Mary.

15. The Cockroach, the Earwig and the Beetle

When Jesus was fleeing from the Jews it happened that he was going through a field where a man was sowing wheat. His disciples told the sower that if anybody asked him had he seen Jesus of Nazareth passing by to give this answer:

'He went by as we were sowing wheat here.'

Next day the farmer went out to look at his field in case the birds of the air were eating the seed. He was astonished to see that the wheat was ripe, the colour of gold and ready for reaping. He gathered his men and they started cutting the wheat. They weren't long at it when the Jews came along. They asked the man who owned the field had he seen Jesus of Nazareth passing by. He answered them and said:

'He passed through the field the day we were sowing the wheat we are cutting today.'

The cockroach stuck his head out of a hole and said: 'Yesterday, yesterday!' to let them know that Jesus had passed through the day before. While they were talking to the cockroach, the earwig stuck his head out of another hole and said: 'Quick! quick! quick!' to let them know that if they followed Jesus quickly they'd catch Him.

'Oh, woe! woe! may you be boiled, burned and scalded!' said the beetle because he was afraid that they would catch Jesus.

To this day it is the custom in the western parts of Mayo that, if an earwig comes into the house, someone takes a red ember from the fire with the tongs and puts it on top of him saying:

'May the sins of today, the sins of my life and the sins of seven generations before me be on you.'

They also kill the cockroach, saying: 'Yesterday! yesterday!' when they are killing him. But the beetle suffers no harm because he had pity on Our Saviour when he was fleeing from the Jews.

16. The Hen's Pain

When Our Saviour, may He be ever praised, was fleeing from the Jews and could find no hiding place from them, the pig hid Him. The pig rooted up the clay and covered Him with it. The hen came along and scratched away the earth that was covering Him. That is why the hen has the pig's pain. The pain was taken from the pig.

17. The Elder, the Holly and the Ivy

Another time, when Our Saviour was fleeing from the Jews and they were gaining on Him, He had nowhere to go, but He came upon an elder bush and He went in under the bush. But the bush shed its leaves. So He went on and hid under a holly tree and the holly hid Him.

He put a curse on the elder bush so that it would be the last tree to get its leaves and the first to lose them. He gave His blessing to the holly so that its leaves would remain green all year round. The holly and the ivy hid Him so they stay green all year. That favour was given to them. Nobody ever puts a piece of elder in a boat and it is never burned in the fire.

18. Miraculous Plenty; the Passion

The Blessed Virgin and Our Saviour were at a wedding and the wine had run out early in the night. Mary told her Son to do something, and in a short time all the vessels in the house where the wedding was were filled to overflowing. There never was such wonderful wine. They left the wedding the next day and as they were going the road they met a farmer. The Blessed Virgin asked him why he hadn't sown any oats in the field he had ploughed.

'I didn't have any,' he said, 'and I had no money to buy some.'

'Well,' said she, 'gather chaff from the ditches and throw it to the wind and then go home and gather a team of reapers, both men and women, for the morning. When you get up in the morning the oats will be ripe.'

When he got up in the morning the stalks were as high as the ditches and their heads were bent down with the weight of the oats on them. Before she left she said to him:

'If anybody comes along enquiring for the likes of us, say that you saw us when you were sowing the oats.'

Next day the Jews came along; they asked if he had seen the likes of them.

'I did,' he said, 'when I was sowing the oats.'

The earwig put his head up out of the ground and said:

'Yesterday, yesterday! Yesterday they went by!'

The Blessed Virgin travelled on and went into the house of a poor woman and asked for shelter for the night.

'I haven't a bit of straw for you to sleep on,' said the poor woman, 'or even a drop of milk for your fine child.'

'Haven't you valuable jewels all around the house,' said the Blessed Virgin, and stayed in the poor woman's house. The poor woman had a great many children and they were all half naked. One of the children was looking around and found a vessel full of milk and shouted out:

'Mammy! Mammy!' said he, 'look at all this milk.'

There wasn't a vessel in the house that wasn't full of milk!

When the Blessed Virgin was leaving next morning, the poor woman gave her a litle roll of cloth from the weaver's house. As her thanks, the Blessed Virgin said:

'Whatever you start in the morning, keep at it until evening.'

That morning she started to measure how many yards of cloth she had and continued measuring until evening. A strong farmer's wife called in that evening and asked her where she had got all the cloth.

'A woman came in to me last night,' she said, 'with a child. When she was leaving this morning she said: "Whatever you start in the morning, keep at it until evening." And I'm measuring ever since!'

'Where did she go? Where did she go?' said the rich wife of the strong farmer.

'She went down that way,' said the poor woman.

The other woman chased after her and, when she caught up with her, she brought her off to her own house. When the woman was leaving in the morning, she didn't leave anything because the rich woman had sinned grievously.

The Blessed Virgin went her way and came to the place of an English tyrant. He had a boy drawing water and watering the oats that he had sown.

'Why are you doing that?' she asked.

'Because the ground is parched from the heat,' he said.

'And what will happen to other people?' said she.

'They won't have a thing,' said he.

'And how do you know that?' she said.

'Because it's not going to rain,' said the boy.

There was never such a night's rain as there was that night!

When Our Saviour came to the City of Jerusalem the Jews put spikes and nails through His hands and feet and a crown of thorns on His head. Some blood splashed out on to the eyes of a blind man standing nearby and his sight was restored at that moment. When Jesus had been crucified, they took Him away. They buried Him seven fathoms deep in the ground and put huge boulders down on top of the grave. When they came home there was an old man sitting in the corner and the old man asked:

'Is there any danger that He'll rise again? '

'No,' said they, 'no more than the poor bird that's boiling there in the pot!'

With that the cock jumped up on to the side of the pot and flapped his wings, scalding them all with the hot water. Next day the Jews went to mind the grave and they all fell into a deep sleep. When they awoke, the mouth of the grave was open.

19. The Thief on the Right Hand

The Virgin Mary and the Child Jesus were out walking one day and they came to a wild wood. They came upon a shack in the wood and there was a woman inside with a boy child. The woman was warming a saucepan of milk for her child. She gave her child some milk to drink out of the saucepan. Then she took the saucepan and gave the rest to the Child Jesus. The Virgin thanked her and went her way.

When Our Saviour was being hung on the cross there were two thieves being hung along with Him, one on either side of Him. It happened that the one on His right side was the child whose milk He had shared.

'Oh, Lord,' said the thief on the right side, 'You are innocent but I am guilty! Remember me when You enter into the kingdom of your father.'

'You will be with me in Paradise tomorrow,' said Our Saviour.

He was saved and he was with Him in Paradise the next day.

20. Conall Cearnach and the Passion

One day, Proinsias Mór Ó Gallchóir asked me did I ever know that there was an Irishman present at the crucifixion of Our Saviour. I said I didn't. He said there was indeed and this is how it came about. He said that there was a big battle in Ireland within the ranks of the Fianna and afterwards the Fianna scattered in every direction but there was one member of the Fianna, whose name was Conall Cearnach, who left the country and enlisted in the army of Rome. Before Conall Cearnach left this country he was a witty, amusing man. But when he returned a few years later he was silent and surly, without a word or a smile for anyone. And people were amazed at the change in him since he went away. Whenever he was asked to account for the change, he wouldn't give them any satisfaction except to say that if they had seen what he had seen there wouldn't be much fun left in them either.

Finally, he confided in a friend what he had seen – about the day he was on Mount Calvary and saw this man being crucified and how, when the crucifixion was over, darkness covered the whole earth and the graves opened and the dead returned, and so people believed that it was a very powerful person indeed that was on the cross. And that is how people decided that it was the crucifixion of Our Saviour that Conall attended that day.

21. Conchubhar of Ulster and the Passion

In olden times when priests were on the run and people were widely scattered they had no particular place to say Mass and had to make do with one night here and another night there. One night, priests came to a house and they told the boy to take a sickle and cut a clump of rushes to make bedding for the night. When the boy approached the clump a voice issued from it saying:

'Don't put me out of my house!'

The boy went back to the priest, who asked him:

'Did you not bring the rushes?'

'No, Father,' said he, 'and if you heard what I heard, you wouldn't either.

'Come on and show me the place,' said the priest.

They went to the clump of rushes and the priest put on his stole and read a prayer. A spirit spoke from it.

'Who are you?' said the priest.

'I am Conchubhar of Ulster!' said the spirit.

'Are you long here?' said the priest.

'I'm here since the Saviour was crucified,' said he.

'And how did you come to be here?' asked the priest

'I was splitting timber one day and got a splinter in my head and then when I heard that the Saviour had been crucified I got a fit of anger. I took my sword in my hand and rushed out through the forest, and didn't the splinter fall out and I died. The Saviour condemned me to remain in my skull until the Day of Judgment!'

'Well I'll baptise you now,' said the priest, 'and you'll go straight to Heaven.'

'And will I have to die all over again?' he asked the priest.

'You will indeed,' said the priest.

'O well, Father,' said he, 'I'll remain in my skull till the Day of Judgment.'

When the priest heard this he shed bitter tears over the clump of rushes and immediately the spirit rose up and became an angel.

'Father,' said he, 'I'm going to Heaven now, for I have been baptised by your tears.'

22. Generosity Pays

A poor girl was going the road one dark night. She had no shoes or stockings and her feet were cut to the bone by the sharp stones of the road. She had no place to sleep and through sheer tiredness she sat down at a turn in the road. Our Lord noticed her and came to her in the form of a man and told her to get up and go to a wake-house that was nearby, where she could find refuge from the night air. She did as she was bid and approached a house where there were candles lighting and was admitted. As soon as she came in she was given enough to eat, and then she was asked to wash the dishes. She did, and she was well able. She was asked to mind the house during the funeral and she did so. When the widower saw how good she was at housekeeping, he asked her to stay on and mind his children and do the washing and cleaning for them.

When the man saw that the girl was so good to work he decided that it would be cheaper to marry her than to pay her, and in due course they married. When the new couple had settled down and were enjoying life without a care in the world the young woman was making bread at the table one day. Our Saviour approached her in the guise of a poor man and asked her, as a charity, for a little of the bag of wheat at the door. The woman looked at him in a surly manner and said:

'Wouldn't potatoes be good enough for you?'

She shouted to her husband to bring a full hat of potatoes for what she thought was a beggar. Our Lord didn't wait for the potatoes but took a couple of grains of the wheat and left. She had barely turned around when she found that the bags of wheat were all empty. The miserly woman understood immediately Whom she was dealing with and ran after Him begging forgiveness. He reminded her that she, too, had been poor once and appreciated charity, but now that she was independent she begrudged a grain of wheat to a beggar. He forgave her and told her that in future she should give charity for His sake.

Good luck follows generosity.

23. Our Lady's Visit

There was a widow once (and indeed there were plenty of them at that time and always will be) and she lived on the side of a hill. She had one little girl. In those days there were fruit trees in Ireland as good as you'd get anywhere in the world today. She and the little girl used to live on this fruit until a day came when the weather was bad and it happened that they had no food in the house. At bedtime that night Brídín was very upset.

'Bríde, dear,' said the mother, 'I think we might as well go to bed.'

'Musha, what chance have we of sleeping?' said Bríde to the mother, 'since we've eaten nothing all day?'

'Don't worry about it, my dear,' said the mother, 'a day and a night's fasting won't do you a bit of harm. God's help is nearer than the door and maybe we'd find plenty to eat in the morning.'

'I don't know so much about that,' said Bríde. 'How am I going to be able to sleep?'

'Don't mind, child,' said the mother, 'with God's help you'll sleep as well tonight as any other night.'

Mother and daughter went to bed and slept soundly. At dawn the mother woke.

'I may as well get up,' she said.

'Musha, Mam,' said Bríde, 'what's the point of getting up when we have nothing to cook?'

However, the mother got up and went down to the hearth and soon had a fine fire blazing. Brídín remained in bed, not at all happy, and outside it was the worst day ever, with thunder, lightning and flurries of snow. The fire was at its best, very early in the morning, when in the door came a little withered old woman who was soaked to the skin.

'God save you,' said the mother, 'come in and warm yourself by the fire.'

The poor woman came in and sat down by the fire.

'Musha, aren't you out very early on such a bad morning?' said the mother.

'Oh, the way it is with me and others like me is that we have to be out, be it cold or wet, late or early,' said she.

'I suppose that's true,' said the other woman.

So they sat on either side of the fine warm fire, with nothing being put down on it.

'Isn't it a pity now,' said the visitor, 'to have such a fine fire going and nothing going on it to cook?'

The woman of the house was ashamed to tell the poor woman that she had nothing in the house and again the poor woman commented that it was a pity to see such a fine fire with nothing cooking on it.

'My good woman,' said the mother, 'I haven't a thing and if I had I'd have put it on long ago to cook for you.'

'Don't worry,' said the visitor, 'but go down there to the little bag I left inside the door and empty it out.'

The mother did so and out came some fine potatoes.

'There now,' said the poor woman, 'get the pot and put them on to boil and we won't be hungry.'

She quickly did as she was told and the fire wasn't long boiling them.

'Now, Brídín,' she shouted. 'Get up now, my girl! I told you last night that God's help was nearer than the door and that we might have His help to-day.'

'What's there, mother?' she asked.

'There's a fine pot of potatoes here and you can eat your fill!'

Bríde got up, delighted to have a fine feed of potatoes. They sat down to eat when the potatoes were boiled.

'Is there anything to eat with them?' asked the poor old woman.

'No, my dear,' said the mother, 'but thanks be to God it's good to have these to eat.'

'Go down to the bag again,' said the poor old woman, 'and empty it out and maybe you'd find something else to go with them.'

She went down and, sure enough, out fell a fine piece of meat.

'Cut it up now,' said the visitor, 'and it won't be long cooking.'

They cooked it and ate it. Afterwards the woman of the house said grace and thanked the visitor most sincerely for bringing the food. They chatted away for a while and then they felt thirsty.

'Have you anything we could heat on the fire to quench our thirst?' said the visitor.

'I'm afraid I've nothing to offer except cold water,' said the mother.

'Oh, put the pan on the fire and boil the water and we'll drink the hot water. It's better than cold water.'

When the water was boiling: 'Go down again to the bag,' said the poor woman, 'and empty it out and see if there's anything there.'

She emptied the bag and out fell a little box.

'Right!' said the visitor, 'put the contents into the water and we'll soon have something to drink.'

She did as she was told and when it was boiled they got their vessels and drank to their hearts' content.

The poor woman stayed with them that night.

'Now,' she said, 'have you anything else you could cook on this lovely fire that is going to waste?'

'Oh, thank you very much,' said the mother. 'We won't ask to eat another thing for two days, we have eaten so much.'

'Get out the hot oven,' said the poor woman, 'and bake us a cake: and empty the bag once more and maybe you'd find the makings of it there.'

She went to the bag once more and out came flour and meal and she made a fine cake for the three of them! They ate it for supper and afterwards they washed their feet and prepared to go to bed.

'You'll sleep along with us,' said the woman of the house.

'No, no,' she answered. 'The likes of me never sleeps with others. I'll just stretch out in the corner on some straw.'

'I won't be satisfied at all unless you agree to sleep along with myself and Brídín,' said the woman of the house.

'I've never done it before,' she answered, 'and I never will.'

They said goodnight and went to bed. Next morning, when the woman of the house got up it was a lovely fine day. Her visitor was getting ready for the road.

'Well now,' said the woman of the house, 'why don't you stay with us and we'd be company for one another?'

'Oh I won't stay,' said the poor woman. 'The likes of me never stays more than one night in any house and I won't either.'

'Here now,' she said as she was leaving, 'take this little bag and mind it and any time you need food you'll find it in the bag!'

Away she went and they said farewell to each other as they parted. And if the woman of the house went to the bag twenty times a day she'd find every kind of food she'd want in it! They say that it was the Virgin Mary who was the visitor and gave them the food.

And that's my tale and if there's a word of a lie in it, so be it.

Priests
'The Priest Clothed As Christ'

The clergy in general were held in high esteem and affection in this country for generations and it is the same today, God bless them. But there were certain priests, from time to time, who earned enduring fame or notoriety for one reason or another, even though they are now long dead and buried. Every parish remembers priests who had exceptional qualities – hospitality (or the opposite!) or deeds of daring, or defending their parishioners in their hour of need. In the old days the poets made poems about them, praising them, castigating them or lamenting their passing, according to their merits in the opinion of the poet. There are hundreds of cases recorded in folklore of remarkable events occurring while particular priests were in the parish and the parts they played in those events. In every case the priest is referred to by both his Christian name and surname.

But these are not the priests mentioned in the following stories – these have no names or surnames usually and even where a name is used in a particular story it is only a passing reference. Usually they are as anonymous as 'the widow's son' or 'the man who lived long ago' that crop up regularly in the old stories. We don't know if these priests ever lived; or where, or by whom, the stories were first told. Whether true or not, they spread from one end of the country to the other, from one generation to another and, judging by the extent to which they travelled, they were very popular with those who heard them. The storytellers of old didn't deal with normal, everyday events, in fact the opposite was the case. The inventors of stories wove oddities, wonders and miracles into their tales as their forefathers in the craft had always done and, as a result, similarities often occurred.

These priests are given certain attributes that should be noted:

(a) They usually have miraculous powers – like turning fish into meat or bringing the dead back from the next world.

(b) These powers are stronger in a young priest than in an old one.

(c) A priest forbidden to say Mass, or wrongly convicted, could do things that would fail an ordinary priest.

(d) These priests could banish spirits and control the devil; however, in these tales, the devil, or a woman possessed by him, can take possession of a priest who must then suffer a severe penance to break the devil's hold on him.

(e) In these tales the priest is more powerful than the minister.

(f) Poor scholars who had studied for the priesthood were wiser and more powerful than ordinary priests.

There are further stories involving priests in other sections of this book.

24. The Priest's Penance

There was a married couple long ago and they were always fighting. They had one son who was able to read and write seven different languages. The son told them that he'd leave if they didn't stop fighting. But there was no use in talking to them and in the end of it all he had to leave. He was travelling on and on and on until he met a gentleman who was looking for a servant-boy.

'That's great,' said the boy. 'I'm looking for a master.'

The gentleman brought him home and set him to tutoring his children for a year and a day. When the year and a day were up the master asked the boy what pay he required.

'Whatever I'm worth and whatever I've earned,' said the boy.

'Right,' said the rich man, and kept him on for another year and a day. Then he asked him what pay he required.

'The same as I told you before,' said the boy.

So he kept him on for another year and a day. When three years and three days had passed, the gentleman called the boy.

'Now,' said he, 'you have educated my sons and I must give you a fitting reward.'

He asked the boy what profession he would like and the boy said he would like to be a priest. The gentleman sent him off to a seminary. When he was ordained as a priest he returned to the gentleman to thank him. Then he set out for his own home and as he drew near he met a woman going to the well for a bucket of water. He asked her how was such and such a man or such and such a woman that he used to know long ago.

'Well,' said she, 'the old man died a few years ago and the old woman is being waked today in a house in the village.'

'God help us all!' said the priest to himself and headed off towards the wake-house.

When he went in he asked the people there to go outside for a few moments until he was ready. When they were gone, he began to read from his book and, very shortly, his mother's corpse sat up in the bed and began to talk to him. He asked her where herself and his father were and she told him that they were in Hell. He asked her was there anything he could do to release them.

'Well,' said she, 'there's only one thing and that would be too hard for you to do.'

'I'll do my best, anyway,' said he.

'Right,' said she, 'when the funeral goes off tomorrow, let you take to the road and there you'll meet a beggar. Get his old clothes from the beggar and wear them, without changing them, for seven years. During that time, don't cut your hair or your beard, don't sleep two nights in the same house and always sleep between two outside doors!'

Next day he took to the road and met a beggar. He got the old clothes from the blind man and set off around the country doing his penance. When he had done the seven years, except for one night, he came to a house where there was only a woman and her daughter. He asked for shelter for the night but they were terrified of him on account of his long beard. When the man of the house came home, he found him lying in the haystack and asked him to come into the house. He went in and when it came to bedtime, he enquired what time second Mass was next day. The man said eleven o'clock.

'Tell the priest that I'll say that Mass,' said he.

'Right you are,' said the man.

In the middle of the night the man of the house woke up to find his house all lit up with the light of glory. He went down to the kitchen and saw the priest between the two outside doors, with twelve bishops from Heaven shaving him. When the bishops left, the priest told the man the whole story from start to finish. In the morning, when he was saying the Mass, his father and mother appeared as two bright butterflies and rested on his shoulders. When he had said the Mass the two butterflies went up through the rafters of the house, up through the sky until they reached Heaven.

25. The Priest who Wouldn't Baptise the Child

There was a poor couple long ago and, one morning, a child was born to them. The midwife said that the child was very weak and that he should be baptised very soon or otherwise he might be lost. The child's father said that he'd bring the child to the chapel and maybe the priest would baptise him before he said Mass. It was a Sunday. They brought him to the chapel and the father of the child went to talk to the priest, telling him that he had a child with him who could die at any moment and it would be as well to baptise him before he said the Mass.

'My word!' said the priest, 'I won't baptise him, you'll have to wait till I've said Mass! I have more to do at the moment and you'll just have to wait. There'll be plenty of time to baptise him when Mass is over.'

So, the priest went off and began to say Mass and before the Mass was over the child had died. When Mass was over the priest called the poor man and asked him where was this child that he wanted baptised.

'He's dead now, Father,' said the poor man.

The priest was astonished when he heard that the child had died and he said nothing for a while.

'Now,' said the poor man, 'the child is dead and which of the two of us is to blame?'

'Well there's no blaming you,' said the priest, 'I'm the guilty one and I'm the one that will have to pay for it!'

The poor man took away the dead child and buried it. The priest realised that he was very much at fault. He went home to his house and the first thing he did was to tell his servant-boy he'd have to leave as he was leaving the district himself and might never again return. He did the same with the servant-girl. He closed and locked every door in the house, put the key in his pocket and took to the road; he was wandering back and over, here and there, for a couple of weeks and one day, on his travels, he was walking upstream on the bank of a river. He took the key from his pocket and threw it into the river.

'That's it,' said he, 'my sins will never be forgiven me until that key comes back into my own two hands!'

He wandered on and night was falling, a wet, cold night, and he arrived at a big wood. He was going through the wood all night, half blinded by the rain, and towards dawn he spotted a light some distance away and headed towards it. There was a little house there and he went in and there was nobody there except a little girl sitting by the fire. He saluted her and they exchanged salutations but she didn't know that he was a priest. They weren't long there when in the door came twelve robbers and when they saw the priest before them they asked him how he came to be there. He said he had got lost in the wood and he had to seek shelter somewhere. They were talking away for a while and the priest asked the leader of the robbers what was their occupation.

'We have none,' said he, 'except stealing and robbing anything we can lay our hands on and bringing it here.'

'Well that's a sorry trade,' said the priest

'There's no better trade,' said the robber. 'How do you think we'd exist here if we hadn't it?'

'You could get a better trade than that,' said the priest

'And what kind of a trade could you give us?' said the robber.

'If you do what I tell you,' said the priest, 'I'll give you a trade that will bring in twice as much money as you're getting now. Out with you to the woods,' said he, 'and bring me in every kind of flower that you find there!'

They all went out and each one brought back an armful of every kind of flower growing on the trees. When they did, he told them to go out again and bring back a fistful of rods, which they did. Then he set to and made a little basket for each man and afterwards fashioned little ornaments from the flowers and put five or six of them in each basket.

'Here, now,' he said to them, 'off with you and into the town and sell them for half a crown each and you'll each have six half-crowns by evening! You'll easily get a half-crown for each ornament.'

They took the baskets and, when they were well clear of the house, the chief robber spoke to the others saying that he believed that the priest was making fun of them. Of course, he didn't know that the man was a priest.

'I think,' said he, 'that he is hoping to get us to go to town and that he has already alerted the soldiers and the peelers to come and catch us, so if we go to town today they'll come and catch us!'

Some of them stopped and decided not to go any further but six of the youngest went to town and sold all the ornaments in each basket for half a crown each. Their companions waited until they returned and the chief robber enquired how they got on.

'Great,' said they, 'we didn't see a peeler or a soldier and sold all the ornaments and got our money and we could have sold as many again if we had them.'

So the others all went into the town and sold all they had and by evening they had plenty of money. The priest asked how they had got on. They said they had done well and sold the lot.

'There now,' said the priest, 'wasn't there another way of making a living apart from robbing. Do the same thing tomorrow and the day after and every day of your lives and people won't be down on you or mocking you, and you'll be making money every day!'

Then they said that it was all very well having money, but how would they get food.

'There's no danger you won't get food,' he said. 'You'll always get food in exchange for money.'

'But still and all,' said the chief robber, 'we haven't a bit to eat now!'

'Get down on your knees now,' said the priest, 'and I'll get you food.'

They all got down on their knees and the priest came over to the table and got down on his knees and stayed there praying for quite a while.

'Now,' said he, 'get up!'

They got up and the table was filled to overflowing with every kind of food you could think of.

'Now,' said he, 'sit in to the table and eat your fill!'

They sat in to the table and ate their fill and when they had finished eating he told them that he was going to make them into holy men. He said he was going to baptise each one and would hear their confessions and give them Holy Communion and they would be holy people from that day on. They were there for a week and he had no idea who the girl was that was with them. One day he spoke to her and asked her who she was and she said that she came from such and such a place and that she had got lost in the wood and the robbers found her and she had been their servant-girl for some time. After a while he found out that she was the servant-girl that he, himself, had before he left his old house.

One day, they were inside. It was a Friday and the priest said that he'd have to go looking for fish as it was forbidden to eat meat that day. The priest got a rod and went fishing in the river near the house, and he wasn't long at it until a trout rose to the bait. He pulled it in and brought it home and told the girl to wash and clean it and put it to boil for the men. She opened the trout and the first thing she pulled out of its stomach was a key with a red tape attached to it. She washed it and cleaned it and handed it to the priest

'There now!' said the priest, 'my sins are forgiven! That is the very key I had the day I threw it in the river and I knew that my sins would not be forgiven until I had it in my hand again!'

The trout was prepared for the robbers and it sufficed for all of them with plenty to spare. After a fortnight or so the priest left them and brought the servant-girl with him back to his own parish. The robbers stayed on in the wood and never stole another thing afterwards, but went on buying and selling and nobody could find any fault with them. Only for that, they would have continued to rob and steal forever. They scattered here and there, each going his own way and in a very short time they were all wealthy men.

That's my story and if there's a word of a lie in it, so be it!

26. The Priest of Ballinrobe

There was a man long ago and he had three sons. One said that he'd have to go to America, and the second son said he'd go to college, and the third son said that he'd stay at home. One of them went off to college. In those days there wasn't any transport: he had to walk from Ballinrobe to go to college, however long it took him. He spent five years there and became a priest. He was coming home and spent the day walking the roads until nightfall. He went into the yard of a gentleman and asked for shelter for the night. He was given it and the gentleman had a hundred thousand welcomes for him. The gentleman and himself spent the time talking until suppertime and after they had eaten their supper they went to bed.

When they were asleep the gentleman's daughter, who had waited on them, decided that she'd like to marry the priest. She went into his room and asked him to give up the Church and marry her. He told her that he wouldn't marry her as he was already married to Our Mother Mary and would not marry any woman till the day he died. When he refused her she left. Her father had a gold plate and she hid it in his bag. When he had gone to sleep she found a piece of meat and put that into his bag along with the gold plate. Next morning – it was a Friday – he got nothing to eat when he was leaving. He left and kept on going until he was about a mile from the house. Then the daughter told the gentleman that their visitor was a bad man. He asked her why she said that.

'Well,' she said, 'this is Friday and I saw him eating meat going down the yard this morning. And, as far as I can make out, he has taken a gold plate with him too!'

The father got some helpers and went in pursuit. When they caught up with him they took the bag and found the gold plate in it and brought him back. He was tried, and sentenced to be hanged the next day. A gallows was erected and he was placed on it. The rope was being placed round his neck when he asked for permission to say a few words. He said that he had been on his way home from college and had called to the house to ask for a night's lodgings from the gentleman, which he was gladly given and got an excellent supper.

'I was barely asleep,' said he, 'when this young girl came into the room and asked me to give up the Church and marry her. I told her I wouldn't,' said he, 'that I was already married to Our Mother Mary and would not marry any woman in this world till the day I die. Then, when I wouldn't do what she asked, she went off and put a gold plate in my bag.'

'You were eating meat in the yard,' said she, 'and it was a Friday!'

'I wasn't eating meat,' said he, 'but I was eating fish. Maybe indeed,' said he, 'that it was meat that you put there but it was fish that I found there.'

They took the bag and examined it and found that it was fish that was in it. So they decided to release the priest and to hang the girl in his place. They put her up on the gallows and when she was up there she told him that she would have him for herself in Heaven or in Hell.

He went off home then and lived there a while until he got a parish. All went well for a while. Then a gentleman sent him an invitation to a dinner and he went to it. After dinner they went for a walk in the garden. When they were crossing a ditch they met a young girl and she gave him a tip on the cheek. He turned back and followed her into a glasshouse. They were in there a good while and when they were parting she told him that she was the woman he had condemned.

'And you can't deny me,' she said, 'I told you I'd have you in Heaven or in Hell!'

He had no idea whatsoever as to what he should do. He felt that he was eternally damned. He went to the Bishop and told him the whole story and the Bishop said that he was, indeed, damned.

'Away with you,' said the Bishop, 'and buy a pennyworth of the smallest needles you can find and then set off in a boat and every hundred yards you go throw out one needle. And when they are all thrown out,' said he, 'you must get them all back again. Then bring them all back here to me and you will be saved!'

The priest went off and bought a pennyworth of little needles and found a boat and went out to sea. He continued to throw out a needle for every hundred yards he travelled until they were all gone. His bread supply was all used up by this time. When he had finished he turned back and instead of looking for the needles he made for the shore. He seemed to be travelling forever before he arrived at a harbour and by this time he was dying with the hunger. He kept on travelling without knowing where he was going and eventually found himself in a wood. He saw a light in the distance. He went on and on until he came to the light. When he came to the light he knocked and was asked who was there. He said he was lost. There were twelve young girls inside and they let him in. He asked them, in the name of God, to give him something to eat. And he was given supper. After supper he asked could he stay the night. They said he could. He sat down and told them every single thing that had happened to him from start to finish. And when he had told it all one of the girls said to him:

'May God help you, but you've plenty to do if there's to be any hope for you! There is a priest who comes here every morning to say Mass for us and if there's any hope for you he will be able to tell you!'

He was very tired and he stretched out on a sort of bed beside the fire and fell asleep. He never woke until the Mass was over and the priest had gone. Then he woke and asked the young girls had the priest come yet and they said he had come and gone.

'If you please,' said he, 'could you let me stay another night so that I can see him tomorrow?'

'You can stay,' they said.

He stayed there till evening. He went out to the wood and brought back an armful of brambles and put them under him in the bed. He lay down on them in his skin hoping that he wouldn't be able to sleep before the priest came. He was overcome by sleep and slept so well that he didn't wake till the Mass was over and the priest was gone again. Then he woke and asked had the priest come. They said he had come and gone. They said they'd give him one more night, and if he didn't manage to catch the priest that night that would be the end. He went out and brought in a harrow and lay on it. He stayed there but if he slept at all it was uneasy sleep waiting for the priest's arrival. He was going to get up before Mass but one of the young girls told him to take his time until after Mass. So he waited until the priest had said Mass and was getting ready to go and then he went in to him. He told him his story and explained the penance that the Bishop had imposed on him.

'Away with you now,' said the priest, 'and go to such and such a town in the morning. There you'll meet a woman,' said he, 'who is selling fish. The first fish you put your hand on, buy it and the price will be fourpence. Here's fourpence and that will buy it. When you've bought it, open it and you'll find all your needles inside. Leave the fish there and take the needles with you.'

The priest went to the town and met a woman selling fish. He asked the price.

'Fourpence each,' she said.

The first one he put his hand on:

'I'll take this,' he said.

He gave her the fourpence, opened the fish and found all the needles inside. He immediately set off home. He had hardly arrived there when the Bishop heard of his coming and sent for him. He went to the Bishop and the Bishop asked him if he had got the needles.

'I have,' said he.

'Well,' said the Bishop, 'I have more sins on my soul than you have!'

Anyhow, the Bishop wrote to the Pope telling him of the penance he had imposed on the priest. He got an answer back from the Pope saying that the priest was a saint and that the Bishop should now do the same penance, casting out the needles into the sea as he had told the priest to do and getting them back again, and that there was no hope of saving his soul unless he did so.

The Bishop went and got a pennyworth of needles. He found a boat and set off out to sea. He threw the needles out and neither himself nor the needles were seen again down to the present day.

27. The Youth and the Priest

(a) Once upon a time there was a man with a good house who used to keep good-class lodgers. A priest stayed there one night. There were sons in the house. In those days it was more usual to say grace after meals than it is nowadays. The husband and wife said grace after the supper and, after the grace, the husband went down to stir up the fire. And there were two angels fighting one another across the hearth, the Angel of the Left Hand and the Angel of the Right Hand, and immediately The Angel of the Right Hand knocked the Angel of the Left Hand on the flat of his back into the fire! If the woman of the house stirred the fire before the man did, the Angel of the Left Hand would overcome The Angel of the Right Hand; but the youngest son of the family was breaking his heart laughing at the pair of them fighting on the hearth. Now the priest had no idea in the world why he was carrying on like this. After the grace was said:

'I'd have thought,' said he, 'that you'd never rear a child without some manners or that wouldn't be afraid of you, at least.'

'Well, it's failing me,' said the father.

Next day as they were having a meal:

'I wonder now,' said the priest, 'would you let me try to teach him.'

That was agreed and the priest asked the boy:

'What are you laughing at?' said he.

'You're not sitting in your confessional chair so that I could tell you,' said the boy.

'I won't be long putting that right,' said the priest.

He put his stole round his neck and sat on the chair and the youth approached him on his knees telling him that the cause of his laughing was that when his father stirred the fire after grace the Angel of the Right Hand would get the upper hand of the Angel of the Left Hand and knock him into the fire.

'And when it was my mother that stirred it,' he said, 'it was the Angel of the Left Hand that did the same thing to the Angel of the Right Hand!'

The priest asked no more. Next day he said to the father:

'You'd better let him come with me,' he said, 'and I'd teach him manners.'

'Musha, I'd let him go with anyone if I thought he'd be taught manners.'

Off went the pair of them and the day grew very wet. They were drawing near to a wood and went in to shelter from a shower under a big tree.

'Well,' said the youth, 'did you ever see such a twisted, ugly wood as this?'

'I did not,' said the priest.

There was a fine plant growing at the foot of a tree there.

'Isn't that a grand plant!' said the youth.

'It is indeed,' said the priest.

'If you went over and pulled it,' said he to the priest, 'you might find something under it.'

The priest went over and pulled the plant and when he had pulled it he found a Sacred Host under the plant. He picked it up and was looking at it.

'Put that in your pocket!' said the youth. 'You might need it where you're going tonight!'

They travelled on until it was getting late and they came to a house. It seems that, in those days, there were no big houses, just little mud cabins with a couple of armfuls of heather for doors. They asked for a night's shelter and the man said the place wasn't good enough for them as there was no woman in the house. Fair enough. He let them stay nevertheless and they were chatting around the fire and after supper, if there was a supper:

'Is there any woman in this house?' said the youth.

'No,' said the man of the house. 'If there is, I know nothing about it.'

'There's a woman in the room,' said the youth.

'There isn't!' said the man of the house.

'Get up,' said the youth to the priest, 'and see if there is!'

The priest got up and put his stole round his neck and there was a woman on her two knees in the doorway of the room!

'And now, maybe, you'll find you need what you found today! That woman was at Confession once and she dropped the Sacred Host and didn't bother to pick it up.'

With that she went to Heaven; that was all that had been bothering her.

After that, everything was alright. Next morning they went their way and travelled onwards; they were passing by a river where a man was fishing but had caught nothing until they came along. When they came he caught a huge trout and then caught two others. The youth took the huge trout.

'Let you take this one,' he said to the priest, 'and I'll take this one and let you take that one!' said he to the fisherman.

'Where is your house?' said the youth.

'It's down there,' said the fisherman, 'but if it is, it's not a fit place for the likes of you.'

'Oh, it'll do us till morning!' said the youth.

They boiled potatoes there.

'Open that fish,' said the youth to the woman of the house, 'and we'll eat it.' (This was the priest's fish.)

She opened the priest's fish, and when she did she found a string tied around its heart and on the string was a key, a door-key. She showed it to them.

'Take that, the string and the key,' said the youth to the priest, 'and put it in your pocket! Maybe you might need it tomorrow!'

He did that. When they had eaten next morning, they went out and there was a low hill near the house. They went up there, themselves and the fisherman, and were looking around them. There was a wood on the other side of the river and a fine house between the wood and the river.

'Did you ever see that house before?' said the youth to the fisherman.

'No indeed,' said he.

When they had talked together for a while, the priest and the youth went across the river as far as the house, and when they got there they walked around the house but the doors were shut.

'Maybe you'd find a use for what you got last night,' said the youth, referring to the key.

He took the key from his pocket and unlocked the door. It turned out that the house was a chapel. There was a priest, wearing vestments, on the altar ready to say Mass and the youth asked him what was troubling him.

'Well,' he said, 'I said a Mass once and couldn't get anybody to serve it for me, and that's what's troubling me. I can't leave this place until I get someone to answer my Mass!'

That was made right and when he went to Heaven, the priest and the youth walked around looking at the chapel. Then the youth said to the priest that was with him:

'Go away with you now,' said he, 'and I'll wait here and, wherever you are in the meantime, be back here at the end of a year and a day! Take the key with you,' said he, 'and throw it into the pool where the trout was caught!'

The priest went off and threw the key into the river and travelled on for the space of a year and a day. He remembered to return to the house of the fisherman. The fisherman was fishing and had caught a large trout. They took it home and did the same thing as they had done a year and a day before. The same key was in the trout. They went out the next morning. They saw the same house across the river. The fisherman hadn't seen it from the last time he had been with the priest until the priest came again. The priest crossed the river and when he came to the door, he opened it with the key and the youth was standing at the altar, as he was when he had left him.

They went off and he threw the key in the river again. When they arrived at the next place, there was a huge crowd of priests gathered and they were arguing and fighting with one another; their Bishop was dying. The youth asked them the cause of their strife and they told him.

'It seems to me,' said he, 'that you are a daft crowd, fighting like this! If you took my advice, you'd get a chair and place it there and give each man a minute or two seated in it, and the person sitting there when the Bishop dies would be the new Bishop.'

So they each took it in turn to sit in the chair, and who should be in the chair when the Bishop died but the youth! He was made a Bishop, and when he returned home to his father he was a Bishop.

(b) A very long time ago, there was a Pope who died and nobody could be appointed except a priest towards whom the papal chair moved when he arrived. Things rested so, and every priest and bishop in the world was invited to come so that they might see which priest or bishop God would choose to be Pope. Priests were coming from every quarter but it was all in vain. Time passed by, but there was one curate in Ireland who decided that he would go.

Fair enough, he got himself ready one day and hit the road. He was going and going but in the end he was getting tired and it was almost night. He went in to a little house by the side of the road. There was nobody there except a couple and their only son. They made him very welcome and invited him to sit down. He sat down and asked for shelter till morning, and indeed they gladly offered it to him. Himself and the man of the house began talking and he was asked where he was going and he told him. The wife prepared a grand supper for him and for themselves too, and the poor priest badly needed it. The priest sat at the top of the table and then the father and the son sat at the bottom. Before the priest ate a bite, he said grace before meals and, if he did, the son began laughing at him. The priest told the father to make allowances for him because the father was red with rage and nearly hit him. They ate and drank their fill and when they were ready the priest said grace after meals and the son got a fit of laughing again.

'Oh,' said the father, 'you're very ill-mannered, son, and stop at once or I'll break your neck!'

'Oh,' said the priest, 'leave him alone. Give him his head, he has no sense.'

Everything was alright then until it was time to go to bed and then the priest asked the lad why he had laughed at him when they were eating.

'O, well,' said the lad, 'it wasn't you I was laughing at then, but I'll tell you the reason. When you first said grace, the Angel of the Right Hand and the Angel of the Left Hand began fighting with one another and the Angel of the Right Hand threw the Angel of the Left Hand into the ashes and won the battle. And when you said the grace after meals they did the very same thing and that is why I laughed!'

'You're a good lad,' said the priest, 'go to sleep now; you'll come with me tomorrow.'

Then they all went to sleep and early next day the priest got up. They all had breakfast and when the priest was about to leave he asked the couple if they would let the lad go with him.

'Well,' said the father, 'he's our only child and we don't want to part with him!' And the mother said the same thing.

'I promise you,' said the priest, 'that if you let him come with me, I'll never take my eyes off him and nothing will happen to him till we return again.'

The man didn't like to refuse the priest and for that reason let him go. The lad and the priest went off and they crossed a huge high mountain and at the very top of the mountain there was a clump of nettles.

'Would you ever know, my boy,' said the priest, 'why there's a clump of nettles so high up the mountain?'

'Well,' said the boy, 'there used to be a chapel here once but it has fallen down, but you'll hear more about it later.'

They went on and on and on and when it was really dark they came across the house of a gentleman, deep in the glen. When they came near it:

'We'll stop here for the night,' said the priest. 'It's too late to go any further; but I'll go on ahead to see will they put us up for the night.'

'Before you go in,' said the boy, 'put a mark on your finger so that you won't forget me.'

The priest put the mark on his finger and went in and the poor boy stayed outside. When the priest knocked on the door the gentleman himself came out and brought him into the parlour and very soon sat him down to a meal. But the minute he sat down, he saw the mark on his finger and remembered that he had forgotten about the boy.

'Oh!,' said the priest, 'that's true. I've forgotten you, my poor boy!'

Straight away, he got up and went out to him.

'I knew right well that this would happen,' said the boy, 'and indeed you very nearly forgot all about me!'

The priest brought the boy in and they all sat down to eat; they ate a good meal, as they were very hungry by that time. When they were finished, the gentleman told them that his daughter was dying and asked them would they have any cure for her. The pair of them went to look at her and she was really ill; the priest could do nothing to cure her. The priest asked the boy had he any idea what could be wrong with the girl.

'Well,' said the boy, 'I know exactly what's wrong with her, and I'll tell you! When she first received the Sacred Host, it fell from her hand, and that chapel has fallen down and there's nothing there now but the clump of nettles we saw there today; and there's no cure for her until she receives that same Sacred Host again!'

'We'll go back to that place again in the morning to get it for her,' said the priest.

Fair enough, they stayed in the big house that night. Very early, the next morning, they set out and they didn't stop or delay till they reached the spot on top of the mountain where the clump of nettles was. They searched high up and low down until they found the Communion and took it with them and went back to the big house without delay. When they got to the house, the priest gave her the Communion and she rose up in the bed better than anybody. Once she accepted the Communion she was completely better. When the gentleman saw how well his daughter was and that she was better than ever he was delighted and gave them a huge load of money but the priest refused to take even a penny; but he said to give it to the boy and this was done.

They bade farewell to the people of the house and set off on the road. They didn't stop or delay until they reached Rome. They went to a boarding house and in the morning the priest told the boy to stay in the house until he, himself, came back. The priest then went to the house where all the priests were gathered but to no avail; he was not fated to be Pope either. He met another priest there and they started talking, and our priest told him that he had this poor boy with him since he left home and that he seemed to have knowledge from God and maybe he should bring him into the Pope's apartment as it might turn out that he was to be Pope. The two priests went back to the boy and brought him to the place where all the priests were gathered. They brought in the boy and instantly the chair moved towards him, indicating that it was the boy that was to be the Pope! Everybody present was astonished, but still, he was a saint, he was so devout. The priest who brought him to Rome was very proud of himself because of what he had done. The priest came home then but the boy didn't, since he had entered a higher service. The priest called in to his father on the way home and told him what had happened. The father was sad that the boy hadn't come home but his wife lost her reason when she heard the story, God save us all!

(c) There once was a priest and he was going to Rome to see the Pope. One fine day, he set out and was travelling for a long time. In the end he came to a house on the side of the road and went in. There was nobody home except one boy, a poor scholar, and he had a cake baking in the oven. The priest saluted him and said:

'Well, my lad, that cake is burning.'[26]

'It is indeed,' said the lad, 'and two twos are four.'

'Upon my soul, you know plenty, my lad, and you'll come with me,' said the priest.

'I won't!' said he, 'there's only myself in the house, and I'm a poor scholar without a penny.'

'You needn't worry as long as I have anything,' said the priest. 'I won't deny it to you. But let me ask you a question: When will the raven be able to talk?'

'Well,' said the boy:

'When the eagles abandon the glens,
When the mist leaves the hills,
When the priests lose their greed,
That's when the raven will talk!'

'You're a right one, surely,' said the priest. 'There's no beating you, so you must come with me.'

Fair enough, they went their way and in a short time they came to a big castle. The priest stopped suddenly and said to the boy:

'You stay here while I go in to the castle to see how is the daughter of the gentleman, for she is very ill.'

The boy said he'd wait and the priest went in. The gentleman gave him a warm welcome.

'Messenger from God, you have great power,' he said, 'and, therefore, cure my daughter because all the doctors have failed.'

'Oh, my good sir, I'm awfully sorry that I couldn't do such a thing.'

The priest went out to the boy and told him the story about the girl who was ill.

'I know what ails her,' said the poor scholar. 'The last time she was receiving the Sacred Host, when the priest placed it on her tongue it fell off on to the ground and she did nothing about it; and from that day to this she has been unwell and there's no cure for her until she receives that Sacred Host again.'

'Oh,' said the priest, 'I'd say she might find it hard to find it again.'

'It isn't a bit hard!' said the poor scholar. 'The Sacred Host is in the same spot from that day to this. The chapel has fallen down since and there are only the ruins left but a clump of grass grew on the spot where the Sacred Host fell and it is still there!'

---

26   *Ag dó*, 'burning', is similar in pronunciation to *a dó*, 'two'.

'Maybe we should go there and search for it,' said the priest.

'It's too late to go now,' said the youth, 'we'll wait till morning.'

Sure enough, they took to the road the next morning and found the chapel and searched the clump of grass and found the Sacred Host.

'Now,' said the poor scholar, 'take good care of it and bring it back to the girl who is sick and hear her Confession first and then she can receive the Sacred Host and in a short time she'll be well again.'

They went back to the castle, and at the very moment they brought the Sacred Host, into the house the girl was cured and said to her father:

'Father,' said she, 'since those two men came into the house I'm feeling a lot better.'

The priest heard her confession and gave her the Sacred Host, and very shortly she was as well as ever she was. When the priest was leaving, the gentleman said to wait a moment so that he could give him a little money.

'Thanks very much,' said the priest, 'I've plenty of my own and wouldn't take a penny from you but you can give it to the poor scholar here!'

So he gave him some money and they went off thankfully and in a short time they reached Rome and when they got near the place where the Pope was waiting, the bell rang three times.

'Oh,' said the Pope, 'there's a blessed saint coming from somewhere today!'

When they reached the place, the poor scholar stayed outside and the priest went in.

'Was there anybody else with you when you came?' said the Pope.

'Oh, there was,' said the priest, 'I had a boy with me.'

'Tell him to come in,' said the Pope.

He went out and at that moment the bell rang three more times.

'Oh, it was easy knowing that there was a blessed saint nearby,' said the Pope.

The poor scholar never came home. He went to college to study for the priesthood. First he became a priest, then a bishop and then an archbishop. Sure enough, God had promised the Pope that he would be released by death when his work was done, and the poor scholar ascended to the throne after his death!

28. The Lost Communion

There was a woman once and she lived to be very old. She was one hundred and eighty years old. Everyone was amazed that she was living so long. They were always trying to find out why she was living so long and, in the end, a priest came to her, asking her could she think of any reason why she was left so long in this world and had anything unusual happened to her.

She said that she was receiving Communion long ago and the Communion fell on the ground and she was too ashamed to pick it up or to tell of it. She said where it happened and the priest searched there, in a place with the ruins of an old chapel, overgrown with nettles and docks. He searched until he found the Communion. The old woman's life was over.

29. The Priest Forbidden to Say Mass

There was a curate in the old days and the parish priest forbade him to say Mass. There was a minister in that place, and the parish priest went to him and said that if anybody of his religion came to him looking for help he should refuse him and send him on his way, because he guessed that the curate might go to the minister for help. The parish priest wasn't long in the minister's house when, who should come to the door but the curate. The parish priest hid from him and the curate was admitted.

'Musha, the reason I came to you,' said the curate to the minister, 'is to ask for your help. I had a very good living,' said he, 'but I was deprived of it, and maybe you might be able to help me in some way.'

'I'll help alright,' said the minister, 'but I can't do it at the moment.'

'Things are very bad with me so,' said the curate. 'I had a very good living by the Grace of God,' said he, 'but it was taken from me; and now I came to ask for help from the devil and I got nothing! I don't know what I'm going to do now.'

He went away and the parish priest followed him and overtook him on the road.

'Here is the key of the chapel,' said he, 'and you have permission to say Mass.'

The curate wouldn't accept the key.

'I won't take the key from you!' said he. 'Unless the chapel door opens for me without any key, I'll never say another Mass!'

The curate walked up to the chapel, and the door was shut and locked. But when he came to the door, it opened of its own accord. The parish priest heard the sound of the lock turning and the door opening. All he did was to go to the curate and throw himself on his two knees and beg his pardon.

30. The Priest and the Evil Spirit

In the old days there used to be a ghost, and anybody who went by the place where the ghost appeared, near the shore of a lake, at any time between nightfall and morning, was found dead next morning, killed by the ghost. Now there was this man whose wife was in labour during the night and he had to go looking for a midwife, past the spot frequented by the ghost who killed people. He was afraid to go on his own but he was afraid, on the other hand that, if he didn't go, his wife and the child she was expecting might die. He decided to go for the midwife, for better or for worse. He felt that either he would die if he passed the ghost or his wife and child would die if he didn't. Anyhow, he set out to go for the midwife. When he reached the spot where the ghost used to be seen, the ghost appeared. Now the name that the local people called the ghost was *Petticoat Loose.*

'You must stand there,' said the ghost to the man going for the midwife, 'until I kill you! I'm not going to let anybody pass here, from nightfall till dawn, without killing them!'

'Well,' said the man, 'if you kill me, on this occasion, you'll be killing three people.'

'Why do you say that?' said the ghost

He told him the reason for his journey, and that three people would die if the ghost killed him because his wife, who was on the point of death, and also the unborn child, would die if they did not have the midwife.

'Well, if that's the case, I'll let you past,' said the ghost, 'but you must come back here again so that I can kill you; or I'll come to your house and kill you there if you don't come back here when you have completed your errand.'

The man went his way and found the nurse, and the two of them went to his house. Next day, when all was in order and his wife and child were doing well, he said that he must go back to *Petticoat Loose*; that he had promised that he would come back so that he could kill him, since he had not done so while he was going for the midwife. That was fair enough. He was ready to go to meet the ghost and said that he'd go and tell the priest beforehand what was happening.

'Did you promise him,' said the priest, 'that you'd go back?'

'I did promise,' said the man, 'but you might as well come along with me.'

'I will not,' said the priest, 'there's no obligation on me to go!'

'Well, if you won't come with me,' said the man, 'I'll send *Petticoat Loose* to you!'

'Rather than have that happen,' said the priest, 'I'll come along with you.'

The priest got himself ready. He blessed holy water, and made all the necessary preparations for the occasion, and anything that he thought he might need, his book and all, he brought it with him. Then he and the man went along the road until they came near the spot where the ghost lived and appeared.

'Can you remember the exact place you were standing,' said the priest, 'when you promised to come back there?'

'I remember it well,' said the man.

'Will you stand there now?' said the priest.

'I will,' said the man.

They walked on until they came to the same spot where he promised *Petticoat Loose* that he would come return. Himself and the priest stood on the spot. The priest had a cane and he used it at arm's length to draw a circle around the place where they were standing and then drew the sign of the Cross in the middle of it with the cane. When that was done he scattered holy water in the area and blessed it. Then he called on *Petticoat Loose* to come and collect the man as he had him here with him. The ghost came and told the man to come to him outside the circle the priest had drawn with the cane.

'He won't go out,' said the priest, 'but let you come and get him,' said he. 'This is where he was standing when he promised he would come to you.'

'Don't you know well that I cannot come in there to take him away?' said *Petticoat Loose.*

'That's not really the heart of the matter, at all,' said the priest, 'but what wrong did you do in this life that caused you to be damned?' said the priest.

'I killed a man,' said the ghost.

'That wouldn't damn you!' said the priest

'I killed two people,' said the ghost.

'That wouldn't damn you!' said the priest.

'I killed a man for payment,' said the ghost.

'Oh, that's what damned you, you accursed spirit!' said the priest. 'Away with you,' said he, 'and let nobody ever see you again, anywhere!'

Petticoat Loose vanished in a flash and nobody, man or woman, ever saw him again, and nobody was ever killed in that spot, at night, ever since.

31. The Young Priest

Once upon a time, there was a priest and he had a lot of workmen. One fine summer's day his hay was nearly saved, only to shake it out and make trampcocks. As he was leaving home in the morning he told the men to have the hay all spread and tramped by evening. Indeed, the morning looked very good, and so they got ready and spread out the hay and they had it almost spread by noon. Before it was all spread, it started to rain. One man stood up and said that it would be a great waste to leave the hay spread out in the rain. With that they saw a young priest coming towards them and he came to the ditch. He spoke to them:

'Who owns the field of hay?'

They said it belonged to the parish priest.

'I'm surprised,' said he, 'if it belongs to the parish priest, that he didn't stay at home to keep the day fine for you!'

One of the men said to the young priest that no priest could do that. The priest asked why ever not, and the man said he thought that no one could do that.

'Now,' said he, 'how come you were turned into a sow in this world? I'm sure you'll have to admit that you did an awful lot of wrong in your time?'

'I never did a thing wrong in my life,' said she, 'except that I had an illegitimate child and I killed it and buried it in the garden.'

'Now listen to me,' said he, 'and don't give me that nonsense! You did plenty more, or the Son of God wouldn't turn you into a sow for just killing one child.'

'I had a second illegitimate child,' said she, 'and I killed that, too.'

'The Son of God wouldn't turn you into a sow in this world if you hadn't done more than kill a second child.'

'I didn't do another thing wrong,' said she, 'except that I had a third child and killed it and buried it in the garden.'

'Now,' said the priest, 'I have you! If you promise me now that you won't do anything else out of the way, from this till the Day of Judgment, I'll leave you as a woman.'

She didn't promise him anything, but still and all he left her as she was. He went back to the parish priest and told him what he had done. She, on the other hand, stayed where she was for a very long time without doing any harm to anybody. Then, after a very long time, she started killing and frightening and chasing everybody. When the young priest heard this, he came and began to pray and summoned her to him saying:

'Didn't I leave you here as a woman till the Day of Judgment,' said he, 'telling you not to do anything out of the way? And now you've started off again! This time I'm going to banish you out into the lake, to come and go with the waves till the Day of Judgment!'

32. The Priest and the Protestant

In the old days, a very long time ago, there was a priest and he had a servant-boy. He lived in a remote area and it wasn't convenient for him to go and get his various necessities, so the boy was always sent for his messages. He had to go through an enclosed field where a Protestant was living, and the boy used a shortcut through the field. But the Protestant told him to go back home and not be interfering with him and trampling his ground. So the boy went home and told the priest what the gentleman had said.

'Go back,' said the priest, 'and tell him that you'll be going back and forth there when he is in Hell with his father.'

Fair enough, the boy went and told the gentleman, who said very little but was very annoyed.

A good while afterwards he gathered a big crowd of people to dinner, and sent invitations to ministers from all quarters, and what did he do but ask the priest to the dinner! The priest thought nothing of it but went to the dinner, and what day was it only Friday! A plate of meat was placed in front of everyone at the dinner, including the priest.

'Take away this plate, if you please,' said the priest. 'My religion doesn't permit me to eat meat on a Friday, and I'm not going to eat it.'

'Well, why wouldn't you eat meat on a Friday?' said the gentleman. 'Mothers give milk to their babies on a Friday, and you drink milk on a Friday and it all comes from meat, so why not eat meat?'

'Well, I won't eat it,' said he, 'since I'm not allowed it by my religion, and I'll bet you anything you like that my dog won't eat it either.'

Fair enough. They put the plate of meat in front of the dog; the priest looked at the dog and the dog looked back at him.

'Bear in mind, little dog, that today is Friday.'

The dog moved his head, hither and yon, over the plate and then went and sat down under the chair the priest was sitting on.

'All I ask now,' said the priest, 'is that you bring me two clean plates.'

The servant-girl asked the gentleman if she could do that.

'Do whatever the priest asks you,' he said.

The two plates were brought and the priest placed one in front of him and the other upside down over it, then he raised his hand over it and, at that moment, there were two fine roasted trout on his plate! So they all ate their dinner and were talking back and forth, each man with his own story and, in the end, the Protestant said to the priest:

'What made you say to the servant-boy,' said he, 'that it wouldn't be long till I was in Hell with my father? You must tell me what brought you to say that.'

'If you give me a chance,' said the priest, 'I'll tell you, but I can't do it this instant. Do you have a cock in the house?' said he to the servant-girl.

The girl asked the master if there was a white cock in the house and he said there was.

'Well, bring him to me,' said the priest, 'if you please.'

'May I do that?' said the girl.

'Anything he asks you,' said he, 'do it.'

The white cock was brought in and put standing on the table. The priest began to pray and it wasn't long until the cock crowed. He began to pray again and in another while the cock crowed again. He began to pray again and in another while he crowed again. At that very moment, the gentleman's father put his head up through the floor, and he as black as soot and suffering pain and sorrow!

'Where were you,' said the priest to him, 'when the cock crowed for the first time?'

'I was on the hobs of Hell.'

'Where were you when the cock crowed for the second time?'

'I was getting ready to come here.'

'Well, now,' said the priest, 'there's no point in asking him where he was when the cock crowed for the third time. You can all see that he was here. Good-bye, now. I've been here long enough!'

The priest got up and left. The gentleman then started on his father, trying to get rid of him. All the others tried to hunt him but to no avail! In the end they had to go and get the priest to come back to get rid of him.

'Be sure to get rid of him properly,' they said, 'because the smell from him is stifling us all!'

'Anyone that wants to say anything to him,' said the priest, 'may as well say it now, while you have him!'

Whether they spoke to him or not, I'm not going to tell you now. The priest sent him back where he came from, without doing damage or harm to anyone that saw him. There wasn't a minister, or other such, at the dinner that day that didn't become Catholics, and they all died as Catholics. The old man's appearance frightened the lot of them. God between us and all harm!

The Devil

When the Devil is weak and not very well,
He is more devout in his heart than a monk in his cell;
But when the Devil is strong and well and again,
No need for him the deeds of the monk in the cell.

In pagan times, people gave thanks to the gods for every good thing that came their way and blamed all evil on bad spirits and, particularly, the devil. The Old Testament makes no reference to the devil as the enemy of man, but there are plenty of references in the apocrypha and the New Testament. The fame of the devil, as Satan, increased considerably in the first six hundred years of the Christian era, to judge from contemporary authors and became ever more widespread since then in the folklore of the Western World. There are thousands of stories about the devil in the folklore of Europe. They don't all come from the same tradition, however, and thus lack a certain unity, so that traits attributed to the devil in some stories are the opposite of those in others. These contradictions are quite understandable when one remembers that the devil of folklore is a mixture of the biblical Lucifer, a cloven-hoofed animal or satyr, like Pan, a demon or *jinn* from the Eastern World, or evil spirits in general.

Tales about the devil multiplied quickly in the Middle Ages. Hooves, horns and a tail were added to him. He often appears as a man in Irish oral tales; a black man is the most usual but he can also adopt the appearance of the Virgin Mary, or the Pope, or a priest on occasion. In more recent stories he can adopt the guise of a fine gentleman but this is a big departure from the earlier pattern. In many stories, the devil tries to get control of a living person by making a deceitful promise and the person then has to seek help from a priest to free himself. Sometimes, the person manages to free himself by outsmarting the devil – in those cases the devil is like the stupid giant that featured in older stories. There are very few stories in Ireland about the devil building bridges or other structures, or seeking a living woman for a wife, even though such stories are common enough on the Continent.

Although, more often than not, the devil is portrayed in Irish folklore as an evil spirit in the form of a human being, there are times when he is treated as an object of derision and scorn, particularly in the longer stories. His dwelling-place is always in Hell, not on earth, in these stories; he has a household to rule, servants to look after him and a mother, wife and family around him. Quite often, the old devil makes one of his offspring release his hold on a human and set him free. In such cases, he resembles more an ogre or giant than the opponent of Our Saviour.

33. The Room in Hell

(a) In the old days there was this couple living in a certain place. They weren't long married when they had a son. The son was still very young when the father and mother both died and he was left a poor orphan, with nobody to rear him. When he was five or six years old, he was sitting by the roadside one day. A gentleman came along and asked him who he was. He told him, saying that his parents were dead.

'I've a letter here in my pocket,' said the gentleman, 'and I'll give it to you. Do you see that man ploughing in the field over there?'

'I do,' said the boy.

'Go over to that ploughman and give the letter to him.'

When the gentleman had said that he went away. The boy crossed over the ditch and made his way to the ploughman. When he reached him he gave him the letter. The ploughman opened the letter and read it. It instructed him to bring the boy home with him to his wife and to rear him.

'Well,' said the ploughman to the boy, 'you'll have to wait here till dinnertime.'

At dinnertime the ploughman untackled the horses. Then he took the boy home to his wife.

'Who is this lad,' said the wife, 'or where did you find him?'

He told his wife the story, how the boy had come into the field and given him the letter.

'And when I read the letter,' said the man, 'it instructed me to bring him home and rear him.'

'Isn't it a great wonder,' said his wife, 'that whatever woman had him didn't rear him?'

The man answered:

'The poor lad is an orphan whose father and mother are dead and he has no one to look after him.'

In the end the woman was agreeable to keeping him and rearing him. Things rested so for a good while. The boy started to go to school and grew up to be a young man. One day, as he was walking the land, he made up his mind to go and seek his fortune. When the man came home that evening, he told him what he had in mind and he, in turn, told his wife. They agreed to let him go. Next day, he got ready. He bade a fond farewell to the man and his wife and then went his way. He walked, and walked, all that day until evening came. He came to a big wood. He had nowhere else to seek shelter for the night so he decided to go into the wood. He got up on top of a double wall. He was barely there, looking around him, when he heard the sound of galloping horses coming down the road. There were three horses with three riders on them. When they came near, he stopped them. The horsemen halted their horses and asked him who he was and what he wanted.

He told them that he was a poor scholar who was looking for work. The eldest man said that they were looking for someone like him and that they were three brothers. The oldest said to get up on the horse, behind him. The poor scholar did that. He got up behind the oldest brother. They went off down the road and told him that they were going home. After a while they came to a big house beside the road. The poor scholar asked the brothers who lived in that house.

'That's the house where we were reared,' said the oldest brother. That's where our father and mother lived but, since our father died, nobody could live in that house ever since.'

'Why is that?' said the poor scholar.

'There's a terrible noise,' said the oldest brother, 'there every night after twelve o'clock.'

'Would you allow me to spend tonight in that big house?' said the poor scholar.

The oldest brother said they wouldn't.

'We won't let you, tonight at any rate,' said he. 'You'll come home with us to our own house.'

On they went. They never stopped till they arrived home. They went into another big new house where they were living. They got their supper. Then they went to sleep and slept through the night. When they got up next morning, the poor scholar asked the eldest brother if he would be allowed to spend that night in the other house.

'All right,' said he, 'but we must have everything ready for the night. We must put in fuel, a table and books and such like for you.'

'Alright,' said the poor scholar.

When the evening came they put everything in order for the night. They put down a big turf fire. They placed a table before the fire. They gave him books and he began reading. Everything was grand until twelve o'clock struck. He heard a noise at the top of the house. Then he heard footsteps. Then a woman came down the stairs towards him and he thought she was the finest woman anyone ever laid eyes on. She came up to him and spoke to him. She asked him to marry her and he told her that he would.

'Well,' said she, 'I've pen and paper here with me and I'll have to have it, written in your own blood, that you'll marry me.'

'I'll do that,' said the poor scholar.

With that, he cut his finger, drew a little of his own blood and wrote down on the paper that he was willing to marry this beautiful young woman. When this was done and the young woman had said a few more words, she started to change in appearance. She began to grow ugly, and he never in his life saw anyone as ugly as her. The poor scholar asked her what kind of a person she was.

'I have been sent from Hell,' said she, 'and now I have a hold on you.'

'That's bad enough surely!' said the poor scholar. 'Things could hardly be worse.'

With that, she went out the door and he saw her no more. He took up his book again and began reading. After another while, he heard a noise upstairs again, and he thought he heard three or four men walking. In a short while they came down the stairs carrying a coffin on their shoulders. They made for him. They put the coffin on the table beside him. When they had done that they walked out the door.

'Well,' said the poor scholar, 'whatever is in the coffin, it won't take me long to find out about it!'

With that, he took the lid off the coffin. There was a man inside, and he sat up and spoke to the poor scholar.

'You're the best man I ever met,' said the man, 'and if you're willing, you'll be able to save me.'

'I'll do that,' said the poor scholar.

'Well,' said the man, 'I'm the man that used to live in this big house. And there's a pocketful of sovereigns under the flag here beside the fire. When tomorrow comes, tell my sons about it and tell them too that when I was alive in this world, I evicted a widow and her poor orphans and I never got forgiveness from her since. That is what is troubling me now. And would you also tell my sons that when they get this pot of money to give a good lot of it to the widow and ask her to forgive me for evicting her. Tell them as well, that I cheated certain workmen out of their pay and ask them to make amends to them too.'

'I'll do all that,' said the poor scholar.

With that the man lay back in the coffin and the lid slid over it of its own accord. The four men came in the door. They took the coffin with them up the stairs and he saw them no more. He sat by the fire till morning. At daybreak the three brothers came to him and asked him was he still alive. He said he was. First, he told them about the beautiful girl who came, and the hold she had on him. Then he told them about their father and the pot of sovereigns under the hearth. He told them about the widow that had been evicted from her house. When he had told them everything they started to search. They raised the hearthstone and found the pot of sovereigns. They went to the widow that he had evicted but it was in vain; she wouldn't forgive him. They offered her a pocket full of sovereigns but to no avail. They asked her why.

'Well,' said the widow, 'the day he evicted me and my orphans from the house, I left my case in the hands of God, and are you asking me now to take it from His hands?'

They said no more but went to the parish priest. They brought the priest to her and, in the end she gave in and forgave the old man. Then they went and paid off the workmen. After that, the poor scholar went to see the brothers. They were very thankful to him and gave him a lot of money. Then he told them that he would head off walking again to see could he find a priest or bishop who could break the hold the messenger from Hell had on him. Next morning, he got ready and set out. He made enquiries along the way. He told people what had happened. He met a man on the road and told him his story.

'There isn't a priest in the country that could say or do that except Father Seán Ó Daibhín,' said the man. 'He lives in such and such a parish. And be sure to go to him before he says Mass in the morning and before he sprinkles the holy water on the people.'

The poor scholar thanked the man for his help and went his way. He didn't stop until he came to a gentleman's house that evening. He went in to the gentleman, asking him for a night's lodgings. He was a fine generous gentleman and gave him the night's lodgings. The poor scholar asked him was he going to Mass the next morning. The gentleman said that he was.

'Do you have any transport to take you to Mass?' said the poor scholar.

'I have my own horse and trap and a driver,' said the gentleman.

'Well,' said the poor scholar, 'I'm terribly tired tonight and I'm afraid that I won't wake in time in the morning. Would you ever give me a call and a lift to the chapel?'

'I'll do that,' said the gentleman.

The poor scholar had his supper and went to bed. He slept well all night. Next morning, when the gentleman got up he told the driver to get the trap ready and to take him to Mass. The two of them set off. He was half way between his own house and the chapel when he thought of the poor scholar. He told the driver to stop, and he did. He told him what had happened. He got out of the trap and sent the driver back to the big house. He roused the poor scholar. He got him into the trap and drove him to the chapel. Just as he was going in the door of the chapel the priest was about to sprinkle the holy water on the people. The poor scholar raised his hand and stopped him. He went up to him and told him his story.

'Well,' said the priest, 'you'll have to wait till I have said the Mass and then I'll talk to you.'

When Mass was over, the poor scholar approached the priest once more. He told him what had happened between himself and the messenger from Hell and the hold she had on him.

'And now,' said the poor scholar, 'can you tell me where I'll find the gates of Hell?'

With that, the priest went out and pointed out such and such a hill to the poor scholar. He told him to go to the south of that hill and there he'd find the gates of Hell. The poor scholar thanked him and left. He didn't stop or delay until he arrived at the huge gates of Hell. When he got to the gates he looked inside. Who should he see, sitting inside at one of the fires of Hell, but the girl! With that he rattled the big gates. Very soon the Head Devil came out to him. He asked him what he wanted. He told him about the piece of paper and the hold the girl had on him. The Head Devil went back in and asked the girl to come out and release the hold she had on the man and to give him back the piece of paper.

'I won't go out,' said she.

'If you don't,' said the Head Devil, 'I'll put you in such and such a room.'

'I won't go out,' said she.

'Well,' said the Head Devil, 'if you don't go out and release this man, I'll put you in the room I have specially reserved for Father Seán Ó Daibhín. If you don't go out at once I'll put you in there!'

'Well,' said she, 'rather than go near the room reserved for Father Seán Ó Daibhín, I'll go out and give back the paper to the man and release him.'

With that, she went out. She handed him the paper he had written on and then went back in again. The poor scholar asked the Head Devil what kind of room he had specially reserved for Father Seán Ó Daibhín.

'If you like,' said the Head Devil, 'you can go in as far as the door.'

The poor scholar went as far as the door of the room, but he didn't ask to go any further. He returned to Father Seán Ó Daibhín and told him what had happened and that there was a certain room specially reserved for him in Hell. When the priest had heard this from the poor scholar, he threw off his clothes and said he would have to go away. He threw off his shoes also.

'I'm damned in this life,' said he, 'and I'll have to leave now on account of a major misdeed I did.'

'I'll come along with you,' said the poor scholar.

The pair of them set out and walked, and walked and walked until they came very near to Rome. There was a narrow inlet of the sea near Rome and there was a small boat on the bank. They went to the little boat. Every time the priest tried to enter the boat, it moved away from him.

'I've gone far enough,' said the priest, 'there's no point in me going any further.'

When the poor scholar went to get into the boat, it didn't move at all. So the poor scholar got into the boat.

'Well,' said the priest, 'I'll be satisfied to let any man cut up my body into little pieces and let the birds of the air snap them up!'

When the priest had said that the little boat spoke up:

'Are you prepared to do that?' said the little boat.

'I am,' said the priest.

'Then, if you are,' said the boat, 'you are forgiven already!'

With that, he got into the boat. He went across the narrow strip of water and into Rome. Himself and the poor scholar spent a week there, fasting. Then they turned for home. They came back to the same parish that Father Seán Ó Daibhín had. The poor scholar stayed there for some time with him. Then, one day, he said to the parish priest that he had to go back to the people that reared him. First, he went back to the three brothers. He spent some time with them. Then he told them that he had to go back to see the man and wife that he had spent his early years with. He didn't stop or delay until he reached the town where he was reared. There was no sign of their house there. Grass was growing on the spot where he thought they had lived. He saw a young lad and he called him. He asked the lad where such and such a man lived. The boy told him.

'In that house over there,' he said.

'I thought,' said he, 'that he lived here.'

'That's right,' said the boy, 'but the landlord evicted him and knocked the house down.'

He went over to the house that the boy had pointed out. When he got there, he went in. There was only the woman of the house there. She was very surprised to see such a fine big man coming in. He asked for a night's lodging.

'I'll give it to you alright,' said she, 'but you'll have to sleep by the hearth.'

'Have you anything for supper?' said he.

'I haven't any food in the house,' she said, 'but that little pot of porridge there on the fire for myself and my husband.'

'Well, that's bad enough!' said the poor scholar. 'Do you remember that you once reared such and such a person?'

'Oh, I do, indeed,' said she, 'but I couldn't tell where in the world he is or whether he's alive or dead.'

'Well,' said he, 'I'm that very man.'

She stood up and made him welcome. She sent for food. He gave them a lot of money. He stayed with them a short time and then brought them into town and bought them a new house. They went to live there. He spent a month with them in their new house and then bade them a fond farewell. He went back again to the three brothers. They gave him a big farm and built a new house for him. He went to live there. After a short time he married a local woman and they lived happily ever after.

(b) There was a monk once and the Pope dismissed him. So he lost his living, you see. He was wandering from place to place and, after spending a long time like that, he came to this county. He climbed up to the top of Errigal to do penance for his sins. When he was a while up there, the devil came to tempt him again. The evil one gave him a castle and court on top of that lonely hill, a place where there never was even a barn or a house before that. He coaxed the monk until he went to live there. He told the monk that plenty of food and drink would come to him, that all he'd have to do was sit down and eat it. And 'twas true for him. So the monk was there and nobody knew he was there or how he was. Everybody knew that he had climbed Errigal to do penance, but that was all they knew and the years were going by.

There was a man in Anagaire who had only one son, who was very fond of playing cards. Every night, he was out playing cards, and not only that, he even carried a pack of cards in his pocket with him every night. One night he was coming home from cardplaying, as usual. He met a girl, a redhead, and as nice a girl as ever he saw.

'Have you got any cards?' said she.

'I have, indeed,' said he.

'Let's have a game!' said she.

'What'll we bet?' said he.

'Oh,' said she, 'the bet will be that whoever wins, wins the other.'

They played a game and the red-headed girl won.

'Now,' said she, 'I own you and you'll have to give me proof of that in your own blood.'

He began to laugh and, said he:

'How will I do that?'

'Draw some of your blood with a pin,' said she, 'and write your name on this bit of paper.'

She handed him a paper and he signed it and she put it in her pocket. Then she gave him a document for himself. She put it in the pack of cards and left. He put the pack of cards in his pocket and went off home, very heavy-hearted, trying to figure out what the whole affair was about. He went to bed but didn't wake up next morning at his usual time. His father saw the cards on the windowsill and said to himself when he saw them:

'You're the cause of his trouble and lack of sense!'

Then he saw the paper in the middle of the pack. He took it out and looked at it and instantly realised that it wasn't written by any human hand. He went to the room and woke his son and asked him what kind of writing he had brought the night before.

'It's none of your business,' said the son.

'If that's the way, you won't live in this house with me unless you go to see the priest,' said the father.

The lad went to the priest, but the priest wasn't able to read the writing and, as a result, the son wasn't able to go back to his father. He walked away with the writing in his pocket without any idea of where he was going. As he was passing the foot of Mucais mountain he saw three priests coming down the mountain after a day's hunting. He waited till they came up to him. He handed the writing to the first priest and asked him to read it but he couldn't. The second priest couldn't read it either. He handed it to the third man then, asking him to read it, if he could at all, as he was in a terrible fix on account of it. He looked very closely at it and said that there wasn't a priest in Ireland able to read it excepting one man who had been in college with him whose name was Bráthair Mór Ó Conchúir.

'Where is he now?' said the boy.

'I don't know,' said the priest, 'but maybe you'll meet him some day!'

The boy walked on with a strange feeling in his heart and in his mind. He came to the foot of Errigal and decided that he'd climb the mountain as a sort of penance on himself. So he set out, sometimes walking, sometimes climbing, until he got to the very top. He walked around with nobody to be seen. With that, a lovely castle suddenly appeared. He went to the door, knocked and walked in. There was a big man sitting by the fire looking very comfortable. He stood up and welcomed the boy and asked him to take a seat. He told him that he had been there for seven years and not a living soul had visited him in that time. He sat the boy down to the best of food, and he ate to his heart's content because he hadn't a bite to eat since he left home. Afterwards, when he had finished eating, he pulled over to the fire. The boy thought that the big man had a keen, clever appearance. He handed him the writing and asked him could he make any sense of it. After he had examined the writing for a while he went to a table and wrote a letter.

'Come on out now!' he said. 'This letter contains your writing. Now,' said he, 'wherever this letter goes, follow it until it stops! Whoever you meet there, give him the letter; but keep your ears open in case you might hear something that would be of help to me!'

He threw the letter on the ground and the wind swept it away. The boy followed it any way it went. It went past Loch an tSalainn until it came to a cross-roads, and the boy hurried to the spot, but there was a big hole with stairs going down, down, into it. Down went the letter and the boy after it until at last it stopped at a gate. He knocked at the gate and a big black servant came out. He handed him the letter and he read it. Then he called on the red-headed girl of the card-game to come out but she wouldn't!

'Well,' said he, 'if you make me call you again, I'll throw you into a bed of coals boiling with red lead waiting for the death of Bráthair Mór Ó Conchúir!'

With that, out she came, the same girl that had played cards with the lad on his way home from Anagaire. The black servant handed her the writing and asked her to give her own writing to the boy, which she did. He left then and didn't stop till he was back in the castle on top of An Earagail. Then he told the man in the castle what he had heard and that it frightened him.

'Well,' said he, 'I'm the very man they were talking about. I'm Brother O'Connor. But you did me a great turn to come and help me. Where is the paper with the writing in your own blood?'

The boy gave it to him. He washed it and cleaned it thoroughly and then tore it up into tiny pieces.

'Here, now,' said he, 'throw these back your throat and you'll have your own blood back inside you again.'

He did that.

'Now,' said the brother, 'take out the iron knife, the hatchet and the saw and sharpen them well on that stone outside.'

The boy did as he was told and then the brother came out to him.

'Now,' said he, 'will you take the castle and all that's in it and you can spend your life there?'

'If it was a hundred times better,' said the boy, 'I wouldn't take it!'

'I knew that,' said the brother. 'Wait till I get my vestments and my book that are in a box in the castle!' said he.

He went in and came back with the box. He opened the box and there were his vestments and prayerbook for Mass, safe and sound. He took the stole from the vestments and put it round his neck and, taking the book, said:

'May the grace of God be about us!'

He opened the book and began to read. With that, the castle vanished and there was no trace of it, no more than if it was never there! Then a flash of fire came and burned the whole top of the mountain. He put away the stole and the book and closed the box.

'Now,' said he, 'you'll have to make three pieces of me!'

'Oh,' said the boy, 'I'll never do that!'

'Well, you'll have to,' said the priest. 'What the knife won't cut, the hatchet will and what the hatchet won't cut the saw will. And make sure you bury me where the wild birds can't get at me!'

He threw off his clothes and the boy made three pieces of him as he was told. When he had done this, he began to shake with fright and ran off down the mountain. He hadn't gone far, when he looked back and saw the birds circling the brother. He remembered that he had forgotten something and turned back. When he got back as far as the brother, he found him all in one piece with no sign that he had ever been cut up. The brother let out a snore, and then another and, with the third snore, he woke up!

'Now,' said he to the boy, 'you've saved me! We won't stay here any longer.'

When he had put on his clothes he took the box and they both left the top of An Earagail. They came down and both continued walking among the hills. At last, the brother said:

'I see smoke coming from a house over there in the glen. There's a chapel and graveyard nearby so the house probably belongs to a priest. Let's go over! I must see a priest as I want him to hear my confession.'

They went over to the house and the priest brought them into his room.

'Now,' said the brother, 'let the two of ye go out to the kitchen while I am examining my conscience.'

The priest and the boy were sitting by the fire and it wasn't long until they heard talking coming from the room. They realised that someone was talking to the brother. The priest listened and the conversation was in Latin, but he understood every word that was said. After a while the priest was called and the brother was lying on a long chair, staring at a picture of Our Saviour, hanging on a wall in front of him. The priest realised that it was the picture that had been talking to him. Then the priest heard the brother's confession. When he had given him absolution, he asked him to anoint him as he was going to die. He asked the priest, as a favour, to keep the boy in his house as long as he lived, and that he'd be good company for him any time he was called out at night. He said that it was he who had saved him from the eternal pains of Hell. Then he died and the priest waked and buried him. He kept the boy then until his father heard where he was. One day he came to the priest to see how he was.

The priest told him, from start to finish, all that the boy had done and suffered and that he was supposed to stay with him as long as he was alive.

'Well,' said the father, 'if that's the way it is, he's better off with you than with me, and we'll leave it so.'

And that's my story now.

34. The Promise of Marriage

When I was a youngster, there was this curate in the parish I lived in. And when he was coming home after being ordained – there were no trains running in the days I'm talking about – he met the finest woman he ever saw in his life and fell in love with her. He promised her that he'd give up the priesthood and marry her. She said she wouldn't believe him and wouldn't pay any heed to him unless he wrote it down with his own blood, otherwise she wouldn't believe him. He drew a drop of his blood with a pin, or some such, and wrote with his blood that he'd do it and marry her. When he had done it and looked at her again, he thought that he'd never laid eyes on an uglier woman. She had two legs like you'd see on a cow or a bullock. He decided that it was the devil that was in it. When he came home he was heart-broken and sighing and feeling very bad. He told them what had happened and they advised him to go to the bishop and tell him the story. He went. The bishop told him that he couldn't do a thing for him, that he was afraid that he had been taken by the devil.

There was a young priest in the college and he said that if the Bishop would allow him he would solve his problem. The Bishop said that he would allow it. He put on his Mass vestments and began to pray and very soon he summoned the devil. Then he said to the devil:

'When I was a youngster at home,' said he, 'my father had a cow and brought her to the fair and sold her. Next morning, when he got up, the cow was outside in the field. Nobody came looking for her and, when the next fair day came, he brought her to the fair again and sold her. And the next morning, when he got up again, the cow was outside on the hill. For a third time, he brought her to the fair and sold her. Now, when she was sold and paid for the first man that bought her came up and said:

'That's my cow, that I bought at such and such a fair.'

And then the second man came and said:

'That's my cow, that I bought at such and such a fair.'

'That's my cow,' said the third man, 'I'm after buying her here today, and paid for her.'

'And which of those three men,' said the priest to the devil, 'would you give the cow to?'

'To the first man that bought her,' said the devil.

'Well,' said he to the devil, 'didn't we buy this man before you did? Be off with you now!'

And that's how he banished the devil.

35. The Devil's Son

(a) There was a poor scholar, long ago, travelling around; that was their only way of living in those times, the poor things. He was out one night and, upon my soul, there wasn't a house in sight, and the night was very far advanced and he had his bag of books slung over his shoulder. He went on, the poor man, putting the road behind him, a dirty, ugly, lonely road, and saw the apparition of a tiny withered old person ahead of him, looking terribly old indeed.

'Yerra, bad luck to you,' said the apparition, 'isn't it late you're out!'

'Isn't it late you're out yourself, you devil!' said the poor scholar. 'At least, I'm able to walk, which is more than you are!'

'Oh, be that as it may,' said he, 'you're out far too late!'

'Alright,' said the poor scholar, 'come on and we'll walk together and be company for one another!'

He wasn't a bit lonely or afraid of him, not like many a one you'd meet today! So he started walking along with him but found that he wasn't keeping up with him.

'Can't you walk any better?' asked the poor scholar.

'I can't, said he, 'you have me worn out! Would you ever take me on your back?'

'I will,' said the poor scholar.

He put him up on his back but found he couldn't carry him even two steps.

'Bad cess to you!' said he, 'aren't you the heavy creature, for such an ugly person that hasn't an ounce of flesh on him, by all appearances! You're the devil himself!'

'I am, indeed, the devil,' said he, 'here on your back now.'

'Come down off it then!' said the poor scholar.

'I will not,' said the other.

'You'll come down off my back, whether you like it or not!' said he. 'May whatever put you in my way, take you away again! Get down off my back!'

He got down. He had to.

'Well, now,' said the old person, 'there's no putting fear or fright on you.'

'No, indeed,' said he, 'and you won't do it, anyhow!'

'Now,' said the old person, 'let's go on. Where are you going tonight?'

'There's a lodging-house, a good distance away,' said the poor scholar, 'where I usually stay, where there is only a couple living.'

'Oh, that's exactly where I'm going,' said the devil, 'I'm there every night of the year. I'll bet you they're always fighting?' said he.

'You might be partly right,' said the poor scholar.

'And they've no family,' said the devil.

'None,' said the poor scholar.

'That's where we'll go together tonight,' said the old man, 'and we'll stay there till morning. And nine months from tonight, that woman will have a son, and he'll become a priest. He'll be sent to school and will grow up and become a priest. And when he says his first Mass, all those that he sprinkles with holy water will be mine!' said the devil.

They spent the night at the house. The poor scholar went to sleep and, when he had slept enough, he got up that morning and took down his bag of books and noted in them the date of the night before and of that day too.

'Musha,' said he, 'now I'll know if you're telling the truth!'

So, the poor scholar went off on his own the next day, travelling around, and, upon my soul, when nine months had passed, he came around again and the boy was there!

'That's one part of the signs,' said he. 'It's you that was in it alright! You told me no word of a lie!'

He was around that area again some years later and heard that the son had gone to college to be a priest

'Well,' said he, 'but it was true for you, and it was you that was in it!'

From that day on he was waiting for fear that the new priest would do damage and, upon my soul, he was near the place, not far away at all, when he heard that the boy had been ordained a priest and was due to say his first Mass the next Sunday.

'If I live,' said he, 'I'll be at that Mass!'

And he was, too! He set off and never stopped until he came to the place where the chapel was and he slept there with his bag of books behind him. Then, when the priest turned round with his brush in his hand to sprinkle the holy water:

'Hold your hand, Father,' said he, 'and don't sprinkle the holy water today!'

The priest scowled at him but, all the same, he didn't sprinkle the holy water. When Mass was over:

'Where's the man that stopped me from sprinkling the holy water on the congregation?'

'Here he is, Father,' said the poor scholar.

'And why,' said he, 'did you stop me sprinkling the holy water?'

'Ah, Father,' said he, 'you must excuse me! This is too public a place to tell you, but I'll tell you in private.'

Then he took the priest up to the end of the chapel and the congregation left and he told him the whole story, from start to finish.

'Oh, God help us!' said the priest, 'I'm damned!'

'I don't know,' said the poor scholar. 'Look at the date,' said he, showing him the dates from the first night to the last and the date he went to school and the date he went to college. He had each date written down.

'There it is,' said he, 'I'm afraid I can't help you!'

The priest left, at once, and he never stopped or delayed until he went to Rome to see the Pope, and, when he was nearing Rome, the bell rang in the chapel.

'Go out,' said the Pope. 'There's a damned soul coming to the house! That bell never rang before!'

Your man came in and told him about the dates.

'It seems,' said the Pope, 'that the poor scholar was right. I think he is, and that you are the son of the devil, and are, yourself, a devil now. I must sack you.'

'Oh, God save my soul!' said the priest.

'Right,' said the Pope, 'I'll give you one chance. Go to Mass next Sunday and, at the Consecration, if you don't fall asleep, I'll give you a chance!'

He went, and fell asleep at the Consecration. Again, on the second Sunday, he gave him another chance and he fell asleep.

'Right,' said the Pope on the third Sunday, 'I'll give you another chance!'

He got them to make a vessel with spikes inside it.

'Now,' said he, 'get into that vessel, in the middle of the chapel, in front of all the people, and don't be a bit afraid! I know you won't like it, said he, 'but, when the spikes go through you, you might not fall asleep. I'm giving you this last chance!'

He got in, and fell down on the spikes and fell asleep.

'Oh, you're the devil indeed!' said the Pope. 'Get away from me! Clear off and take off your priest's clothing and go away, as you were before. Go off, now, from place to place, from town to town! Here, take this key, and find the farthest bit of sea you can find and throw the key into it and if you ever find it again,' said he, 'I'll make a priest of you.'

'That's fine!' said he, 'I'll always be a devil!'

Away he went, the poor man, and he was so upset that he couldn't eat any more than would keep body and soul together. And he went out to a headland, like that at Ceann Sléibhe out west there, and remembered the key and threw it over the edge. He got on with his life anyway, the poor man, but not long afterwards he set out for the east, as though he was making for the harbour over there, and he went into a house. It belonged to a fisherman and he asked for lodgings there and, on my soul, didn't he get lodgings from the man of the house. The woman was trying to send him off but the man said to leave the poor man stay, as he wasn't taking up much room; she tried very hard to get him out but the man wouldn't let her. So he stayed there.

'Put a fresh fish to cook for the stranger,' said he.

She was very surly. She wouldn't prepare the fish for him but the man of the house did and when he opened the fish, there was the key in his belly!

'With the help of God,' said he, 'I've got it!'

He didn't wait till morning to get the key. He asked for the key and the fisherman gave it to him and he set off and never, ever, stopped till he arrived in Rome with the key; and when he was nearly at the house again, the bell rang.

'Your man is coming back again,' said the Pope, 'and he has the key!'

He knew who was coming because the bell hadn't rung since. He gave him the key then and he became a priest from that day on.

That's my story, and if there's a word of a lie in it, so be it!

(b) Once upon a time there was a man and his wife and they had one son and anything the father told the son to do he'd say to go and do it himself. They were terribly poor and the father said that he'd have to go and earn some kind of living for his wife and son. He went off and was travelling always until he came to a place where four roads met. There he met a man who asked him where he was going. He said he was going to look for work.

'Wouldn't you think,' said the man, 'that it would be fitter for your son to go looking for work than you!'

'My son,' said the man, 'wouldn't cross the road if I asked him.'

'Throw your stick down there,' said the man, 'and tell your son to come for the stick. He'll refuse to come for the stick. Tell him, once more, to come for the stick,' said he, 'and he'll refuse again. The third turn, tell him that you'll give him a shilling for drink, if he goes for it and I'll bet you that he'll go for your stick!'

The father went back home and sat down. He told his son that he missed his stick at such and such a place and would he please go and get it for him.

'Get away with yourself,' said the son, said he, 'and go for it yourself if you want it.'

'Musha, would you please,' said the father, 'go and look for it for me.'

'I won't go for it,' said the son.

'If you go for it,' said the father, 'I'll give you a shilling for drink.'

'Put it there!' said the son, 'and I'll go for it for you.'

He got the shilling and went off. He kept on going till he came to the place where the stick was lying. The other man was still there. Both of them reached for the stick at the same time.

'That's my father's stick,' said the young lad.

'And I say it's not,' said the other man, 'it's my stick.'

'And I say it isn't,' said he, 'that it's my father's stick and I'm going to get it too!'

'I'll give it to you,' said the other man, 'if you'll carry me to such and such a house.'

'Hop up on my back, then,' said he.

He got him up on his back and went along until they reached the house.

'Down with you now!' said the young lad.

'I can't get down here,' said he, 'you'll have to carry me to the next house.'

They went on and when they came to the second house:

'Get down now,' said the young lad.

'I can't get down here,' said he, 'you'll have to carry me to the next house.'

When they reached the third house, he got down.

'Now,' said the young lad, 'why didn't you get down at the first house?'

'They had thrown out the foot-washing water and the river was between me and the door.'

'And why,' said the lad, 'didn't you get down at the second house?'

'They were saying the rosary,' said he, 'and I didn't want to go in.'

'And why,' said the lad, 'are you going in here?'

'The man and wife in this house are fighting,' said he, 'and falling out with one another and I am allowed go in here till morning. There'll be a young son in this house,' said he, 'after nine months, and he'll be a priest when he's twenty-one, and at that time he'll be saying Mass over in that chapel. And there won't be a man or woman in that chapel who won't be mine if he sprinkles holy water on them!'

The young lad made a note of the date of the day and went off home. Next morning, he travelled on and on until he was forty miles away from that house. There he began to work for a gentleman. He wasn't long there till the daughter of the gentleman fell in love with him. They married and he was then as good as any gentleman ever. He lived there for years and years until it was about a fortnight before the time that the priest was due to say Mass at the chapel. Then he said it was about time he went to see how his father and mother were. He told this to his wife, that he had to go home, that he hadn't seen them for such a length of time, and that he'd like to see how they were. He got a horse and saddle, took plenty of money with him, and off he rode. He never stopped until he arrived home. He went to the door and his mother came out and asked him what he wanted.

'Would you give me a night's lodgings?'

'I certainly wouldn't,' said she, 'for I've no time for the likes of you. You've a much better place of your own.'

'Would you please let me in till morning?' said he.

'I won't,' said she, 'I've no room for you or for your horse either.'

'Did you ever have a son?' said he.

'I did,' said she.

'How is he,' said he.

'I don't know whether he's dead or alive,' said she, 'I haven't seen him for almost twenty-one years.'

'I'm your son,' said he.

'Certainly not,' said she, 'you are joking me.'

'Do you remember the day,' said he, 'that my father sent me for his stick?'

'That happened, alright,' said she, 'but you're still not my son,' said she.

'I am, indeed,' said he, 'and there's a young priest due to say Mass in that chapel over there next Sunday. I've come back to be at the chapel that day.'

He went into the house. From the way he told her all sorts of things she was convinced, in the end, that he was her son. Himself and herself had a great night with the neighbours.

Anyway, he went to the chapel on Sunday and went to the parish priest. He told him not to let the young priest give the first blessing with holy water – that it should be the parish priest who'd sprinkle it – and then they'd see what would happen. The parish priest took the holy water and sprinkled a drop on the young priest and he went in a shower of sparks through the sidewall of the chapel. Then he sprinkled the whole congregation. When that was done the parish priest said that he was the best young man that was ever born in the parish as he had saved the entire congregation. He went home then and afterwards went off to his own place, and he's there ever since.

36. The Devil and the Candle

There was this man, who was a sort of gentleman with plenty of money. He was always drinking and spending, without any interest in religion, but spending his time carousing. One night, he was out travelling, and it was a wild and bitterly cold night and he met a priest with his horse stuck in a bog. He managed to rescue the priest, but the poor horse had drowned. It seems he was a good man, after all. He took pity on the priest and gave him his own horse. The priest was going on a sick call.

Things rested so, and eventually the priest died, but the gentleman continued his drinking and carousing. One day he was out hunting on the day before Christmas. He was hunting, as I said, with his horse and was a long way from home when the horse cast a shoe. Nightfall came and he came to a forge and asked was the blacksmith in. The wife said that he wasn't, he was down in the public house drinking. He went looking for the public house to get the blacksmith but, on the way, he met up with this tall, black, strapping fellow. They spoke to one another and the tall man asked him where he was going. The gentleman told him that he was going to the public house to ask the blacksmith to shoe his horse.

'Yerra,' said the other, 'I'm a blacksmith too and I'll put on the shoe for you.'

'That'll be grand,' said the gentleman.

They went back to the forge and the smith prepared the shoe and fixed it on the horse. The horse was very cross all the time he was working on him.

'Oh,' said the blacksmith, 'every horse is cross when I am shoeing him!'

When the job was done the gentleman offered to pay for it.

'Let's go and have a drink,' said the long black man, the blacksmith.

'Fair enough,' said the gentleman.

They went off and found the public house and it was full. The blacksmith went down the back and I don't know whether he drank or not, but when some of the people had gone he pulled a pack of cards out of his pocket and asked the gentleman would he play a game. He said he would. They went into a back room and the blacksmith had a fine, deep pocket and it wasn't too long before he had won everything from the gentleman. Then he played for his horse, and if he did, by Jove, the blacksmith won the horse too. He was broke then and he was very upset.

'Will you play for yourself now?' said the blacksmith.

The gentleman said he would. They started off and, if they did, the tall black man beat the gentleman.

'I've won you now!' said the blacksmith to the gentleman.

With that, he scowled and began to look very nasty. The gentleman realised that it was the old boy himself, the devil. He was ordering him to get up and come with him and, naturally, the gentleman wasn't inclined to go. Just then, who should come in but the priest that he had rescued a long time before, the priest that was almost drowned, and the gentleman recognised him.

'What's all the commotion about?' said the priest when he heard the noise between them.

'Well,' said the long black man, 'I've won this man here. He wagered himself in a game of cards and now he must come with me!'

There was a stump of a candle lighting on the table, an inch or two long.

'Give him time,' said the priest, 'until this bit of candle is used up.'

He agreed. And if he was there from that day to this, the candle wouldn't be used up or shortened. The old boy had to go off on his own and leave the gentleman after him.

'Take that bit of candle now,' said the priest, 'and put it somewhere that no one will ever find it and take good care that nobody lights it or uses it.'

The gentleman took the candle and he became very religious. He gave up his bad habits. He gave his wealth to build a chapel. The chapel was built and the candle was buried beneath it and it's there still where no one could ever get it. They say that the old boy, the devil, is seen on Christmas Eve walking round the chapel, as if he surmised that the candle is there somewhere but he doesn't know where. He doesn't know everything!

37. Patience Beats Destiny

In the olden days poor scholars used to wander around Ireland. They'd spend, maybe, a week in a house they liked, and oftentimes they'd stay two weeks, but if they didn't like the house, or if it didn't come up to their wishes in respect of lodgings or food, they might only stay the one night.

Anyhow, the story goes that a poor scholar was going the roads one time and came to a farmer's house. He used to call there regularly, any time he was going that way, and usually spent a week or two there. On this occasion a boy was born in the house, the night after he arrived. Before the child was born the scholar went out and he was able to tell from the stars, or maybe it was the moon, the fate that was destined for the child from that day till the day he died. When he came in the child had been born so he sat down and wrote a letter and gave it to the mother of the child. He folded it up small and told the mother to make a small cover for it of cloth, or maybe leather, so that it would never get damp or the writing fade until the boy would be old enough to read the letter for himself.

One day the boy was coming from school, when he was growing up, about ten or twelve years old, and was running home in a hurry when the little bundle on its cord, which was hanging round his neck, came loose and began to hit his face as he ran. He grabbed it and tore at it. He felt it was an encumbrance, hitting him on the mouth and the eyes as he ran quickly. He tore the covering that was on the outside and saw the paper and the writing on it. He took out the paper, and opened it up and began to read it. And what was written on the paper was that on a certain day, month and year Destiny would kill him. When he got home he asked his mother how it came about that it said in the letter that was concealed around his neck for as long as he could remember that it was Destiny that would kill him, and who had written it and why. His mother told him that, on the night he was born, a poor scholar was in the house, that he went out at the time he was being born and that when he came back in again he wrote the letter and gave it to her; and he told her never to let anybody read it until he, himself, was educated enough to be able to read it for himself.

'If that's what's in it,' said his mother, 'God help us! I don't know what we're going to do or how we can save you.'

When his father came home he was told the story. The father told him that he'd make him a house with nothing for walls except glass and the timber frames to hold the glass in place; and nothing in the world would be able to get in at him except his mother, to look after him and prepare his meals.

The years passed until the year came when it was forecast that Destiny would kill the young man. He had grown up by this time and was twenty-one years old. It was the very day that the letter said that Destiny would kill him and he was seated inside his little house, on his chair before a table, reading a book. On looking out through the glass wall of his house, he saw a worm, not very big, climbing up the wooden frame of the window. Then it made a hole and came in through the frame into the house to the very place where he was. It came towards him and he never stirred. It walked on his boots and then up his legs and then up his chest and then went into his mouth and he never raised a hand to stop it. It came out of his mouth and then went up each of his nostrils and still he did nothing. Then it came down out of his nostrils and went into one eye, came out again and went into the other eye and came out again. Then it went into his ears and still he didn't move a hand to stop it. When it had walked and searched every part of his body and he hadn't raised a hand, either to stop or hurry it, it climbed down on to the floor. And became a man.

'You're the best man in the world,' said he. 'Patience has defeated Destiny, and you have beaten me. I am Destiny, and if you had as much as raised a hand against me or impeded me anywhere I went in your body, I'd have killed you. But now Patience has defeated Destiny,' said he, 'and you are the most patient man in the world today. Therefore, you shall have a long life: Destiny will never kill you, for your patience has defeated Destiny.'

38. The Fisherman's Son and the Devil

There was a fisherman long ago, and there often was, and always will be, I suppose! He was fishing from the rocks one day and a man came up to him.

'If you give me,' said he, 'your first-born son, you'll never see a poor day again.'

He kept at him until, in the end, he promised him his first-born son. He came home, and went fishing again the next day, and he was hard put to bring home all the fish he caught. It took him till the middle of the night to bring home his catch. He began to prosper and to escape from poverty. Everything went well for him and he soon had a fine young son to be baptised; but he would have to give away the boy when he was twenty-one.

Now, the way it was in those days, when they were going to school, the masters were referred to as poor scholars. Every pupil would keep the master for a week but the fisherman had no space in his house to put up the poor scholar. But the fisherman's son came home one evening and told his father that he'd better do up the house so that he could bring home the poor scholar and keep him for a week, just like all the other pupils, and he had no intention of being different from all the others.

'I won't!' said the father. 'The house is good enough as it is!'

When the father made the deal with the man who came to him while he was fishing, the man gave him the conditions written on a piece of paper and said to put it away safely. He did put it away safely, and the place he put it was under the rafters. Well, the son came home from school another evening and told the father to knock down the old house. The father refused.

'Well, if you don't knock it down,' said he, 'I'll knock it down myself when I come home from school.'

That's how it turned out. The son came home from school and the father wasn't knocking it down. When he had eaten his food – whatever it was, he ate it – he climbed up on top of the house. He started to throw down the roof sods and laid bare the rafters. When he came to one rafter and began to move it, he found the piece of paper under it. He stopped and read the piece of paper. Then he climbed down off the roof.

'Right, father,' said he, 'I'm leaving you!'

'Where are you going?' asked his mother.

'I'm going,' said he, 'to seek my fortune for myself.'

'Why so?' asked she, 'aren't we well off as we are?'

'I don't care,' said he, 'I must be off!'

He didn't say another word to her. He took to the road and entered service with a man in County Cork. There was already another servant-boy in the household before him and there were girls in the house too, daughters of the farmer. They were keen on the fisherman's son and the other boy didn't like that at all.

'I'm telling you,' said the other boy to the master, 'if you don't send him away, you'll have trouble! That fellow is the devil and you'd better send him out of your house!'

'I don't see anything devilish about him,' said the farmer. 'I see him going about his business, fair and honest, as good as anyone.'

'Well, you'll find out soon enough,' said the boy.

'How could I send him away,' said the farmer, 'without any cause?'

'I'll tell you how to get rid of him,' said the other. 'There's a house to be burned on such and such a hill tomorrow, so give him a letter to take to the hill and say in the letter that it is to be burned, and it will burn!'

'Is that the way it is?' said the farmer.

Anyway, he gave him the letter and the fisherman's son went on his way.

'I'd do anything for you,' said he, 'because it's worth my while to do it for you.'

He went on his way and it was a Sunday morning. He was going past a chapel and people were going to Mass there.

'"Twas ever said,' said the fisherman's son, 'that it's not right to turn your back on the House of God.'

There was a priest in the yard before him as he was going in. He went inside and heard Mass and when he came out the priest was outside. He put his hand in his pocket and gave the shilling he had to the priest. He wasn't three or four yards from the priest when he put his hand in his pocket and there was the shilling in his pocket! He turned back to the priest.

'I'm afraid that I wronged you just now,' said he. 'I never gave you the shilling after all, even though I thought I did. Here it is now!'

He handed it to the priest

'That's two shillings you've given me,' said the priest

He was hardly gone a couple of yards from the priest when he put his hand in his pocket again and there was the shilling once more! He went back to the priest again.

'Ah,' said he, 'I'm making fun of you!'

'You're not,' said the priest, you gave me two shillings.'

'Here's another shilling for you,' said the fisherman's son.

He had hardly left the priest when he saw a man before him with a fire between his two hands. The man walked past him. He followed him on account of the fire between his two hands and he never stopped, the man with the fire between his two hands, until he came to the farmer's house. He followed him there. When he went in the farmer was beating his wife and they were both killing one another and the servant-boy was sitting on a chair in the corner, goading them on.

'There you are now, my bold farmer,' said the fisherman's son, 'you had me down for a devil by this fellow here and now look who's the devil! There's your servant-boy now and look what he has done to you! He has put yourself and your wife quarrelling!'

The farmer came towards the fisherman's son as if to strike him.

'Don't hit me anyhow!' said he. 'It's the truth I'm telling you and I'll prove to you he's a devil!'

He showed him that he was a devil and that he had fire between his two hands.

'As long as water flows and grass grows,' said the fisherman's son to the servant-boy, let me never see you near me, ever again! And don't make trouble between me and anybody else! You made me and the farmer fall out with one another.'

By Jove, that made the farmer pause and he stopped and thought a while and had a change of heart.

'Yerra,' said he to the fisherman's son, 'where would you be going?'

'Oh, I'll be leaving you now,' said he, 'since I never got one with from the first day.'

He went off down the road and night was catching up on him. He came to a house and there was nobody there but the woman of the house and six or seven children, scattered here and there around the house, half-naked. Some were crying and others were lying there, weak with the hunger. He knocked at the door and asked the woman of the house for shelter for the night.

'Musha, *a ghrá gil*,' said she, 'it wouldn't do you any good to let you in, because, if I did, you'd get no peace! The man of the house will come home drunk, and my poor children are without food for three days. He comes home, drunk like that, bringing nothing for them to eat.'

'Don't worry about that!' said he. 'Just let me stay till morning!'

'*A ghrá gil*,' said she, 'he's likely to kill you!'

'Don't worry about that,' said he, 'even if he does!'

He went in and sat down by the fire and told her to waken the children.

'Yerra, musha, what's the point in waking them, they'll only start screaming?'

'Don't worry,' said he, 'just waken them!'

So she woke them up and they started crying, looking for food.

'Have you anything you could give them?' said he.

'Nothing,' said she.

'Search,' said he.

'Oh, I've nothing,' said she.

'Try the cupboard,' said he.

She tried and out came the smell of baking from white bread! She took it to the table and they ate their fill and they were delighted. They had barely eaten it and the children were just asleep when the man of the house came in, blind drunk. Straight away, he went for his wife and attacked her! The fisherman's son got up and told him to behave himself.

'I won't, said he. 'And get out of my house, whoever ordered you to come in here! Get out of my house!'

'I won't, said the fisherman's son, 'I know what's wrong with you. The devil is behind you and I'll show you the devil!'

'The devil is not behind me,' said the man, 'and get out of my house! You've a cheek to talk like that.'

'I'll prove to you that the devil is behind you,' said the fisherman's son, 'by showing him to you!'

He took out his book and read a small bit of it and caused him to see the devil clearly, with the fire between his hands.

'I think I told you before,' said the fisherman's son, 'that no matter where I was, ever, you were not to come there; but here you are, following me, trying to stir up trouble, everywhere I go!'

He drove him out through the sidewall in a shower of sparks. By Jove, the man of the house was terrified. Not one drop of drink remained in him until he became cold sober. Then they couldn't figure out how they'd find somewhere for the fisherman's son to sleep. So they gave him their own bed. He said he'd be all right in the corner, but they wouldn't agree. So they made up their own bed for him. That was a Saturday night, and the next morning was Sunday. The fisherman's son wasn't inclined to get up. A voice spoke above him.

'Get up,' said the voice, 'and it's about time for you! Don't eat or drink anything!'

He got up, as the voice directed and then he didn't know what to do next when he got up. He went to the door and saw a bird outside the door, on the doorstep. The bird moved off and he followed it; the bird made every second hop in front of him until he led him on to the altar. The Mass vestments and other necessities were laid out fresh in the chapel before him. He put on the vestments and said his first Mass there. And from that he went on to be the parish priest there.

That was good and it wasn't bad. His mother and father had fallen into a decline after him. They were left destitute after he left the house and his mother was beyond help, crying and screeching every day, wondering where had her son gone, and he the only one she had. One day, a poor woman came to her at the door asking her for a drink.

'I haven't any,' said she, 'although, time was when I could have given you a drink!'
The poor woman said to her:

'If you knew where your son was, would you go there?'

'I would indeed,' said she, 'if my two legs would carry me there!'

'He's in such and such a place,' said the poor woman, 'and he's a parish priest, and you might as well go there, yourself and himself.'

They went off next morning, herself and himself, and they weren't gone far when a man came up to them.

'Where are you going?' said he.

'We're going to our son,' said they, 'to such and such a place.'

'How do you know where your son is?' said he.

'Oh, an old woman who came to the house to us told us where he was and to go to him,' said the old man.

'Yerra, wasn't this woman only making a fool of you, so that she'd have the house to herself after you?'

'He's right,' said the old woman to the old man. 'She was fooling us!'

They went back to the house again and the old woman was there before them.

'I see you came back!' said she.

'Yes,' said the old man, 'because a man told us that you were fooling us.'

'Don't mind,' she said, 'what that man says! I wasn't fooling you. Go there!'

They went and the same man was there in front of them but wearing different clothes.

'Where are you going?' said he.

'We're going to our son who is in such and such a place,' said the old man.

'Let's go home!' said the old woman.

'I won't,' said the old man. 'You go home, if you want to.'

Well, they went ahead down the road.

'Right,' said the man, 'I'll follow you!'

And he did, too. Shortly before the priest's house there was a deep creek at the side of the sea. If you went near the top of the creek, the creek would suck you down into it.

'Come this way,' said the man, 'this is the road!'

The priest was up in his room and saw the three through his window, making for the creek. He called for his servant-boy.

'Hurry,' said he to the boy, 'and whistle at those down there, for fear they'd go near the creek! They're not far from the creek, whoever they are.'

The boy went out and let a whistle and beckoned to them to come up.

'Yerra,' said the man who was with them, 'he's only joking you!'

'He's not,' said the old man, 'we'll do what the man that's calling to us says, whatever business he has with us.'

'I'll come after you,' said the other man.

And he did, too. They went up to the boy and the priest recognised his father and mother through the window but he didn't recognise the man that was with them at all. He told the servant-girl to call them in. The servant-girl called the three of them in, and all three came in. The priest came down. The priest asked them what they wanted. They said they were going to such and such a place enquiring about their son.

'And would you know your son?' said he.

'We would,' said they, and he talking to them!

Then he told the girl to get them their dinner and the girl prepared the dinner.

'And then,' said the priest to the girl, 'when it's ready, make the Sign of the Cross over it.'

The priest went back to his room. He was sitting in his chair looking out. When the girl had prepared the dinner she made the Sign of the Cross over the food and the man jumped up and went out the door. The priest jumped up out of the room and went to the door.

'Aha, you devil!' he said. 'There you are. Didn't I tell you a long time ago that, as long as grass would grow or water flow, you were not to come near me and yet you are still trying to get your hands on me!'

Then he banished him through the air in a shower of sparks.

The father and mother ate the food and had no idea where they were.

'Come on,' said the old woman when they had eaten the food, 'let's go and see can we find him.'

'Where are you going?' said the priest.

'We're going to our son who is in such and such a place,' said she.

The priest went and called the servant-boy. He told him to go down to the store and bring up a set of clothes for his father and his mother. He got clothes for each, and shoes and everything.

'Now,' said the priest, 'am I not your son and you didn't recognise me!'

'Are you, really?' said the mother.

'I am,' said he. 'Did an old woman call to you at the house?'

'She did,' said the mother. "Twas she who told us you were here and that man that was with us came up to us twice trying to get us to go home.'

'He was the devil,' said the priest. 'And it was the Virgin Mary who came to you to send you to me. Stay here now as long as you live. You'll be near me. I'll get you a house!'

He found them a house there and they're there, as good as ever, ever since. That's my story. If there's a word of a lie in it, then so be it !

39. The Old Hag's Hope

There was a woman around here, once, and she was terribly pious when she was young. You never saw anyone as well mannered, meek and gentle as she was. She was of a very sunny disposition entirely. She was calm and easy-going and pleasant, and no trouble to anyone, but the old people used always say: A pious youngster is the makings of a right old devil! And there's no word of a lie in it. As she was getting on in years, she was getting peevish, difficult, angry and argumentative. She got stuck into anyone who crossed her path. No one escaped her, but no one was to be pitied as much as the poor man who married her. He got it all! She never stopped nagging him. She was harping and talking from morning to night and from night to morning again. Her tongue was going like a windmill. She wasn't too bad while she enjoyed middling health but towards the end she took bad and went to the devil entirely. You couldn't stand her at all, once she began to fail. She had the poor man turned inside out, and, not merely that, but he was ruined by her. All his worldly wealth was spent on her. There was no doctor or quack, far or near, that she ever heard of that she didn't send for. Every man gave her his own kind of remedy but it was no use; they couldn't get her back on her feet. She'd have been dead long ago, if she had been a right person, but it's hard to kill a bad thing, and still, no matter how bad she was, there was nothing wrong with her tongue!

Now there was a beggar in those parts and he had the name of being very knowledgeable. One night he called on this old couple and asked for shelter for the night. The old man said he was very welcome but, in return, he'd have to do his best to find out what was wrong with the old woman. He said he would, indeed, and welcome. He went up to the bed and stared very hard at the old woman and, indeed, it wasn't the good word that was on top of her tongue for him. He stood a while looking sharply at the old woman, while she went on like a windmill, tearing away at him. He listened to her for a good long time. In the end, he shook his head and walked down through the house. The old man asked him what he thought of her.

'Not good,' said he. 'The devil has gone in between two of her ribs and it would be hard to get him out.'

'Can she be cured at all?' said the old man.

'There's no cure for her,' said he, 'but the one cure and that cure is very far away.'

'Tell me what it is,' said the man of the house,'and I'll do my best to get it.'

'There's an aspen tree that grows in Norway,' said he,'and if you got three slivers of that to burn under her nostrils, you'd get rid of the rascal!'

Next morning, a fine strapping neighbour was sent off for the slivers. On the way to the port he met a man who was repairing an old boat. They started to talk and in the course of the conversation the messenger related the errand he was on.

'If I were you,' said the boatman, 'I'd take a short-cut. I'd take a fistful of shavings of this old boat to her and maybe they'd cure her as well as any other shavings you'd find anywhere.'

The messenger took two or three slivers and headed for home. When he thought it was about the time he'd be back from Norway, he went to the old woman, bringing the slivers with him. He told her to sit up. She sat up and he lit the shavings under her nose. When the last of the shavings was almost burned up, the rascal jumped out of her mouth!

'Well, you're not up to much,' said the messenger, 'if the shavings of an old boat can put the run on you!'

'Oh,' said he, 'it wasn't the shavings of the old boat at all, but the hopes of the old hag!'

40. The Devil as a Cat

There was a time, once, when a young priest came out from the college. His father and mother were well off. On that account he felt that it would be no penance on him to stay with his father and mother; that he'd be better to travel round the country like any other poor person and say Mass every Sunday wherever he found himself. He walked away and went everywhere, as well as he could until one misty day. The day came down heavy with mist and rain. He got very hungry. He came near to a castle and said to himself:

'I'll go up to the castle to see would I get anything to eat, or would I get anything at all.'

The maidservant saw him coming and, when she did, she said to her master:

'Oh, there's a Catholic priest coming,' said she, 'and when he comes, what will I do?'

'Oh, bring him in!' said he. 'It's almost dinner-time and bring him in so that he can have his dinner.'

When he knocked on the door the girl came out and asked him to come in, as the master was inviting him in to have his dinner.

'Great!' said the priest.

When he came in it was the gentleman, himself, who was cooking. When he was preparing the meat, there was a black cat there and the cat jumped up on a chair that was nearby. The master carved the first slice of meat and gave it to the cat. Then he carved the rest of the meat and, finally, put it on the plates and gave another slice to the cat. When he gave the second slice to the cat, all the young people, the gentleman's children, sat down together with the priest and the gentleman. When they had eaten their dinner all the young people got up and went off their several ways and the priest and the man of the house stayed in their seats, talking.

'What kind of a cat is that you have?' said the priest to the gentleman.

'Musha, now,' said the master, 'that's a wonderful cat. That's a family cat.'

'That's an interesting word,' said the priest, 'a family cat. How do you mean he's a family cat?'

'Well, I think he belonged to my grandfather, and before that to my great-grandfather and before that again to my great-great-grandfather and now I have him,' said the master.

'Oh,' said the priest, 'a cat as old as that must have some name that he will answer to.'

'Certainly, he has,' said the gentleman.

'Well, call the cat,' said the priest, 'till we see does he come.'

He called the cat but the cat wouldn't come. The priest said to the girl:

'Maybe he'd come to you?'

'He never ate a scrap of food,' said she, 'that I had prepared, and anything I ever offered him, he wouldn't even look at it.'

'Oh, he wouldn't! You're not of his class,' said the priest.

They started to look for the cat but the cat was not to be found, high up or low down. The priest lit a candle and went up in the attic and there was the cat, sitting in the corner. When he saw the candle coming towards him he jumped up and spat at the candle and put it out.

'That's not my loss,' said the priest, 'it's your loss.'

'Well,' said the cat, 'it's because I didn't watch myself that you were able to do that.'

The priest went down, bringing the candle, and spoke to the girl:

'Give me some water,' said he, 'and some salt.'

The girl returned with some kind of vessel and the salt and water; the priest put on his stole and blessed the water and the candle and went up to the cat again. When the cat saw the light of the candle coming towards him, he wasn't able to stand. Then he came down and stood at the feet of the priest. The priest prayed for a while and then said to the cat:

'How long are you here?'

The cat said nothing. The priest prayed for another while.

'How long are you here?'

The cat said nothing.

'How long are you here?' said the priest again, 'I am your master now!'

'I'm here since the time of his great-grandfather.'

'Where is his great-grandfather?'

'I have him.'

'Where is his great-great-grandfather?'

'I have him.'

'What are you waiting for?' said the priest.

'I'm waiting for himself,' said the cat.

'Well, you won't get himself,' said the priest. 'He's too charitable. Are there many changes in the castle since you came here?'

'There are three changes,' said he.

'Well, whatever door you came in,' said the priest, 'that's the door you must go out.'

He put the cat out through the wall in a shower of sparks.

When the priest was leaving the gentleman was standing there.

'Well,' said he, 'you must stay now.'

'I won't,' said he. 'There's no point in a person who's doing penance staying in a place where there's plenty to eat and drink. I'll just keep on going until I find a place like this for myself.'

'Well, if you're ever around these parts again,' said the gentleman, 'don't call in here. You might come in, but you won't find me here. If I stayed here and became a Catholic, everyone in the place would be saying, "There's a turncoat!" They'll never get the chance to say that to me. I'll go away to a foreign island, somewhere nobody ever saw me before, and I'll become a Catholic; and that's the reason why you'll have no business coming here looking for me, but maybe you'd find someone else here.'

41. The Devil in the Form of the Virgin Mary

There were these two priests, a parish priest and his curate, living in a place like Baile an Fheirtéaraigh. Late one night, a sick call came for the parish priest and, believe it or not, he refused it, he wouldn't go. The curate asked him why he wouldn't go. He just said he wouldn't, it was too late for him.

'Are you really not going?' said the curate. 'Then, I'll go.'

The curate went on a saddle horse and found the sick person. He gave her the last rites and he had hardly put the Holy Oils on her when she died. Afterwards he went home. On his way home, he saw three lights coming towards him, and one was very weak by comparison with the other two. He approached them and they approached him. He asked the weak light why it was so weak by comparison with the other two.

'Ah, I only got lay-baptism,' said he. 'That's why I'm so weak.'

'If only I had someone to act as godmother for you,' said the priest, 'I'd act as godfather myself and then I'd baptise you properly.'

'Ah,' said the Virgin Mary, suddenly appearing, 'I'm here!'

Then he baptised him and when he was baptised his light increased until he was as strong as the other two. They were three children of the woman he had prepared for death. They were angels from Heaven, come for their mother who had just died.

'You have done very well now,' said the Virgin Mary, 'and it comes better from you than from the parish priest, for he refused to answer the sick call. And what stopped him from coming to give Extreme Unction was that he thinks that it's me he sees in his room every night; and it's not me at all but the devil, God save us all! who can appear as anybody he chooses.'

Well, the priest went home, and if he did, he went in and the parish priest asked him had he anointed the woman. He said he had and that the sick person had died.

'I'll stay in your room tonight,' said he to the parish priest.

'You won't,' said the parish priest.

'I will,' said the curate.

'You won't!'

'I will!'

Well, he had to let the curate come to his room. They both went to the room and weren't long there when the devil came in and sat on a chair in the form of the Virgin Mary. The curate put on his stole and prayed for a while, then he prayed for a second time, and then he prayed for a third time. He sprinkled holy water and the devil vanished in sparks up the chimney.

'Look at that now,' said he to the parish priest. 'Who had you but the devil in the form of the Virgin Mary? And you thought that it was the Virgin Mary herself!'

That's all.

42. The Devil and the Man with the Scabs

There was a poor man, long ago, and he was covered in scabs. His children all died. His entire body was covered in scabs and his wife spent every day out seeking a drop of milk for him to drink.

One day a poor man came to him looking for alms.

'I've nothing at all I could give you,' said he to the poor man, 'unless I could give you a fistful of scabs.'

'Give me that, even,' said he.

He put up his hand and scraped them off and gave a fistful of scabs to him, and if he did, the poor man found it was a handful of gold he had! The poor man went off then and there was a river ahead of him with stepping stones to cross it. When he had crossed the river, the wife of the man in the house came towards him, carrying a mug of milk which she had got. He asked her where she had been. She said that she had been looking for milk for her poor husband, who was very ill, covered in scabs and confined to bed.

'Yerra,' said he, 'he's not a poor man at all, but a very rich man. Look,' said he, 'I asked him for alms just now, as I came by, and look at the fistful of gold he gave me.'

'Ho! Ho! Indeed,' said she. 'By my body and soul, he wouldn't give me as much as a penny to buy a drop of milk, but making me get it as alms, begging it from the neighbours!'

She took the mug and turned it upside down by the side of the river where there was a whirlpool and lumps of foam floating around, and then she went on home. The house was about forty spade-lengths from the river.

'Did you get anything that would slake my thirst?' the husband asked her.

'I did,' said she, 'and I spilled it out. I met a poor man who told me he asked you for alms and you gave him a fistful of gold! And you wouldn't give me as much as a penny to buy a drop of milk for you!' said she.

Ah, it must have been the devil that was there!' said he. 'I gave him no alms but the alms of some of the scabs on me. Go out again, and bring your mug with you, and go to the place where you spilt the milk!'

She went there, with her mug, and the milk was in the foam, floating in the river where she had spilt it. She put the mug, upside down, on top of the milk and put her hand underneath it, and the milk returned to the mug as it was before she spilt it. From that day on she used to get milk in the foam and they both knew that it was the devil that had passed by.

43. 'My Skin to the Devil!'

Long ago people were given very heavy penances. They were made to spend three nights praying in the corner of the churchyard.

There was this man who hadn't been to confession for a long time and he was ordered to spend three nights in the corner of the churchyard for his penance. The same day a man was buried in that churchyard. During the night he saw this big, black, strapping man coming and digging for the body. In those days many people were buried without coffins. It didn't take him long to get the body over ground. Pulling out a knife, he skinned it and put the skin to one side while he buried the body again. The other man was watching this and he had a stick and a bottle of holy water with him. Using his stick, he pulled the skin towards him and sprinkled holy water round about it while the other man was burying the body. When the body had been buried by the big black man:

'Give me the skin,' said he.

'What are you doing to that person's skin?' said the man with the stick.

'Well,' said the big black man, 'the only bit of that person that I have a claim to is his skin because he had a habit of making an oath while he was alive, "My skin to the devil!"'

'There it is for you!' said the man with the stick.

'You've put a boundary between me and it,' said the big black man.

He let him take it when he asked him who he was. The long black man told him that he was the devil.

Penances

'Praised be the people who suffered the hardship
And now are at ease in the Heavens of grace.'

Long ago penances imposed on sinners were very much more severe than they are today. Things have eased off a lot since those days. There are many tales told about the severe penances performed by monks, voluntarily, or in atonement for particular sins. The following stories are based on those practices.

Whether the sins were big or small, it is usual in these tales for difficult, or almost impossible, penances to be imposed for all of them. The priest, the bishop and even the Pope, in turn, cannot grant forgiveness, so the poor sinner is forced ever farther from home to complete his penance and obtain forgiveness. Occasionally, the person imposes a penance on himself for the sake of a soul in Purgatory.

It would appear that the stories assumed their present form in the Middle Ages. However, it is evident that their origin goes much farther back than that. There is some resemblance to ancient tales where a person is honour-bound and must perform certain feats as a result.

There are a few other stories in other sections of this book in which penances are involved.

44. The Poor Scholar

There was a poor scholar long ago and he lost his position and had to go away. In the evening, he came to the house of a gentleman and asked for lodgings till morning. The gentleman agreed, so he got himself ready and went to sleep. At midnight, the daughter of the gentleman got up and tried to get into the bed with him. He told her that he wasn't having any of that and that he'd never marry. She told him that, if he wouldn't marry her, she'd make life hard for him, and he told her that he wouldn't marry her, no matter what happened to him. When he wouldn't marry her she put a golden cup, belonging to her father, into his bag and waited until he had left next morning; after a while she told the gentleman that the golden cup was missing, taken by the poor scholar.

'Ah, stop,' said he, 'why would he do a thing like that?'

'He did it, anyway,' she said to her father.

The father went and sent his horsemen after him and when they caught up with him they said that he had stolen the golden cup. He told them he hadn't stolen it and that, if he had it, he was guilty and if he hadn't then he was innocent. They searched him and found it in his bag and, having found it, they brought him back to the house. They brought him to court and they got a consent to hang him. The day came for the hanging. The girl asked her father to be allowed to go to the place where he was to be hanged.

'Why not?' said the father.

At one o'clock in the day he was to be hanged. The rope was put round his neck and when it was in place the stage was pulled from under him and the rope broke. The second time, another rope was put round his neck and the stage was pulled and the rope broke again.

'There isn't a rope in Ballinrobe today,' said he, 'that can hang me.'

'If there isn't,' said the hangman, 'there's a chain that will hang you.'

By Jove, they found the chain and put soap and all sorts on it to make it slippery. When it was good and slippery, they put his head in it, but the chain wouldn't run on his neck. Then he said that there wasn't a chain in Ballinrobe that would hang him, because he was an innocent man.

'But,' said he, 'try her head in it and see will it run.'

By Jove, they agreed to try her head in the chain and the moment the stage was pulled she was hanged. He was allowed go free. He went on and on for a world of time and when he stopped he went to confession. When he went to the priest and told him his sins, by Jove, the priest wouldn't give him absolution until he had bought sixpence worth of pins and embarked on a ship and tossed them overboard, one at a time, until they were all gone, and then got them all back again and brought back to the priest. Then he would grant him forgiveness.

The poor man set off and kept on going, throwing out a pin every inch of the way until he had thrown out the last one and the ship turned back for port. When he came ashore, he said that he wouldn't go any further until he had had a good rest. As night was falling, he stopped at the edge of a wood. He saw a light in the distance, and went towards it and when he reached the house he found a little girl and a young lad there. He asked for a night's lodgings and sat down and after a while he asked them how they made their living. They told him they had no means of livelihood but that the Son of God came every day at twelve o'clock and brought them sufficient for their needs until twelve o'clock the next day.

'Do you think,' said he, 'that He'll come tomorrow?'

'I'm certain he'll come,' said they.

'If He's coming,' said he, 'would you mind if I stayed to see?'

'You can,' said the girl, 'and welcome.'

He stayed there till the next day. But, next day, when the Son of God came, he was asleep and never noticed the Son of God till He was gone again. When He was gone, he awoke and asked the girl had He come yet. She said that He had come and gone while he was asleep.

'Do you think He'll come tomorrow?' said he.

'I'm certain He'll come,' said the little girl.

'Well, if He comes tomorrow, will you wake me if I fall asleep?'

'I will,' said the little girl.

At twelve o'clock the next day a terrible tiredness came over him and he fell asleep. The Son of God came and the little girl tried to waken him but couldn't. When the Son of God had gone again, that was the time he woke and asked the little girl had He come yet.

'Oh, He's gone again,' said the little girl.

'Ah,' said he, 'why didn't you waken me?'

'I was pushing you and tapping you,' said she, 'and trying every way I could to waken you but there was no way I could waken you.'

'Oh,' said he, 'may God help me! I'm in terrible sin! Do you think He'll come again tomorrow?'

'He will,' said the little girl.

Next morning he got up and found a hatchet and went out cutting thorn-bushes until around eleven o'clock and brought them in to the corner. When he had placed them in the corner and it was getting near twelve o'clock, he stripped down to his skin and threw himself on to the thorns in his bare skin.

Who should come in but the Son of God.

'Oh,' said he, 'young man over there, get out of that! You've suffered enough for your sins. Who gave you such a penance?' said the Son of God.

'Such and such a priest told me that I hadn't a hope of forgiveness ever until I had gathered up the sixpence worth of pins again and brought them back to him.'

'Away with you now,' said the Son of God, 'and keep going again tomorrow until you arrive back at the same port that you sailed from. And here are eleven pence for you, in case you wouldn't have it yourself, and buy the first fish you see from the woman there. She'll ask you for eleven pence for it and don't do any bargaining but give it to her at once. Take your penknife and open up the fish and there isn't one of the pins that you won't find in its belly. Then take them back,' said He, 'to the priest who gave you that penance. And he'll grant you absolution and tell you that you are forgiven. But may God help the priest who gave you that penance!'

45. The Two Sons

There was this couple long ago and they had two sons and there was no day since they were born that the parents weren't in disagreement. They were always fighting and throwing things at one another and beating each other. When the two sons grew up they took such a dislike to their father and mother that they both said they might as well leave and never come back. One day they went off and walked away until they came to a crossroads, and the two decided that they might as well separate and each one should go his own way. They went away and the elder son wasn't long travelling when he met a gentleman. The gentleman spoke to him and asked where he was going. The young man said that he was looking for a good master. The gentleman told him that he was on the look out for a good servant-boy and it was lucky that he had found one at last.

Himself and the gentleman went home to his place and he worked for him for a long time. When himself and his brother were parting, they promised one another that they'd meet again in seven years. When he had been working for the gentleman for almost seven years, he told the gentleman that he'd like to go looking for his brother, that he hadn't seen him for seven years, nor his father or mother either. When he was about to leave the gentleman asked him what pay he wanted. He told the gentleman that he'd accept any pay he was offered, that he wasn't going to haggle, but that anything he chose to give him, he'd accept. The gentleman then said that he might as well stay on for another seven years. He was satisfied with that and agreed to stay on for another seven years. When those seven years were up, he was going to leave again and he was told that he might as well stay for a third seven years. So he stayed until he had spent twenty-one years there. When that time was up he was going to leave and the gentleman said that he must pay him well and he'd give him whatever in the world he'd like. He asked the boy would he like to be a magician and the boy said that he would, that there was nothing in the world he'd like better. So he brought him to a place where they taught magic and he was there a long time until he had learned the art of magic. When he came back to the gentleman, he started out for home and when he got to the crossroads there was no sign of his brother. He walked and walked until he arrived at the place where his father and mother lived and, when he came to the place where their house had been, the house had fallen down and there was no sign of them. He remembered that, when he was a youth, there was a spring-well near the house and that everyone in the village used to come drawing water from it; so he decided he'd sit by the well for a while and it wouldn't be long before someone came for water who could tell him where they were.

He wasn't long sitting there when he saw a young girl coming to the well, and he asked her had she any news about the pair who used to live here long ago. She said that she didn't know them but had heard the old people talking about them and that the old man had died a long time ago and that his wife was being waked in a house in the village that day and would be buried tomorrow. He asked her would she show him the house and she said she would, and welcome. He went along with her to the house and, when he went in, nobody there recognised him. He asked the people in the house would they leave for half an hour. The people went out and, when they were gone, he went down to the room where she was laid out and spent some time praying over her. It wasn't long until she rose up, as alive as ever she was. He spoke to her and asked her where she was now and where was his father. She told him they were both in Hell and were no more pulling together than they had been in this world, but fighting and killing one another as they had been when they were alive. He asked her was there anything in the world that could get them out of there and she said that there was only one thing, but that he wouldn't be able to do it. He asked her what it was and that he'd try it anyhow. She told him that he'd have to go for seven years without shaving and not sleep two nights in the same house and when he would go to sleep that it would have to be on a handful of straw between the two outside doors.

He went away and the first poor person he met, he exchanged clothes with him and he went from house to house until the seven years were up except for one night. He came to a big house at the side of the road and it was Christmas Eve, and when he got to the house he knocked at the door. There was a father, mother and daughter living in the house. The father had gone out shopping or something and when the girl saw him – for it was she who answered the door – she wouldn't let him in. He said that she should let him in for the night and she said that she wouldn't and to get out of her sight quickly! All he did was to go out to a corner of the garden and lie down there. It was a night of snow and rain. When the man of the house was coming home he saw this man lying in a corner of the garden and when he went in he asked the girl and her mother what sort of a man was there. They said that he was a man who had called earlier asking for shelter and that they had hunted him away from the house. He told them that they had done wrong, that it was Christmas Eve and that it was wrong to turn anyone away on that night. He turned around and went out to the man and brought him in and began to make up a bed for him. But he said that he wouldn't get a wink of sleep on any bed but that he'd sleep on a handful of straw between the two doors. The man got him the handful of straw and he lay down on it and slept on the floor.

When the man of the house got up next morning he found the man so well-dressed that he hardly recognised him. He asked him was he going to Mass and the man of the house said that he was. He said that he would go with him to Mass. They went to the chapel and when Mass was over the priest noticed the stranger and came to talk with him after Mass. When he came down, who should it be but his brother that he hadn't seen for twenty-one years and he was now a priest! And while they were talking together, two white doves came down and stood, one on each of his shoulders, and after a while they saw them going up out of their sight into Heaven. They were the souls of their father and mother. He had saved them.

The blessing of Almighty God and of His Church be on the souls of the dead!

46. The Man who Beat his Father

There was a man of the name of Ó Sé living in Fionntrá and he hadn't a pick of land. He was a poor man who went from place to place earning his pay. He used to go visiting every night in Baile an Chalaidh and in Baile Eaglaise and a lad who used to go visiting with him every night said:

'Wait for a year,' said he, 'and I'll go with you,' for he was always saying he'd go to America if he had the fare saved up.

'Fair enough,' said Ó Sé, 'I'll wait two years, if you'll come with me.'

'I'll come with you, for sure,' said he.

When the two years were up, they went, the pair of them, down to Queenstown on a jingle, and when they got there they found lodgings. They went into a tavern there and spent a while talking, the man from Fionntrá and the man from Baile an Chalaidh. When the servant-girl, who was working for the sister of the tavern-keeper, came in, she saw Ó Sé and lost her mind completely with love for him, he was such a fine man. The girl had come looking for soap and when she got the soap she just couldn't leave for looking and looking at the lovely man. When she got back her mistress asked her what kept her so long and she said that she just couldn't come because there was the finest man anyone ever laid eyes on up in the pub.

'And,' said she, 'I just couldn't take my eyes off him.'

She kept telling her mistress about him like that.

'Well,' said the mistress, 'if he's as fine as all that, up with you and ask him to come down here till I see him.'

She herself was a widow. She was a sister of the publican and had a grocery shop herself, selling meal and flour and anything else she could. She told the girl to bring her brother down too.

'The woman in the shop wants you,' said the girl when she went in again. 'If the three of you care to go down, she'll stand you a drink.'

'*Mo ghrá, mo shúil*,' said the brother. 'My sister is a fine woman and I'll bet that she has seen Ó Sé. Let's go!'

'I'm not going there, anyhow,' said Ó Sé.

The other two were going and Ó Sé was set to stay but in the end it was put up to him and he went down too. The minute he went in she sent for a pint of whiskey and put it on the table.

'There, now,' said her brother to the widow, 'if it's a fine man you're after, you've got him now, as fine a man as ever an eye was laid on.'

'I'm sure he is,' said she. 'If he stays with me now, I'll marry him as he stands and he'll inherit all I have, my store and my houses.'

Ó Sé said he wouldn't. They kept at him and at him until in the end he changed his mind and he said, at last, that he would. His pal went off the next morning and Ó Sé stayed on and married the widow. He was spending his life with her while the man from Baile an Chalaidh went to America. He never dropped a line to his father or mother and they were amazed that their son didn't write to them. A year passed and still the son never wrote to them. So his father set out for Baile an Chalaidh to the relatives of his pal and asked them was it long since they had a letter.

'No,' they said, 'it's not a fortnight since we had one.'

'Have you any idea is my son alive at all?' said the father.

'He's alive, alright,' said they. 'He's married down in Queenstown.'

'Musha, that's news to me,' said the old man. 'That man must be gone to the next world, because he'd have written to me if he was alive.'

Well, he went home and he told his wife that he had news of their son and that he was alive and where he was living. The wife said he was surely dead. The husband said that he'd find out before long; that he was going to walk to the place to find out if he was there, as they were saying.

'Prepare some food for me,' said he to his wife.

'I'll do that,' said she.

He put the food in a knapsack and took his stick in his hand and started to walk, sleeping the odd night here and there till he arrived in Queenstown. He had no idea where his son lived there. He met a policeman and asked him was such and such a man living in the town, a man of the name of Ó Sé.

'What do you want him for?' said the policeman.

'He's my son, if that is enough for him,' said the old man with his knapsack on his shoulder.

'If you're any connection of that man,' said the policeman, 'you'll never again have to look for charity. He's the richest man in this town. 'I'll show you the house, and welcome.'

He went along with him looking for the house and directed the poor man to Ó Sé's. He made his way in towards the house. It was a summer's morning and the son was going up to his sunroom. When he saw his father coming as a beggar to the door he jumped up and came out and grabbed a whip that was hanging by the door. He ran out to his father and caught him by the arm and gave him four lashes of the whip as hard as ever he could draw.

'Go now,' he said, 'and never again come to your son's house in the form of a beggar. Be off with yourself!'

'Since you've done that,' said the father, 'remember that it will be many a long day before you see me again. That's all the thanks I get for rearing you since you were a child!'

He went off and never stopped till he got back to Fionntrá again and left his son where he was. Things rested so and he was very sad and downcast at what his son had done to him. Around Michaelmas, his son was due to have the stations. The two priests were hearing confessions on either side of the fire, with the people further down the room, and the priest noticed that Ó Sé was letting every other man go ahead of him. He got up from the confessional chair and asked him was he going to confession. He said he was.

'I'm watching you all morning,' said the priest, 'letting everyone else go before you, so what have you done that you can't take your turn.'

'I won't come,' said Ó Sé, 'till you've heard all the others.'

'Fair enough,' said the priest.

When the priest had heard all the others he asked him would he like to go down to the room to make his confession and he said he would. He brought him up to the room, or maybe it was down, and asked him what he had done wrong. So he told him about his father.

'I can't give you absolution,' said the priest. 'You're chained to the devil. Think of the father who reared you from childhood and the way you repaid him when he came to visit you! The devil has you on a chain and you've fallen into mortal sin. Eat your meal with us now and as soon as you've finished go to the bishop. As soon as we leave, you should leave too, for if you don't you'll lose your soul!'

'I'll do that,' said Ó Sé.

They had their meal. Ó Sé sat at the end of the table with the two priests beside him, counselling him. His wife never knew that it was his father he had beaten until that day, so she said:

'If I had only known,' said she, 'that it was your father that was outside that day, it would have been a very long time before I'd have let you hit him! I'd have treated your father a lot better than that since it was the first time he came to visit me.'

He took a fistful of money when he had finished eating and away with him, walking, and never stopped till he arrived at the bishop. He made his confession to him but he got no absolution from the bishop.

'Go as fast as ever you can,' said the bishop, 'and find the Pope. Your soul is damned. You've fallen into mortal sin on account of what you did to your father.'

'Oh, God save my soul!' said Ó Sé.

That put the fear of death in him. He travelled on with plenty of money in his pocket and not wanting for anything and never stopped or delayed until he reached the Pope. And there wasn't a single bell in the Pope's monastery that wasn't ringing as Ó Sé was approaching the door.

'There's a man coming to the house who is either a saint, a sinner or damned,' said the Pope. 'There isn't a bell in the monastery that's not ringing.'

He went to the door. He was let in and, the very minute he was inside, the head-man came up to him and asked him what he wanted and who he was. He said that he was a man who wanted to confess to the Pope and he was told that, if that was what he wanted, that was what he'd get, and welcome. The Pope came out to him and asked how many priests and bishops there were between there and the place he came from that could give him absolution, besides himself, and he told him in his confession what he had done.

'I couldn't give you absolution or remission of your sins, no more than any of the others,' said the Pope. 'You are in the clutches of the devil on account of what you did to your father and you're a great pity, such a young man to be damned in the next life, out of pure ignorance. After all your journey, I can't give you absolution or Holy Communion,' said he, 'but there's to be an ordination in my own monastery next Monday and a newly ordained priest has more power than I to give absolution and Holy Communion to the first person that speaks to him after ordination. I'll give you food, drink and a bed from now till Monday and I'll put you in the way of being the first person to speak to him after ordination. There are twelve people suffering from paralysis waiting on their knees for a newly ordained priest, hoping he'll cure them. I'll slip you in ahead of them all.'

'Thank you very much,' said Ó Sé.

He put him in a room and while he was in the room he never stopped praying for two or three days until Monday came. The Pope came in to him on Sunday evening and put him at the doorway where the newly ordained priest would come out.

'Get down on your two knees there before him,' said the Pope, 'and ask for forgiveness.'

'Right,' said Ó Sé.

When the ordination was over, the young priest came out and, when he opened the door, there was Ó Sé on his two knees before him.

'What are you doing there?' said the priest

'If you please, I want absolution and Holy Communion from you.'

'I couldn't have given it before this,' said the new priest, 'but I can and will give it now, and welcome.'

He brought him into his room and gave him absolution and Holy Communion.

'If you promise me this,' said the priest to him during confession, 'I'll give you Holy Communion afterwards and, if you won't promise, I won't.'

'Anything you ask me to do, I'll do,' said Ó Sé, 'I'll do it with a glad heart to make atonement for my sins.'

'I'll give you absolution and Holy Communion so,' said the priest.

And so he did.

'Now,' said the priest, 'there's many a crossroads between Queenstown and Rome.'

'There are, indeed,' said Ó Sé.

'The first crossroads you come to,' said the priest, 'you'll meet a serpent, letting dreadful screeches out of her and you must lick her three times before you go past her. At the second crossroads, you'll meet another that's seven times bigger and you'll have to lick her three times before you go past. At the third crossroads you'll meet another, seven times bigger than the other two put together and you must lick her three times. Until you've done that,' said he, 'you won't have made atonement for your mortal sin.'

'I promise you I'll do that,' said Ó Sé.

So he took the road towards Queenstown, having got forgiveness for his sins and reached agreement with the priest. He wasn't long gone till he came to a crossroads, and there she was before him, a serpent, making dreadful screeches as if to eat him.

'I don't like you at all,' said Ó Sé, 'and I'd be as well off to keep clear of you!'

He hopped into the field and came out at the other side of the field. He left the crossroads behind him and didn't go near the serpent. Away with him down the road and at the next crossroads he met a serpent that was seven times bigger than the last.

'The other one was grand, compared to you!' said Ó Sé. 'I'd better get away from you fast, for fear you'd eat me alive.'

He went in to the corner of the field and out the other side and didn't go near her. When he got to the third one, he was afraid that she'd eat him alive.

'Whatever about the other two,' said he, 'you're the master of them all! I'd better flee.'

He sneaked past her.

'That's great!' said he. 'I've got past the three of them, but to no avail. I might as well go back again, in the name of God, and do what the holy man told me to do.'

He went back by short cuts to the first of the three and went up to her and licked her three times and she didn't stir.

'God help us!' said he, 'I lost more than I gained the first time!'

He licked the second one three times and she never stirred.

'That's better again,' said he, 'I almost lost it.'

He licked the third one three times and she made a knot around his neck. He put his hand in his pocket and drew out a silk shawl and covered the serpent. He felt himself grow very heavy, very weak, almost unconscious. He turned back towards the town the Pope was in and he was barely able to walk. The first house he met in the town, he went in. He asked the woman of the house if she kept lodgers and she said she did.

'Are you looking for lodgings?' she said.

'I am,' said he. 'I'm very tired. I've made a long journey since morning. Show me my bed and my room.'

'Alright,' said she.

She brought him down to a room with a window overlooking the street.

'That's your room,' she said, 'and your bed, and here's a lock and key for when you want to be by yourself.'

'I think I'll lie down,' said Ó Sé. 'I'm getting very tired.'

'You may do so,' said the woman.

He lay down on the bed. The landlady had a maid and, later on in the day, whatever look she gave, she saw that the room was as dark as if there was no window in it at all. She tried to open it, and when she looked in she let a scream.

'Yerra, what's wrong with you, you foolish girl,' said the mistress.

'Oh, Virgin Blest,' said the maid, 'the room that was as bright as the sun is dark, so dark that you couldn't see a thing in it!'

'Yerra, whist!' said the mistress.

'Oh, come down,' said the girl, 'till you see for yourself!'

She went down and as soon as the mistress saw the room:

'Go,' said she, 'and bring the priest quickly.'

The maid went off. The priest was in that same town and she told him to come to such and such a house. The priest went, and he was the same priest that had been ordained the day before. When he came he asked who was sick or ailing there. The mistress said that there was nobody sick or ailing but that this stranger was down in the room and that she had no room!

'Show me the room,' said the priest.

She showed him. The priest took out his book.

There was nothing in the room but black flies – the room was full up to the top with black flies! He read from his book until every one of them flew out the door of the room and the room was as bright as the sun. The priest went in and there was nothing in the bed, not a bit of flesh and blood, that hadn't been devoured, except for his four bones.

'Well, now,' said the priest. 'That's alright! I've saved his soul but his flesh and blood have been devoured by the devils from Hell.'

They buried him, and Ó Sé never returned home from there.

And that's the story as I heard it.

47. The Man who Divided the Corpse

A long, long, time ago, there was a man living down at the other end of this parish in a place they call Bréachmhaigh. He married a woman from a place down near Dún Fionnachaidh. When his wife died the man wanted her buried at the end of the parish where his own people were buried and the wife's people wanted her buried down near Dún Fionnachaidh, with her own people. When the funeral got to the crossroads, the wife's people tried to bring her up and the husband's people tried to bring her down to their own graveyard. They went on arguing until they came to the main road and in the end they left the coffin down in the middle of the road. There was a man named Mac Fhionnlaoich living in the big house, which is now a ruin outside the town, in a place they call Fochair. He was a sort of chief who had great power. He came down to them and they let him decide what was the right thing to do. Both parties were completely divided and his decision was that the only thing he could do was to divide the corpse between them and give half to each. With that, he took out his sword and made two halves of the body. The wife's people took away their half of the body and buried it in the graveyard down at Dún Fionnachaidh and the man's people took their half of the body and buried it in their own graveyard at the top of the parish.

Mac Fhionnlaoich began to be troubled about what he had done, dividing the body, and he couldn't sleep at night, getting up and walking around without rest, night or day. He went round from place to place asking advice from the Church about what was the right thing to do or what penance should be imposed on him for what he had done. He was going round like this and he was a rich man with plenty of money. He went up to Donegal, to where the monastery was and where the monks were living and the advice that a monk there gave him was that he'd have to build three churches and when he had completed the third he'd get forgiveness.

'Now what kind of sign will I get when that is done,' Mac Fhionnlaoich asked, 'to show that I've completed my penance.'

'Well, when you have completed the three churches, lie back on your back and spread out your two hands and you'll see what happens. If you are pardoned, a bird will come and build a nest in your right hand and lay three eggs there and hatch three young birds. Then when the three young birds are fully fledged they'll fly away, and then you'll know that you've completed your penance! Each of the three churches must be built in a town whose name begins with 'Cluain', and you must travel the country to find out where those towns are without ever asking anybody where the towns are.'

Fair enough, there was a town down here that they called Cluain Beag and he built a church there. He built another church near Dún Fionnachaidh at a place called Cluain Dá Chorcach (Clondahorky). He had to search for a third Cluain and he travelled the country to see could he find a third Cluain. He had plenty of money to build a third church so he went down to Inishowen and there's a town there called Cluain Maine (Clonmany).

He said to himself:

'I'm on the way to finding the third Cluain now.'

A boy told him that there were monks living in Cluain Maine and that he was bringing sacks of potatoes to them; that it was the custom of the neighbours to give sacks of potatoes to the monks for their upkeep. He followed the boy until he came to Cluain Maine and so he found out where the place where the third Cluain was and he built a church there. He came back then to the first church he had built at Cluain Beag, half a mile from An Craoslach, and lay down on his back and fell asleep. The bird came then and laid the eggs on his hand and hatched them and when Mac Fhionnlaoich woke, the little birds had flown. He knew then that God had pardoned him.

48. The Boy who Killed the Girl
Once upon a time there was a boy and a girl and they were very great with one another but then there was a falling out between them. They had a small cabin in a wood where they lived and the boy was tempted and killed the girl and then

knocked the hut down on top of her. Afterwards he was full of remorse. He had a brother, a priest, so he went to the brother and told him the story.

'Oh! you're damned,' said the brother, 'and there's no forgiveness for you unless the Pope gives it!'

He went to the Pope and the Pope told him that he couldn't grant forgiveness for his crimes, they were too great.

'Is there a saint in the world,' said he, 'who could grant me forgiveness?'

'No,' said the Pope, 'but there are three saints at such and such a place in the South Pole,' said he, 'and if they can't grant you forgiveness, I don't know anyone else that can.'

'That's very far away!'

He went to his father and told him the story and said that he'd have to go and get a vessel and the cost of the trip would be a thousand pounds. The father had to gather a thousand pounds for him. He set off and went to the South Pole. The saints were some distance apart. He went to the first saint and, if he did, he was given a night's shelter but there was no food sent from Heaven.

'There's no food coming to me,' said the saint, 'and if you're the cause of it, go outside the house and God will send the food to me!'

He went outside and the food came. The traveller got some food from him and the other man asked as he was giving the food:

'What happened you or why didn't the food come to me?'

'I did such and such a thing and I came seeking forgiveness.'

'Oh! I can't grant you forgiveness, you accursed man! Get away! There's a greater saint than I am such and such a distance away and go to see him.'

He went. He sought out the second saint, and, if he did, he went in and there was no food coming to the saint; and he asked him to go outside so that the food could come and that he'd then give him some of the food. He went outside and he got his share of the food when it came.

'What did you do out of the way to stop the food coming to me?' said the saint.

He told him what had happened.

'Oh! you accursed man! You can't be forgiven! There's a saint that's greater than I am a little distance away. Go to him and if he can't forgive you then nobody can forgive you.'

So he went to the third saint. The food didn't come to him when he went inside and he was told to go outside so that the food could come. He went out and, if he did, the food came to him.

'What did you do out of the way, that the food didn't come to me?'

He told him the story.

'Oh, you accursed person! Stay there for a week and then go to the chapel on Sunday.'

He went to the chapel on Sunday and he heard Mass.

'Wait there for another week,' said the saint.

He waited.

'Now, go to the chapel next Sunday and carry this rosary between your two hands and go into a corner of the chapel and if it happens that nothing interrupts you during Mass, you've a chance!'

He went. He took the rosary and went into the corner of the chapel and he heard Mass and, if he did, nothing interrupted him while he recited the rosary that day so he went to the saint.

'You succeeded today?' said the saint.

'I did,' said he.

'Go now,' said the saint, 'back home again and you won't be able to put your two feet on the ground for however long or short a time it takes you to get to the hut you knocked down on the girl. That's the place you'll be able to stand on your feet again, but until that time you won't be able to go on your two feet but on your knees! That girl is still alive under the hut, if you dig it up. And it isn't the killing of the girl that's the cause of such a severe penance on you but the child she was carrying. She's still alive and will arise as much alive and well as the day you buried her, so go to her.'

He had to go, and it was a mighty journey. It was also a great penance. He had to go on his knees until he reached the hut he knocked down on the girl.

49. The Saint and the Robber

There was a saint long ago and, if there was, his meals came from God. He used to spend the day praying and thanking God for everything. One morning, when he woke, he stuck his head out of his cell and it was a cold, wet, morning. He drew in his head and said:

'It's a cold, wet morning, this morning.'

He sat in his chair and waited like that till the evening, when the day was clearing. No food was coming from Heaven to him that day. He was getting hungry and thirsty and he couldn't think why in the world his food wasn't coming to him from Heaven today, as it used to come every other day.

'I've done something out of the way,' said he to himself, 'and I can't figure out what it is.'

He was there till nightfall and he spent the night cold and hungry, and he got neither food nor drink. When he got up in the morning he was very hungry. A voice came to him in the middle of the next day:

'You'll get no more food from Heaven,' said the voice. 'Do you remember the other morning when you got up and said that it was a cold, wet morning? You never thanked God for it,' said he, 'and as a result, you'll get no more food from Heaven.'

'I remember it well,' said he. 'Is there no remedy for it?'

'There's a remedy alright, but if there is, it will cost you dearly.'

'If I have to pay for it,' said the saint, 'I'll pay. I'll be satisfied. Whatever work or hardship or trouble you will lay upon me, I'm prepared to suffer it.'

'You'll have to go out into the middle of the river,' said the voice, 'and stand there with your staff stuck into the riverbed and stand there until green moss grows on your staff.'

He went out next day to the river with his staff. He stuck his staff in the middle of the river and stood beside it. He stood there the first day, and the afternoon, and when it was night, around one o'clock in the morning, he saw a man coming towards him with two beasts. The man made straight for him.

'Get out of the way of the beasts!' said the man.

'I won't,' said he, 'because I must stay here.'

'Yerra, what's keeping you there, you fool?' said the man. 'Wouldn't you leave that place and get out of the river?'

'I couldn't,' said he. 'I must stay here.'

'Yerra, what are you doing there?' said the man. 'Or what did you do out of the way to make you stay there?'

'It was a wet day that came and I never thanked God for it, and I was made to come here to complete my penance.'

'Ever and always,' said the man, 'my trade was robbing and looting and stealing and these are two beasts that I've stolen, and I never thanked God in my whole life. Since you're there, I'll go on the other side of you and that's the end of my robbing. I'll take my staff and stick it down on the other side of you, and myself and my staff will stay there till green moss grows on it.'

He stuck his staff down on the other side of the saint and the next evening there was green moss on each staff. The voice came to them, saying that their sins were all forgiven and to sin no more.

Visits to the Other World

'Heaven is a blessed and wonderful place;
From which no one returns to meet friends or their spouse;
Free of mist and sin, and troubled minds,
Only glory and happiness and perpetual harmony.'
— from the poem *An Sotach is a Mháthair*.

'Cold, wet, Hell.'
— from an old poem

'Remember the sinner who's feeling unwell,
Remember, he's boiling forever in Hell,
Remember the soul that is damned now, I fear,
Lamenting below there with many a tear.'
— from a poem ascribed to *Donnchadh Mór Ó Dálaigh*.

'As deep as *Poll Tí Liabáin*.'
— old Connaught expression.

From time immemorial people have tried to imagine for themselves what kind of place the other world was and where was the kingdom of the dead. There is probably no other question that exercised the interest and imagination to the same degree. It was best, they thought, to go and see it for themselves and this resulted in accounts in the literature of many countries of how mortals visited the otherworld and what they saw there (Väinämöinen in the *Kalevala*; Dionysius, Orpheus, Hercules and Odysseus in Greek literature; Dante in the *Divina Commedia*). It is the same with the folklore of many countries, such stories abound there too.

In our own country, neither the written literature nor the folklore are lacking in similar accounts. We have a plentiful supply of stories and poems describing visits by living people to the other world and returning to tell the tale, and of cases where the dead returned to this world to tell how they fared there. There is a significant difference between the accounts of the pre- and post-Christian eras; Christianity put a new slant on the old ideas but the change was gradual and not readily perceptible. It appears that some of these stories and poems were composed in the Middle Ages. Traces of paganism are easily discernible in many of them. For example: Hell was cold and wet in the older accounts while later versions speak of a place of pain or of the fires of Hell. And yet, one often finds in these stories that a person in Hell can escape from it just as we, nowadays, believe that a soul can be released from Purgatory.

Very little research has been done into this subject in Ireland by comparison with that done in other countries. If reading these stories encourages our own scholars to undertake this research then our efforts in publishing them will have been all the more worth while.

50. The Queen of the Planets

There was this couple, long ago, and the man was held in high esteem but the woman wasn't because she was so unkind. The man died first and, if it wasn't for the regard of the neighbours he wouldn't have been buried at all, it was such a bad day. The woman died some time later and she got two of the finest days that ever were. Everyone was amazed that she got such a blessing because nobody liked her. Well, their son decided that he wouldn't sleep in the same bed two nights in a row, nor eat two meals at the same table until he found out why his father, who was liked by all, got such a bad day while his mother, who was disliked by all, got such a fine day.

He went away, anyhow, on foot. He was a good way from home when he came to a house and got lodgings for the night there. A widow lived there with her three daughters. That night, the widow asked him where he was going. He told her about his father who was as good a man as ever was, who was liked by everyone, but no worse day ever blew from the skies than the day he was buried; and about his mother, who was never liked by anyone, and nobody wished well, who got the finest day that ever came from above for her burial.

'And I won't sleep the second night in the same bed and I won't eat a second meal at the same table till I find out the reason why,' said he.

'Well,' said she, 'if you find the answer to your own problem, see if you can find out anything about my daughter's.'

She had three daughters and nobody had any regard for the eldest and she couldn't figure out why.

'Well,' he said, 'I've enough problems of my own without taking on anybody else's but if I find out anything I'll let you know.'

He went off in the morning and kept walking till nightfall. He went into a house. A blacksmith lived there and during the night the smith asked him where he was going, just as the widow had the previous night. So he told him about his father and his mother.

'Musha,' said the blacksmith, 'if you find any answer for my own problem, let me know on your way back.'

'What problem is that?' said the boy.

'Well,' said he, I'm working from early till late, from Monday to Saturday, and I can't save anything. I haven't a penny left after all my work!'

'I'll do what I can,' said the boy, 'but I'll probably never return.'

He went off next morning and walked all day. He went into a farmhouse for the night and got lodgings there and sat down by the fire. During the night the farmer asked him where he was going, just as the other two had the previous two nights. He told him how things were, giving an account of his father and mother.

'If you can find an answer to my problem at all, let me know,' said the farmer. 'There's a damp patch over the door of my house that I can't stop dripping; no matter how good a thatcher I get, he can't stop it.'

'Well,' said the boy, 'I have plenty of problems now, anyhow.'

He was getting no answers, only fresh problems.

'I'll let you know if I hear anything,' said the boy, 'and welcome.'

He was walking and walking all day and not a house in sight. It was getting late and still there was no house. Finally he saw a light some distance from the road. He went towards the light and found a house. The door was wide open. There was a fine warm, tidy kitchen before him, a fine big fire on the hearth, a grand chair beside the fire, and not a soul in the house. He sat down in the chair beside the fire and he wasn't long there when in came a very fine woman who greeted him in a pleasant, civil way and he greeted her the same. She prepared a meal for him and it lacked for nothing. He sat down at the table and ate his fill. Then she gave him water to wash his feet after his walking. He sat back by the fire and they chatted away – as nice a woman as ever he met.

When they had been talking for a long time she told him it was time he went to bed, that he was tired out after the day. There was a big pot of water on the fire and the water was almost boiling over. The room was off the kitchen with a door in the middle and the bed facing the door. He could see the hearth from the bed. He went to bed, and a very fine bed it was, but he wasn't able to sleep. He wasn't long in bed when the pot began to boil on the fire. When it boiled, the woman didn't take it off. She put her head into the pot and started to go down, down, into it and gradually disappear until all he could see were her two feet.

Then her two feet vanished and he couldn't see her at all. He had a clear view of the hearth and the poor man wasn't thinking of sleep. The whole thing amazed and frightened him. When you'd think she'd have melted in the pot, she came up out of it again, as alive as she went in. He was terrified; he thought he'd be the next into the pot! Then she slung a rope over the rafters and made a noose on it. She stood on a stool, put her head in the noose and hung herself. There she was, kicking and choking, until she finally stopped. When he thought she was definitely dead, with her tongue hanging out a foot and a half, she came out of the noose, as alive and well as she had ever been. Then she took a razor and cut her throat. Out came the blood, as it would come from a slaughtered beast. She fell on the floor and was kicking her feet and moaning and groaning. In the end she stopped and there wasn't a stir out of her.

'Right,' said the man in the room below, 'she's really finished now!'

After another while, she got up again, and she stood up as healthy and well as she ever was. He was wondering; he didn't know what to do. He was surprised at what had happened. It wasn't long before she pulled another trick. She went off and brought back a bag and put it on the table. She took the table out to the middle of the floor and started counting gold and silver for a very long time. When she had a lot of it counted she gathered up the money again and put it back in the bag. Then she took a silk dress, put it on her and took a book and spent a long time reading the book. About the same length of time as she had spent in the pot, and the length she spent hanging, and the same length as she had spent lying on the floor with her throat cut and the same length as she had spent counting the money, that was the length she spent reading the book. When she had finished reading the book she went down to the room.

'Are you asleep?' said she.

He didn't answer.

'Ah,' said she, 'you can't sleep! Don't be a bit afraid! You saw,' said she, 'everything I did tonight?'

'I did,' said he.

'Did you ever hear,' said she, 'of the Queen of the Planets?'

'I did,' said he.

'That's me,' said she. 'Did you see how long I was in the pot?'

'I did,' said he.

'Any child that was born while I was in the pot, that's the death he's destined for. And did you see how long I was hanging?' said she.

'I did,' said he.

'Any child that was born while I was hanging, that's the fate he's destined for,' said she. 'Did you see how long I was lying on the floor bleeding, with my throat cut?' said she.

'I did,' said he.

'Any child that was born while I was lying on the floor, that's the death he's destined for,' said she. 'Did you see how long I was counting the money?'

'I did,' said he.

'Any child born while I was counting the money,' said she, 'that's the life he's destined for. And did you see the length I was reading the book?'

'I did,' said he.

'Any child that was born while I was reading the book, that's the life he's destined for. I know what brought you here, it's because of your father and mother. Nobody ever disliked your father, everybody thought well of him,' said she. 'Your father's purgatory was only those two wet days. No poor person ever had a good word to say about your mother, and that was the only welcome she got, that fine day. Your mother will be here for you tomorrow,' said she. She had a brass ball in her hand: 'She'll have her mouth wide open with two curs chasing her. If you don't get her with this brass ball and stuff it down her throat, she'll eat you so that you won't be able to go back to tell the tale.

Now, the widow you met the first night and begged you to tell her about her daughters, tell the girl to carry her mother on her back to Mass on two Sundays and everyone will admire her. Now, the blacksmith you met on the second night who asked you to find out why he could save nothing, tell him that he is the first at work on Monday and the last at work on Saturday and that the likes of him never had any luck. And the farmer you went to on the third night who asked you to find out why he couldn't cure the leak over his door, tell him to give back the straw he had stolen.'

He stayed in the house till morning and then went off down the road. Very soon he saw his mother, followed by two curs, coming towards him with her mouth wide open. He attacked her with the brass ball and shoved it down her throat. No sooner had he done that than she collapsed in a heap of slime on the road and the two curs ran away.

He told what had happened to the farmer, and to the blacksmith, and to the widow, and they did what he told them and everything turned out well for them.

That's the Queen of the Planets for you now.

51. The Beam in the River

There was a woman here in Ireland long ago and she and her husband had a lot of property and money. And plenty of poor people were coming around collecting alms. The man always gave them plenty to eat and drink and gave them charity whenever he was at home. Whenever the woman found that the man was away she turned the dogs on the poor. Things rested so. When the woman of the house died she left one son, and since they had plenty of property and money he spent a huge amount on food and drink and all sorts of the best at her wake and funeral. When the father died he hadn't as much as a candle to light at the wake. The son vowed that he wouldn't stop or rest, ever, till he had walked the world to find out what was best: to be good or bad. He went off on foot one day and he was walking till nightfall when he went into a house and asked for a night's lodgings.

'We can't give you lodgings unless one of us goes without food,' they said. 'We are the three best cobblers in the world and we're working six days a week and every Saturday night until it's almost Sunday morning.'

One of the men fasted and they gave him supper and they said that if he was ever going that way again and he was able to tell them, to tell them why they could never save anything, despite being the three best cobblers in the world. Fair enough. He got up next morning and went off, and when evening fell he came to a house and asked for a night's lodgings there. They gave him a great welcome and gave him lodgings. And they asked him where he was going and he said that he was going to see whether it was better to be good or bad.

'Ah, come on, you idiot,' said the man of the house, 'don't you know well that it's better to be good than bad!'

He saw a drip of rain falling from the rafters of the house and asked why it was leaking.

'There's no rain falling tonight,' said he.

'If I put all the slates in Ireland on the house,' said the man of the house, said he, 'there'd still be rain falling from those three rafters. And may God send you luck,' said he, 'if you ever find out, be sure to let me know why the rain comes in.'

'I'll tell you, if I ever find out,' said he.

On the third day he was walking he had covered quite a distance when he came to the banks of a river and he saw a beam out in the water. There was a woman standing up on the beam and three dogs on this side of the water and three dogs on the other side, and all the dogs were trying to grab the woman who was on the beam. He sat down and watched the dogs trying to catch the woman out on the beam. Then he heard a bell ringing. He thought there must be a chapel nearby. He went towards the sound of the bell and came to a chapel and there was nobody inside the chapel but the priest. The priest said Mass and when he had said Mass he turned around and asked him had he walked far. He said he had walked a fair distance.

'What's the greatest wonder you saw since you left home?' said he.

'I saw wonders in plenty,' said he. 'The first house I came to on the first night had the three best cobblers I ever saw in it. One of them had to fast to provide me with my supper,' said he. They were working six days of the week and even on Saturday night until it was almost Sunday morning.

'Well, when you go back home,' said he, 'if you spend a night in that house, tell them that it's the working on a Saturday that is spoiling what they are doing; that they are overworking on Saturday and affecting the work they do on the other days. If they give up the Saturday work, they'll have more strength. What other wonder did you see since you left home?'

'Well, the second house I was in,' said he, 'I remarked to the man of the house that there was no rain falling outside and still rain was falling on me from the rafters. He told me that if he put all the slates in Ireland on the house the rain would still come in.'

'Well, you can tell that man,' said the priest, 'when you are going home, that he stole those three rafters from his godfather and he'll never see a fine day without rain coming in on him until he gives back the three rafters or their value to his godfather or until he makes some similar restitution. Did you see any other wonders since you left home?'

'Well, I did,' said he. 'I saw from a riverbank, east the road a bit, this woman out on a beam and there were three hounds this side of the river and three hounds on the other side of the river, all trying to grab the woman on the beam.'

'Did you not recognise the woman?' said the priest

'I didn't,' said he.

'That's your mother who used to turn the dogs on the poor.'

'Oh, musha, do you think it's her?'

'It is,' said the priest.

'Is there anything in the world that could save her?' said the son.

'Nothing,' said the priest, 'except a place up there where there's a cascade of poison falling down and there isn't a drop falling from it that wouldn't go through iron.'

'Oh, musha, even that same,' said he, 'I'd do it sooner than have my mother any longer out on that beam with the dogs watching to catch her.'

'Well, you can stop right there!' said the priest to him. 'You have saved your mother by taking the penance on yourself. Your mother is saved now. And I'm your father,' said he. 'Go on home now and carry on the same as your father did every day of his life. And you'll never see a day that you'll want for health or wealth. And you'll get to Heaven in the end. It was the Son of God that put myself and the chapel in your way, before you walked any further.'

52. Donncha Mór Ó Dálaigh

It's many a score of years since there was a man living at Mín Mhór, a village near Taobh an Mhuilinn, who was called Donncha Mór Ó Dálaigh. And he was always good to the poor. As good a man never lived, and he'd never let anybody go past his door without giving them lodgings for the night, or food if they were hungry. His wife wasn't nearly as good as him. Sometimes when he gave them lodgings, she'd put the run on them.

Fair enough. Eventually she died and Donncha Mór lived on afterwards and he was ever and always good to the poor and giving them lodgings. On the day she died, the neighbours at the funeral were so lucky that they were able to walk home in December, with their coats slung over their shoulders, pouring sweat. Every last one of them was remarking on the weather, it was so very good for the funeral of this old hag.

Fair enough. The time came round when Donncha Mór Ó Dálaigh himself died. On the day he died, at the beginning of the month of June, from the day he died till the day he was buried it blew a gale, with lightning and thunder; and the neighbours who came to the burial had to go back home, the storm was so bad and they were nearly killed. Any and everyone remarked on the dreadful day that Donncha Mór got and he so good-hearted, as against the wonderful day his wife got and she not half as good as him. The son was listening to the neighbours talking about this and wondered why it was so. Fair enough. One day he said to his two sisters:

'I'll not sleep another night here till I find out why it was that my father got such a bad day for his burial and my mother got such good weather the time she died. Would you ever pack some food for me and I'll walk away until I find out the reason.'

'They made up some food for him, the son. Donncha Óg was his name. He walked away until nightfall and he came on a little house by the side of the main road. And he decided that he'd go in there to see who lived there or what news they might have. He went in. There was a man sitting inside who was preparing food from morning to night and by evening he was no more able to satisfy his hunger than he was in the morning. He saluted Donncha Óg and Donncha Óg saluted him.

'You're a stranger around these parts,' said he.

'I am,' said Donncha, 'I was never down this way before.'

'Stay here with me,' said the man, 'and make a fresh start tomorrow.' 'Whatever chance you have, you've no business going on now, with the night falling.'

Donncha Óg stayed till morning. Next morning, when the old man had provided a bite of food, Donncha thanked him and wished him well as he went off.

'Now,' said the old man, 'while you're on your way, enquire about my problem if you can. Maybe you'd find the solution. I'm preparing food from morning till night and I just can't get rid of the hunger.'

'I will,' said Donncha.

He walked on till night came, enquiring at every house he came to. He went into another house and there was a man and his wife inside with an awful lot of children. The children looked very hungry and half-naked and the man looked terribly young and so did the wife. He saluted Donncha and Donncha saluted him. Donncha told him the business that brought him that way.

'Stay here till morning,' said he, 'and make a fresh start tomorrow, and you'll have a better chance.'

Donncha stayed there till morning. They made him a bite of food in the morning and he wished them well as he left.

'Now,' said this man, 'if you find out about your own business, maybe you'd enquire about mine. There's no place in this house that I can lie down but that a fresh drop of water doesn't fall on my face and no matter what roof or shield I put over me that same drop falls on my face. Maybe you'd find out the reason for it.'

'I'll enquire,' said Ó Dálaigh.

Ó Dálaigh walked on till late evening, going from house to house, asking at every house about the reason for the different weather on the occasions of the death of his father and mother, and at nightfall he went into another house. There was a woman there with three of the finest daughters he ever laid eyes on. She saluted him and he replied in the way they used to in those days.

'You're a stranger around these parts,' said she.

'I am,' said Donncha.

'Stay here till morning,' said she, 'and make a fresh start tomorrow and you'll find out more about your business.'

'Donncha stayed till morning. When she gave him food in the morning:

'If you find out about your own business,' said she, 'would you enquire about my business. I have three of the finest daughters that ever the sun shone on and no man has ever proposed marriage to them and would you ever find out why.'

'I'll enquire,' said Donncha.

He walked on until he came to a big field that had a high wall all the way round. He looked in over the wall. A cow couldn't stand in that field, there were so many there and their eyes popping out of their heads with anger for one another; with grass growing up above their eyes and they weren't as well fleshed as ravens they were so distressed – each one pucking the other with his horns and fighting, and a very aggressive look to them all. He was very surprised considering how much grass was there. He walked on another little bit and came to the wall of another field and looked in. The field was crowded with cattle with the flesh falling off them and not a bite of grass on the ground, which was so bare that you could pick pins off it. Some were lying down and licking one another while others were standing up and shaking with flesh. He thought that this was the most surprising thing he had seen since he left home.

He walked on another bit and came to a place where there was a big river coming down from a hill, and a stream nearby with a bridge over it. He sat on the wall of the bridge and looked up the river, and the water coming towards him was as white as buttermilk. He decided that this was the most amazing thing he'd seen so he'd go up to see where the river came from. He walked up by the river and over a hill until he got half-way up to the top. When he got to the half-way stage of the hill there was a big heap lying over the river like a huge reek of turf, but made of human skulls entirely, and with a white juice coming out of them and making its way down the river. He stood looking at this and it amazed him. With the second look he took to the other side of the river, who did he see standing on the other bank of the river but his father who had died the year before, Donncha Mór.

'Oh, father, is that you?' said Donncha Óg.

'It is, indeed,' said the father. 'Where are you going?'

'Well, musha,' said the son, 'everyone in the village was very surprised at the awful day you got for your burial and the fine day my mother got and she not anything like as good as you.'

'Oh, you have little to do,' said Donncha Mór, 'if that's all that's bothering ye! On the day I was buried, all my sins were transferred to the crowd at the funeral and they had done their penance by the time they got home. Now, on the day your mother died the words she always used were "May I never see God!" and she never saw God since then. She hears the music and happiness of Heaven but she hasn't seen God, and won't till the Day of Judgement. I'm in Heaven ever since, but I came back here to tell you how things were.'

'Tell me, father, why is that river coming out white like buttermilk from those skulls?'

'Well,' said Donncha Mór, 'those are the skulls of all the priests that ever lived, doing their penance for the sins of their flock and they'll be there till all the penance is done and they won't see Heaven till the Day of Judgement.'

'Well, father,' said the son, 'the first day I left home on this journey I was with a man and he asked me if I found out about my own business could I find out about his. He was preparing food from morning till night and could never get rid of his hunger.'

'Well,' said Donncha, 'when you go back to him, tell him to say grace and then the food will nourish him.'

'Well, father,' said the son, 'I was with a man on the second night and he had a houseful of children and a wife and he told me that if I found out about my own business to try and find out about his. There's nowhere he can lie, no matter where, in his house that a cold drop doesn't fall on his face. It doesn't matter what roof or shelter he puts over him.'

'Yes, that's a man,' said Donncha Mór, 'that didn't do right by orphans that he evicted. And let you tell him when you go back to give the orphans their due and the drop will cease.'

'Well,' said the son, 'I was with a woman and she had three of the finest daughters I ever laid eyes on, and she asked me if I found out about my own business to try and find out why no man had ever proposed marriage to any of them.'

'Right. When you go back to her again,' said he, 'tell her that she had too much of an opinion of the girls when they were young, thinking that they were lovelier than the Virgin Mary; and God turned the people against them, and there they are, without any husbands. And when you get there ask her will she give you the eldest. And if she says she will, then marry that woman and before the wedding feast is over the other two will have found husbands.

'Well, father, I saw a field with lots of cattle, with grass up to their eyes, and they weren't as well-fleshed as ravens and their eyes popping out of their heads with hate for one another and pucking each other with their horns.'

'Right. Those were neighbours,' said Donncha Mór, 'who didn't behave well in this world and were always fighting and were never great with one another and there they are, and there they'll be, till the Day of Judgement.'

'Well, I saw another field,' said the son to the father, 'and the cattle in it were shaking with flesh and still you could pick pins off the ground; some of them lying down and others licking one another so you'd think it was summer.

'Right. Those were good neighbours,' said Donncha Mór, 'who were great with one another in this world and did no harm to one another or to anybody else and everyone was great with them. And there they are, and there they'll be – they are in Heaven and will always be there.

When he looked around, Donncha Mór was gone; there was no one to be seen on the other side of the river. He went back and when he came to the man he was with on the first night he told him that he wasn't giving thanks for his food – to give thanks and the food would nourish him. He went to the second man and said that if he made reparation to the orphans he had evicted wrongly the drop would cease. He went back to the woman and told her that she had thought too much of her daughters when they were growing up and had thought that they were lovelier than the Virgin Mary and that God had turned the people against them.

'But, if you give me the eldest, I'll marry her, and if you don't give her to me that is alright too.'

She said she'd give her. Donncha Mór's son and the eldest woman were married and, before the wedding feast was over, each of the others had a husband. Donncha Mór's son went home with his wife and all the news to his sisters and from that day to the day he died, he was a contented upright man and good to the poor.

That's all I ever heard of him.

53. The Woman who Went to Hell

Long ago, there was a widow, as there often was and always will be. She had only one daughter whose name was Máire. The daughter decided to marry, anyhow, and the man she married was called Micí na Muc. They weren't long married when Micí wanted to get rid of the poor old woman out of the house. She asked for time, the length it would take her to spin seven pounds of wool, and was given it, and it was seven years before she had it all spun. When she had spun the seven pounds, Micí told her that her time was well up by now and to be off in the morning. Next morning, she put her daughter up on her back and they set off and travelled the road until they came to a farmer's house. They asked for lodgings for the night and were given them. That night the young woman asked what kind of house was it that was built on the farm.

'Would you go and mind it for the night?' said the man of the house.

'I would,' said Máire.

'I'll give you twenty pounds,' said the man of the house, 'if you stay there till morning.'

'I'll go, as long as you look after my mother.'

'There's no fear that she won't be well minded!' said the man of the house.

Away she went and went into the house. She kindled the fire, she swept the floor, sat on a chair and opened a book. She started to read. It wasn't long till a woman came up through the floor, driving a cow and carrying a spancel and a can. She told Máire to get up and milk the cow. So Máire got up and milked the cow. The woman told her to drink three sups of the milk, to wash her hands and face with the remainder, and then throw it against the wind. Máire did as she was told. The woman went off and Máire sat as before. The woman was hardly gone when a big strapping man came up through the floor, looking very fierce. He sat at Máire's side until the cock crowed. Then he went off. Next morning, when daylight came, Máire went off and came to the farmer's house and the first thing she did was to enquire about her mother. The mother said she was alright if Máire was alright.

'I am,' said Máire.

She began to work and never pretended a word until night came. The farmer asked her would she go again that night. She said she would if her mother was well cared for. The farmer said he'd give her forty pounds. That night she went to the house and went in. She kindled the fire. She swept the floor and lit a candle. She sat down and took up a book and began to read. It wasn't long till the woman came, carrying the spancel and the can and driving the cow before her. She told Máire to get up and milk the cow. So she got up and milked the cow.

'Drink three sups from the top of the milk,' said the woman, 'wash your hands and face in the rest of it and then throw it against the wind!'

She did as she was told. The woman went off and she had hardly gone when the man came, and as fierce as he was the first night, he was seven times worse this night. He sat opposite Máire on his chair and Máire never pretended to see him until the cock crowed. Then he went away. As soon as it was daybreak Máire went to the farmer's house. The first thing she did was to enquire about her mother, and the mother said she was fine and strong as she hoped that Máire was too, and she said she was. She set to work until night came. The farmer asked her would she go there again that night. She said she would if he took good care of her mother, which he said he would and welcome.

'And you'll get sixty pounds for tonight,' said he.

Off she went to the house that night and went in. She lit the candle, kindled the fire, swept the floor and sat on a chair, reading a book. She wasn't long there when the woman came to her with the spancel and can and the cow before her. She told Máire to get up and milk the cow. She got up and milked her.

'Now, drink three sups from the top of the milk,' said she. 'Wash your hands and face in the rest and then throw it against the wind!'

Máire did as she was told.

'Well now,' said the woman with the cow, 'he'll come again tonight to you and, as bad as he was the last two nights, he'll be seven times worse tonight, and he'll threaten to eat you alive tonight; let you tell him that he won't, as there's a fine barrier between you!'

She went off and Máire sat down in her usual place, reading her book. She wasn't long there when the man appeared to her through the floor and, however he looked the previous two nights, he was seven times worse this night. He sat down on a chair and wasn't long there when he spoke.

'I'm going to eat you alive tonight, Máire!'

'Ah, you're not,' said Máire, 'for there's a fine barrier between us!'

'Welcome in your life and your health, Máire!' said he.

'Yerra, you devil,' said Máire, 'what has damned you?'

'Oh, what damned me was,' said he, 'that when this house was being built, my father made me the ganger over all the men and then, when they had earned their money, I came and kept all their money. That's what damned me. And now,' said he, 'when you go back – my father is prepared to pay you – don't take a penny from him, but tell him to give you a certain room in the house to sleep in instead, and he'll give it to you and welcome, even though my mother won't like it.'

She went back, and, as soon as she went in, she asked how her mother was. The mother said she was fine and strong if she was too.

'I am,' said Máire.

She started off working and never let on a word. The people in the house were amazed that she wasn't saying anything. At dinnertime the man of the house came to pay her and she said she wouldn't take anything but to give her a certain room in the house to sleep in instead. The farmer said she was welcome to it.

'That's my child's room,' said the old woman in the corner. 'You can't have that.'

'Ah, she can,' said the farmer, 'think of all we're saving.'

So she got it and went to sleep there and she was sleeping there for a while. Some days she slept late and she and the woman of the house fell out with one another. The woman of the house told one of the servants to go and look through the keyhole, and she went and looked; and didn't she see her inside with a child in her arms and a fine strapping man sitting at the other side of the bed with them. She ran down and told the woman of the house.

'Ah, it's true then!' said she. 'She's a saint and I'm damned! That's my son! Go up to her now and tell her that there are some things here that people are after and would she oblige me by letting me hide them in that room because no one else is allowed in there!'

She went up and asked the woman in the bed would she allow them into the room. She said she would. They came, and they disguised the old woman every way they could and hid her in a corner of the room. That night it wasn't long before she saw her son coming and sitting on the side of the bed beside the woman with the child! She couldn't contain herself and threw off her disguise and grabbed hold of her son.

'Oh, God protect us always, mother!' said he. 'If you'd only waited another two hours, I'd have been free forever for you, but now, I must spend another seven years in Hell on account of you!'

'You needn't, my love,' said she, 'for I'll go in your place!'

'You won't go, mother, because you couldn't do that.'

'I certainly will,' said she.

So she went to spend the seven years in place of her son and, begor, if she did, it wasn't long before she was back burnt and scalded!

'I knew,' said the son, 'that you couldn't go there!'

'I'll go, then,' said the father.

'You can't,' said the son, 'it just isn't possible.'

The father went and he was hardly gone when he was back again.

'I'll go,' said the woman with the child, 'if you'll take good care of my mother till I come back.'

'Oh,' said the farmer, 'you'll do the job alright!'

He gave her a ring and told her not to eat a bite of food that came from Hell but to give it to the dog that was lying on the doorstep and that her own food would come through the ring. And that's how it was. She went to Hell and completed the seven years; and every time she was given food she gave it to Caesar who was lying on the doorstep. When the seven years were up she asked for her pay. She was told that her pay went to pay for her food. She said she owed them nothing for food, that she had given it to Caesar. They asked Caesar did he get the food and he said he had. They told her then to do seven more years and she said she would. She did the seven extra years and when the seven years were up she asked for her pay. She was told that her pay would have to pay for her food. She told them to ask Caesar about it, and Caesar said it was himself that got the food. Then she was asked what she wanted. She said that she wanted every soul that was suffering most to be released to her and put on her back. They were all piled up on her, as many as she could carry and she left. And, just coming in the gates of Hell was Mící na Muc, her husband of long ago!

'Will you bring me with you, Máire?' said he.

'Well now, I don't know,' said she. 'But it was ever said "Render good for evil". Find a place on me!'

She went off and in a short while she met a gentleman.

'You've a heavy load, my good girl!' said he.

'I have,' said she, 'but I'll put up with it!'

'Would you sell them?' said he.

'I would,' said she, 'but who might you be?'

'I'm Saint John.'

'I wouldn't sell them to you at all,' said Máire, 'for I bought them more dearly than you did!'

She moved on and it wasn't long till she met another man.

'You've a heavy load, my good girl,' said the man.

'It is,' said she, 'but we'll manage!'

'Would you sell them?'

'I would,' said she, 'but who might you be?'

'I'm Saint Michael.'

'I wouldn't sell them to you at all,' said she, 'for I bought them more dearly than you did!'

She went on and in a short time she met a third man, and they saluted one another.

'Your load is heavy, Máire,' said he.

'It is', said Máire.

'Would you sell them?'

'I would,' said she, 'but who might you be?'

'I'm the Saviour,' said He.

'I'll sell them to you,' said Máire, 'because, whatever price I paid for them, you paid more dearly!'

She released them to him and they flew up to heaven as white doves. Then she went off and was walking until the dew came down at nightfall and she met a poor man. She asked the poor man where he was going to spend the night.

'I'll go up above here,' said he, 'to the wedding of a man who was a widower for the past fourteen years.'

'I'll go along with you, so,' said she.

They went up to the house and went in and sat inside the door; and this tall, supple youth came up to Máire and stared very hard at her. Máire thought she recognised him as the child she had left behind her when she went to Hell. He kept staring at Máire. Máire asked him why he picked on her above anybody else there.

'You'd be better off going down to your father,' said she, and telling him that there's a poor woman down here and to give her something to eat.'

The lad went off and told the story and, begor, didn't he come back with a dish of meat! Herself and the poor man ate and drank their fill, and as they were drinking Máire told the poor man to leave some at the bottom of the vessel. He did, and she took the ring from her finger that she had got from the man who was going to Hell, and dropped it into the vessel and handed it to the boy.

'Here,' said she, 'take that to your father now and tell him to drink it for your mother's soul.'

The boy went and told his father what the poor woman had said. He drank the drink and, if he did, didn't the ring fall into his mouth, and he recognised it at once because his name and surname were on it.

'Musha, my boy,' said he, 'would you ever show me that poor woman?'

'I will,' said the boy.

He took him by the hand and led him through the crowd until he brought him in front of her. He held out his hand and made her most welcome. He told her that he had thought she wasn't up to her word and that she was long since dead. He took her with him and dressed her up in finery and it was badly needed after fourteen years. He told the wedding guests to go home and that he'd pay any expenses incurred for the wedding; that his own wife had come back and he wouldn't have any other wife, as she was the one who most deserved him. He married her and they lived happily ever after.

That's my story, and if there's a word of a lie in it so be it!

54. The Son who Sought his Sister

There was this couple long ago and they had only one son and a daughter, and there were never two people more fond of one another than the son and daughter. There wasn't a living woman better than the daughter, and they loved each other dearly, and I believe, God help us, the father and mother were the same. This day, the son was gone out and a man came to the father and mother and asked them to let the daughter go with him. The father, mother and daughter took such a liking to the man who came in that the father and mother allowed the daughter to go with him. When the son came home and found his sister missing he asked his father and mother where she was. They told him.

'You'd think,' said he, 'that you wouldn't let her go with a man you never saw before!'

That's how it was. The son was very sad and lonely after her. When she was gone a while with the man he asked his mother to prepare some food as he was

going to look for the daughter, however near or far he had to travel. He had no
idea whether his sister was dead or alive or where she was. He walked on, from day
to day and from day to day until one day he met nobody, not even a house. Just
at sunset he looked ahead and saw, in the distance, two trees so he made for them
as darkness fell. There was a gate behind the two trees and a house beyond it. He
went in. There was a woman inside and, anyway, when she saw him coming she
made him welcome and set out a chair for him. He was sitting in the chair, and
while she went back and forth, he kept his eyes on her. And the woman who gave
him the chair was his sister.

He wasn't long seated in the chair when he heard the finest and sweetest music
he heard in his life coming towards him, and what was coming towards him
but three or four milch cows. When they stopped in the yard outside the music
stopped. The dog came in and, after him, the dog's master; and when the master
came in he took his hand and shook it. He pulled up a chair and sat beside him
and began to chat and talk.

'You've covered a lot of ground on your journey,' said he. 'You must stay here
and pay a visit. That's your sister and the reason I took your sister here was to
preserve her from sin, to save her.'

'You can take your ease now,' said he, 'and there won't be any hurry on you for
two or three days.'

When they had eaten their supper they went to bed. Next morning, when the
master had milked the cows, he told the dog to bring the cattle and leave them in
the garden they usually went to. The dog went out to the street and, the minute he
did, the cows began to move, with their horns making the sweetest music he ever
heard; and he listened with amazement until the dog left the cattle in the garden
they were kept in every day. When evening came, the master told the dog to bring
the cows home. The dog went off and the same music they made in the morning
accompanied them home and it was a great pleasure to listen to them until they
ended up in the yard and the dog came into the house.

When the cattle were ready on the second day the master told the dog to drive
them, and the boy said he'd like to go with the dog to see the place. The master
wasn't a bit inclined to let him go with the dog.

'Well now,' said he, 'if you're going with the dog, leave the dog alone, don't
stare at anything, don't stand still, and don't tell the dog what to do or the dog will
hurt you.'

He drove out the cows and the music of their horns started again and he was
watching the dog and the dog was constantly moving. He was walking by a broad
river, along a path by its side. He saw a rock lying across a precipice and there was

a hole where the water was stagnant and he stopped to look at the rock and the hole. He saw a white dust scattered over the top of the water and what he thought were minnows down below trying to catch the dust. When the dog saw the man standing and looking he fairly bristled and came up to him looking very angry. But the man began to walk on, and there was a steep cliff below him and water falling over the edge; and what was down below but a black dog with his mouth open hoping to catch anything falling from above, like the dust. When the dog saw him staring, he bristled again. The boy didn't bother about him and all the dog did was to turn his back on the cows and rush off home. The boy went back home and the dog was there a good while before him. The master looked at him when he came in.

'You annoyed the dog,' said he.

When the cows came home that evening there was no music from them. When the master saw the cows coming without any music:

'Aha,' said he, 'you vexed the dog so much that he didn't put the cows in the right place. What did you do to the dog?'

'I did nothing,' said he.

'You must have done something wrong,' said the master. 'Didn't I tell you not to stand nor to stare at anything and you didn't do that and the dog didn't leave the cows in the right place. Can't you see,' said he, 'that the cows have lost their music? What did you do to annoy the dog?'

'I did nothing,' said the boy, 'but when I came to a big hole that was on the way there was something like dust sprinkled on the water and I stopped to look at it.'

'Is that all you did to the dog?'

'Nothing,' said he, 'except that when I came to a cliff a bit further on there was water going over the edge and there was a black dog down there with his mouth open trying to catch the dust in his mouth.'

'Was that the time the dog turned home?'

'Yes,' said the boy.

'That's when the dog had cause to be angry,' said the master. 'Do you know now what you were looking at in the places you saw those things?'

'I've no idea,' said he.

'Those were the children who died in this world without baptism. And the dust you saw is the dust that was sent from God in Heaven to nourish them. The minnows were the children.'

The boy asked him then about the dog.

'That was the devil that was down there hoping that the dust would fall into his mouth, but he wasn't able to get it. You stopped to look at him, said he, 'and that's what made the dog turn for home. You committed a sin and on account of that the cows have lost their music.'

The master did no more till the next day when he said to the dog to drive the cows and leave them in the usual place. Indeed, the dog didn't need a second bidding, and didn't need any helper either. That evening, the cows came home and their horns made the sweetest, finest music ever as the dog drove them home. When that was done and the boy had spent three days there the master said:

'Your three days are up. There's your sister now,' said he, 'and you can take her away with you. She is free from sin and you can take her home. I brought her here to save her from sin.'

55. The Wonder Competition

There was this boy long ago, as there often was and will be forever, and he set off to look for work. He met a farmer who took him on. They agreed on terms of five pounds for a year's work. There was only a month left to run when the boy went to town one day and met a ship's captain and he enlisted with the captain for a year and a day.

'But,' said the boy, 'I've still a month of my year's contract to go.'

'That's alright,' said the captain, 'for it'll take me a month here to unload my vessel and to take on a new cargo.'

He went back home and every now and again he would remind the master to have his pay ready for him. The master said he would, until the very last day, and then the master told him to clear off or he'd shoot him. The poor lad left after his year's work and went to the town where the captain was, weeping and lamenting. The captain asked him what was wrong and he told him what the master had said, after his year's work.

'Don't bother about him!' said the captain.

He embarked with the captain and worked hard as a sailor for a year. When his year and a day were up and they were returning home they saw an island in the sea that they never saw before.

'Well, upon my word,' said the captain, 'that's a real wonder! There's an island and, in all my comings and goings, I never saw it before.'

He told nine of his men to go ashore and find out what kind of an island it was. While our sailor didn't need to go, because he had done his year and a day, he said he'd go as a tenth man. So in they went and were walking through the island when they saw an enormous load of timber in a cart with a white horse, and two men on either side beating it. Our sailor spoke up:

'Don't you know right well,' said he, 'that he'll never be able to pull that load?'

'Well if he doesn't,' they said, 'he can stay here forever.'

'I won't have to,' said the horse, 'if that man there forgives me.'

The horse was the master who had kept the five pounds from the servant boy.

'How could I forgive you?' said the boy.

'Oh, if you don't forgive me,' said the horse, 'I'll be stuck here forever.'

He forgave him from his heart and, as they left the island in haste, the sea was at their heels all the time till they came aboard the vessel. They were telling the captain what had happened and he believed them when he saw that, where he saw an island at first, there was now nothing but sea. They reached port and the sailor had a hundred pounds after his year's work and he had it hidden in a belt tied around him. He didn't like to stay in the town in case he'd be robbed. He went out a bit into the country and went in to an old man and asked for a night's lodgings. The old man agreed and made him welcome. He gave him supper and they spent the night talking together.

'Well, my sailor lad,' said he, 'I'm sure you saw many wonders during the year?'

'I did, indeed,' said the sailor. 'I saw a wonder that no one ever saw before.'

'Would you like to bet on your wonder, my sailor lad?' said the old man.

'I've a hundred pounds for my year's work,' said the sailor, 'and I'll bet you that.'

'I'll match it with another hundred,' said the old man.

So the sailor told him his story first about the island and the horse and everything.

'Oh, my sailor lad,' said the old man, 'that's not a patch on my wonder. I was here and I was married, and my wife was the meanest person anyone ever saw, and although there was nothing to stop her giving alms, she'd rather throw it out the door. In the end, death came and swept her off. I went into town to get stuff for the wake and my people and I were here keeping watch during the night when we heard a horse approaching and its saddle creaking. The rider dismounted at the door. He came in. He went over to where the dead woman lay and poked the dead woman with his stick. She sat up and talked to him and they spoke for a while and when he turned his back on her she lay back down again and you'd think she had never stirred. He went out the door and nobody had the courage to talk to him. Everyone was saying that I hadn't done this right or that I hadn't done that right but I made up my mind to keep her there for another night. Everybody that was there that night didn't come the second night, but people who weren't there the first night were all gathered there the second night. Everybody was listening and, sure enough, they heard the horse coming at the same time. The rider came up to the door, came in to where the dead woman lay and poked her with the stick he had in his fist. She sat up and they were talking together and when he turned his back on her she laid back and you'd think she'd never stirred. He went off out the door and nobody had the courage to speak to him. Since the matter had gone so far, I kept her for a third night and went to town and got a coffin for her. And there was not a tinker or traveller that didn't gather that night with the exception of those who had been there the previous two nights. They were all listening and, at long last, when the time came, they heard the rider coming on his horse. He got down at the door and came in, carrying his saddle and he poked the woman lying there and she jumped down on the floor. He put the saddle on her back, mounted it and rode her out the door and I never saw her since. And look you! my sailor lad, which is the greater wonder, mine or yours?'

There was the poor sailor after his year's work, with his hundred hard-earned pounds and he couldn't eat a bit or drink a sup for worry. The old man could see well how troubled he was and after a while said:

'Now, my sailor lad,' said he, 'I don't want your money and I'm not going to take it off you. Keep it for yourself, but never again make a bet with anyone, because you never can tell what the other person saw!'

The sailor left and came home and lived a long, full life from that day on.

That's my story, and if there's a word of a lie in it, so be it!

56. The Farmer and the Ship's Captain

A ship's captain came to An Daingean once and met a farmer. If he did, they began to talk and went off drinking. While they were drinking:

'I suppose,' said the farmer, 'that you've been at sea for a very long time?'

'Musha, I have,' said the captain, 'I've been at sea for forty-odd years.'

'I suppose, so, that you've seen some marvellous wonders,' said the farmer, 'being out there night and day?'

'I saw,' said he, 'something you never saw.'

'Let you have the first word,' said the farmer to the captain.

'I will,' said he. 'One fine, sunny day I was out in the middle of the ocean and there wasn't a puff of wind, and if I was, there wasn't a sight of land or anything else, for that matter. There was nothing to fill the sails, the day was so calm. Myself and the men were up on deck and, when we looked around, we saw a hare racing over the sea and a pack of hounds after him and a man on a saddle-horse after them. The hare made straight for the ship, just as the hounds were about to catch him, and jumped into the ship and went down into the hold. He came to me, the man on the horse, and told me to put out the hare or he'd sink myself and the ship! I told him to have patience. The men were disinclined to do anything. They went down into the hold to see the hare and she was there as an old woman but nobody wanted to catch her. The captain said they'd be flogged if they didn't put her up on deck. They went down and she was making music with her nails on the ship's side, trying to stay put. Eventually the men got her up top and threw her overboard and, if they did, she went off as far as my eyes could see. I watched her till she vanished over the sea with the hounds and the man on the saddled horse after her.

'Now it's my turn,' said the farmer.

'It is, indeed,' said the captain.

'We have a custom,' said the farmer, 'when a person in the neighbourhood dies, to have pipes and tobacco, tea and bread, and we all, the neighbours, go to the wake-house. I was in a wake-house once, my good sir, and I can swear to you that I was there. During the night a man on a saddled horse came to the door and, if he did, he left the horse outside and came in himself wearing a big coat. He started talking to the corpse, laid out on the table, and he sat up, as he always would when he was alive; and, if he did, the man on the saddled horse did nothing but go off out the door. Nobody bothered him. The relatives said that he wouldn't be buried for another day so that they could consult the parish priest. They went to the priest but the parish priest wouldn't come there.

"If you'll allow me, I'll go," said the coadjutor.

"You may," said the parish priest.

"There's no use in me going there unless I have a free hand to do whatever I think is needed," said he, "and I couldn't do it without your permission."

"You have my permission," said the parish priest

"Out you go then," said the other priest to the messenger, "and I'll come along with you."

They went and when he got to the wake-house he took out his book and read from it, from the hearth to the door. He asked the people who were there would it be long before he was due again. They said it wouldn't be long, that it would be less than an hour. After another while he asked again.

"He's outside now," they said.

The curate stood at the foot of the coffin and, if he did, the man on the horse came in and the corpse spoke to him, as he had done the previous night.

"Tell me, my good man," said the priest, "you're not going, just like that, without telling me your business or what brought you here after this corpse which is dead."

"Well," said he, "when he was in this world, poor, and nobody interfering with him, he was always saying 'my body to the devil.' I'm the devil and I have him!"

"You won't have him," said the priest, "for I'll give you something else to do. The body is no use to you and I'm going to have his soul!"

He took out his book and prayed some more and drove him up through the chimney in a shower of sparks.

"Away with you now," said he, "and don't be showing off!"

Next day, they buried the body.'

'I'll leave you be the judge,' said the farmer, 'as to which of us won the bet.'

'Oh, you've won!' said the ship's captain. 'Your story is much more wonderful!'

57. The Farmer, the Priest and the Schoolmaster

There was a farmer going to town one day and, if he was, he was going to do some business there. Who did he meet but a priest as he was walking on the road to town. Priests did not have horses in those days because times were bad. The farmer told the priest to get up on the cart for a bit of the road. He was very glad of the lift. He was worn out from the road and they were company for one another. Along the way they came upon the schoolmaster who was also going to town about his own business. So there were the three of them in the cart without meeting anyone, but being company for one another. They started to discuss which of them had the best way of living. The priest said that he had a better life than either of the other two.

'Oh, you haven't,' said the schoolmaster. 'My life is better! Sure I'm the one that teaches you, and only for me you wouldn't be there at all.'

'Ah! That doesn't matter!' said the priest, 'I have more power than either of you.'

Well, they were tired of one another in the end, with neither able to solve the problem. When the farmer saw them getting tired, that's the time he spoke up.

'Well, you're tired now,' said the farmer, 'and you have to give up, but it's my opinion, listening to you all this time, that my way of living is better than either of yours!'

'Right,' said the priest, 'it's hard to figure it out between us! Still and all,' said he, 'we'll leave it to the next man we meet to decide which of us has the best way of living.'

They were travelling along and never met a soul until they came to a bridge. Who should they see but a fine elegant gentleman with his elbow resting on the coping of the bridge!

'Stop the horse,' said the priest to the farmer. 'We'll leave it to this man. He's the first man we met.'

They told him the story and, if they did:

'Oh,' said the gentleman, 'it's hard to decide between you! Still, I'll solve the problem. Leave the horse here with me and I'll keep it safe. Let the three of you go up that hill and keep on walking till daybreak tomorrow and whichever of you sees the greatest wonder, let him bring it back here and I'll have the horse for you safe and sound.'

They went off, one walking to the east of the hill and another going west. Then, when night fell, the schoolmaster wasn't long walking until he came, at the top of the hill, upon the finest garden he ever saw, with everything you'd ever want to eat in it.

'I've seen something wonderful,' said he, 'and I little thought that such a lovely garden would be found on the top of such a wild hill.'

He had a pocket handkerchief and he filled it up with all the different fruits of the garden so that he'd have proof the next day, such as apples, and gooseberries and so on.

Well, the priest went off and he hadn't gone far that night till he reached the top of the hill and there was a large standing-stone, taller than himself, and everyone who had ever, ever departed this life, big or small, seemed to be round the stone, each with a ball, and as each one came up with the ball they struck the stone with it.

'I've seen a wonder,' said he, 'the likes of which I never thought I'd see in my lifetime, and it seems that everyone that ever lived, big or small, boy or girl, is there!' said he.

The farmer went his way and seemed to meet nothing; but in the end, very late in the night, he came on a fine mansion of a house on the very top of the hill.

'Who in the world,' said he, 'would live in such a fine house on top of such a wild hill! I'll go in and maybe they'd let me stay the night! I'm worn out from walking.'

He went in and there wasn't a living soul to be seen inside; but there was every sort of food that anyone could ask for laid out on the table, between food and drink.

'I'm hungry and thirsty,' said he, 'from walking all day and all night, and I'm sure they wouldn't be hard on me for taking a bite to eat, since there's nobody here to invite me to eat.'

He drew up a chair and sat down at the table and ate his fill, and no-one came to tell him stop, and he saw no-one. Still nobody came, so he got up and began looking here and there into the rooms around him. But he saw nothing. He saw one room with three of the finest beds anybody ever lay on, all neatly prepared.

'Musha, God help me,' said he, 'I'll get into one of these! No one should blame me and I'll be refreshed after a hard day!'

He got into the nearest bed but he was hardly lying down when the bed turned upside down and tossed him out on the floor again.

'You're the queer bed,' said he, 'and isn't it the queer thing you've done to me! Musha, I'll try this one,' said he.

He tried the next one and didn't it do the same trick on him.

'Well, then,' said he, 'I'll try the third one.'

He got into the third bed and found it as comfortable and peaceful as he could wish and he fell into a deep sleep. Next morning was fine and bright and when he woke he felt as fresh and well as ever he'd been. He got up and the same food was ready for him and he ate his fill of it. He asked for God's help and went out the door to go back to the bridge to see was his horse waiting for him. When he arrived the gentleman was there waiting for him with his horse and cart, safe and sound. The other two were there as well.

'Well, now!' said the gentleman, 'you've come back, but which of you saw the greatest wonder?'

'This is the wonder that I saw,' said the schoolmaster, 'and I brought proof of it. Look!'

Apples – that's what he had.

'Oh, you've proof, alright,' said the gentleman, 'and you didn't do too bad! What did you see?' said he to the priest.

'I saw this strange vision,' said the priest, 'of everyone that ever lived, big or small, each carrying a ball and striking it against a stone which was on top of the hill.'

'And what did you see?' said he to the farmer.

'I saw such and such a wonder,' said the farmer, 'and tried to go to sleep there but two beds tossed me out but the other one let me be and I slept soundly till morning.'

'Oh, yours is the best life of all!' said the gentleman. 'Those were the kindnesses you show to the poor,' he said to the schoolmaster, 'when they call to you at your schoolhouse door. Your only concern is to have sweets and little toys to give to the poor. But you,' said he to the priest, 'are the standing-stone on top of the hill, and all the people you saw were the people you allowed die without giving them the Holy Oils, and the children that were there are those you let die without baptism through lack of interest and procrastination when you were needed. When you were sent for, people had died without being anointed with the Holy Oils before you came; and now they all hate you and that's why they are all belting you with every blow they can give!'

'You went into the House of God,' said he to the farmer. 'There your food is always waiting for you any day you leave this world for that is the way you treat the poor. You give every one of them the best you can to eat and drink, and even give them your own bed to sleep in if you have nowhere else for them to sleep and so a bed is ready for you. Your own bed is the one that's most like the bed of the Son of God, and it's that one that let you sleep because it's prepared for you for the day you leave this world. Now your life is better than anybody else's. Away with the lot of ye now! I'm the God of Glory and there was nobody else able to solve your problem for you on your way but Myself!'

58. The Landlord in Hell

There was a landlord in Letterkenny long ago, a very long time ago, and he was the first landlord to collect rent on a yearly basis. The other landlords before him used to collect rents from the people but this one named a certain day, and on that day all the tenants used to have to go to him with the rent. He had a lot of land down around Letterkenny and a lot of land below Letterkenny. But there were a lot of poor tenants inside in Corrán Liath and around Cnoc na mBroinn. There were poor tenants in those parts, and on rent day they went in together with their rents and there was this man who went in to pay his rent after all the others had paid their rent. He was short six shillings and the landlord wouldn't give him a receipt until the six shillings were paid. The tenant said he hadn't got the six shillings.

'Well, whenever you get the six shillings come in here and pay them over and I'll give you a receipt from my hand.'

The tenant went home and went about his business, working every day, and from day to day, till one day death came for the landlord and he died. The tenant said that he had made a big mistake when he had paid the money but not got a receipt. When rent-day came the following year, the tenants went in to pay their rent again; and again he waited to pay until almost everyone else had paid. He went to pay the rent and the landlord's son, the eldest one, who had inherited from his father, said that there was rent due for two years and he must pay both. The tenant said there was not, that he had paid all the rent last year except for six shillings which he had forgotten about, but had not got a receipt from his father.

'I don't care what you did or what you didn't do,' said he, 'you are down for two years' rent and two years' rent you must pay; or else you must get a receipt from my father for the rent you say you paid.'

'Where would I get a receipt from your father?' said he.

'If you have to go to Hell for it,' said he, 'then you'll have to go and get it!'

The tenant set off home and set about trying to get the money to pay the rent. There was a long avenue from the rent-house to the main road and when he got to the main road there was a man on a white horse waiting there who greeted him by his name and surname. He asked him where he had been and the tenant told him that he had been down paying the rent, and that the young landlord wouldn't accept the rent from him until he got a receipt from his father, and he asked him where he could get that and he had said that, if he had to go to Hell for it, he'd have to go and get it.

'Hop up here behind me,' said the man on the white horse.

He jumped up behind the man and the pair of them rode out above Letterkenny until they came to a wood. The man on the white horse turned into the wood and continued till they came to a cliff, and in the cliff-face there was a big iron door.

'In the name of God,' said the tenant, 'where are we now?'

'You're at Hell,' said he. 'There's the gate over there, and when you dismount go over and bang on the gate and a messenger will come out and you can tell him your business and he'll show you where to find the landlord.'

He got down off the horse and went over and banged on the gate. The messenger came and the gate was opened and when he went in he saw the landlord sitting facing him. He walked over to him. The landlord made him heartily welcome and asked him how he was. The tenant said he was fine, how was he himself? He said he was only middling. He asked him what he wanted.

'Well,' he said, 'I paid you the rent last year, but I was six shillings short, and when I went to pay the rent this year your son refused to give me a receipt unless I paid two years' rent. I told him I had paid the rent to you last year, except for the six shillings, and he told me that I'd have to get a receipt from you that I had paid it. I asked him where I'd get it and he told me that if I had to go to Hell for it I'd have to go to Hell, and here I am now.'

The landlord took out a pen and paper from his pocket and wrote a receipt for two year's rent.

'Here you are now,' said he, 'and go to my son and show him this and he'll recognise my writing.'

As he was leaving the landlord he turned round and looked at him.

'My lord,' said he, 'Hell can't be as bad as people make out!'

'Why do you say that?' said the landlord.

'You look very happy and comfortable sitting in your chair there,' said he.

'Come over here beside me,' said the landlord.

He went over.

'Now,' said he, 'pull this cloak away from the side of my neck till you see the kind of place I have.'

He pulled the cloak. A blast of fire came up between his body and the cloak and severely burned tenant's cheek.

'I'm well paid for coming back!' he said.

He went off out, and when he got to the man on the white horse:

'I see,' said the man on the white horse, 'that you got paid for your journey; there's a mark on you, and everyone will know from it that you were in Hell. Get up behind me!'

He jumped up behind the horseman and they went off to the rent-house. When he got inside he threw the landlord's receipt on the table and the landlord's son asked him where he got it.

He said he got it in Hell.

'Is my father in Hell?' said he.

'He is,' said he.

'Well, if my father is in Hell,' said he, 'it doesn't look good for me!'

'Oh, well, whatever way you are or will be, your father is in Hell.'

He cancelled the two rents.

'Now,' said he, 'tomorrow at ten o'clock go to the parish priest and ask him to come here with you till we see what we should do.'

The tenant went and called on the parish priest and the pair went to the young landlord's house. The tenant told him the story from start to finish and the man became a Catholic and the family are Catholics to this very day.

The Other World:
The Rebellious Angels

'Don't ponder, my friend, on useless things,
  But ponder often on our last ends.'
  – opening lines of devotional poem 'Our last ends'.

'People of ill-will, the unbaptised, and the rebellious angels – three groups who will never see God's Heaven according to the story people tell.'

There is a very rich fund of religious poetry and story in Irish literature describing events on the Day of Judgment and our last ends. Some are poems of repentance giving dire warnings of the sad fate that awaits sinners who fail to repent in this life. They present a view of Heaven, Purgatory and Hell and the lives of the dead there.

The same sort of imagination is involved in the belief expressed in folklore about the fairy folk: they'll never see Heaven unless they have sufficient blood in their veins to enable them to write their names with it. Some stories say that they'll go to Heaven on Judgement Day if they have that much blood in them but, alas, it seems they haven't. That causes them to be dissatisfied, troubled and harmful. According to some stories they are fallen angels. Among the other groups who will never see Heaven are the unbaptised, the evil-spirited, short-changers (people who give short measure in this life to people buying from them) and women who are paid to get rid of unbaptised babies. These were regarded as grievous sins, it seems, when these stories were composed.

59. War in Heaven
The cause of the war in Heaven was that the Eternal Father had a parlour and none of the angels was allowed to look into it. Lucifer was the highest angel of all and he looked into the room when he got the chance. The Mirror of Glory was inside and a picture of the Blessed Virgin who was not born until two thousand years afterwards. That's what caused the war in Heaven. If the angel hadn't done that, there would have been no war in Heaven, but the servants began to back him and they annoyed the Eternal Father.

It was a terrible war. They say that, before that, the sun and moon and everything else could talk. The Eternal Father allowed the sun to shine as before – the sun escaped punishment. He put the moon in decline when she was in her prime so she faded away till she was no more than a silken thread. Then He restored her until she waxed full again. The sea, which we see ebbing and flowing, was stationary in its own shape then but he made it retreat, six hours going out and six hours coming back and beating itself on the rocks. He expelled the angels from Heaven and there wasn't a snow-storm from that day to this that was thicker than the angels leaving God's Heaven. While that was happening God was asked not to expel them all.

'As it is now,' said He, 'so let it be!'

All those who were on the earth are on the earth still, and those who had not reached the earth have not reached it since. Those who were flying through the air in gusts and whirlwinds were called the Storm Host. The remainder were on the earth and had no chance of escape. The Archangel, who is called the Devil, is in a hole and cannot leave it unless called by a human being, but when he is called he comes because he has that power.

When the Eternal Father had done all that in anger He closed up Heaven for two thousand years. While Heaven was closed during that two thousand years, when anyone died their souls went to a place called Limbo. When the Son of God suffered the Passion for them and was crucified and hung on a cross. He was buried. He rose again, praise and thanks to the Lord! And from Good Friday to Easter Sunday He went down to Limbo of the holy fathers bringing freedom to the souls who had died over two thousand years.

60. The Fallen Angels

There are three groups of the good people or the Fallen Angels. When Lucifer, their Archangel, fell out with God, God threw him, and those who helped him, out of Heaven. Some fell on the earth, some fell into the sea and some of them are in the air. Those are the air-demons who are in the sky. As they were being thrown out Heaven was getting empty and Saint Michael said that Heaven was becoming empty – that there'd be no one left if they didn't close the doors. The Eternal Father gave the order to close the doors and that was done.

'Let everything remain as it is now!' said the Eternal Father.

And so it was. Those who fell to the ground are still there; those who fell into the sea are still there; and those who were still in the air stayed in the air and are still there. Those are the air-demons. They expect that they will be allowed back into Heaven again on the Last Day. If they didn't, they wouldn't leave a person or four-legged animal or anything that grows on the ground. That's the reason they don't do more damage.

61. The Priest's Judgement

In the old days there was a man, we are told. We don't know if it is true or false but this is what we were told. It was a Sunday and, in those days, a long time could pass between one Mass and another. In some places it was said once a quarter and in others it might be once a year. Priests weren't so plentiful then as they are nowadays. At this particular time there happened to be a priest at hand and he was saying Mass in a miserable little cabin hidden in a valley in the mountains. There weren't so many people going to Mass in those days as there are now; they were indifferent about it. There happened to be a man going for a load on the side of a hill and the time he was collecting the load was when Mass was being said. A man came up to him whom he had never seen before or since, he was hardly better off for seeing him. He spoke to him and asked him:

'Why aren't you at Mass?' said the stranger to him.

'Musha,' said he, 'I had to gather this load and I don't see much benefit in it.'

'Well now,' said he, 'you'll have to do what I'm going to ask you.'

The poor man was overcome with fear because the man who spoke to him looked very fierce, and he said he would.

'Go at once to the priest,' said he, 'and ask him what are the three groups that will never see Heaven.'

'Oh,' said the man, answering him, 'he won't tell me now! He's saying Mass.'

'Put the question to him,' said the stranger, 'just as he is changing the book – you will be in time if you hurry – and he'll have to answer you!'

He was so afraid that he went off and drew near to the priest. There weren't many people gathered there but he made his way through them. Just as the priest was about to change the book he asked him: 'Who are the three groups that will never see Heaven?'

The priest turned round and said:

'The Fallen Angels,' said he, 'the unbaptised, and people of ill-will.'

The priest asked him to wait until Mass was over and he did. When the priest was ready he asked him who had sent him. He told him.

'I understand!' said the priest. 'Go back at once,' said he, 'as fast as ever you can and don't go near the place you were before. Take a spade and shovel from the house as you go and see can you find a soft spot near that place and make a hole in the ground. There's no need to make it deep, just big enough to allow you to lie down flat in the hole; then lay the spade and shovel over you. You must make the Sign of the Cross with them! If that doesn't save you, there's no saving you!

The man did as he was told and came near the place where he had met the man in the beginning. He made the hole as quickly as he could. When he thought he had made it deep enough and that he'd be able to lie down in it, he lay down on his back and put the spade and shovel in the shape of the Cross over himself. He had hardly done that when the big fierce man appeared above him and asked him: 'what are you doing down there?'

He told him that he had come to give him the answer to his question.

'Who are the three groups,' said the stranger, 'who'll never see Heaven?'

'They are,' said he, 'people of ill-will, the unbaptised and the Fallen Angels who were banished from Heaven.'

When he heard that he turned into a shower of sparks. He lit up like lightning or a fire and there wasn't a soul within a mile of him that wasn't frightened by the noise he made! There wasn't a living thing on the side of the hill, right down to the rocks, that he didn't leave bare with the dint of the noise and flames he made until he vanished in red sparks!

And that is the reason I've been told for putting the spade and shovel in the shape of the Cross over a grave from that day to this. I don't know if it's true but that's what I heard. I always heard that from the old people and it sounds like it could be true. But if it's not, I didn't invent it!

62. The Piper

Towards the end of the famine times, there was a man living in Baile na Bó whose name was Seán Mac Aoidh. One night he was taken ill suddenly and it was necessary to send for the priest. The parish priest was awake when the call came and he called on the curate. He got up but was afraid to go out on his own and he asked the parish priest to go with him. The pair of them set out, walking quickly in the direction of Baile na Bó. As they went over the brow of Ceathrú Ceanainn a man appeared ahead of them with a set of pipes. He began to play the pipes on the road before them. He walked ahead and they followed him until they came to Droichead Ráithe. The priests were very surprised to see a piper playing so late into the night but they enjoyed the music and they were neither tired nor afraid when they caught up with him at the bridge. The priest then put his hand in his pocket to see had he any money for the piper but he spoke up and said:

'I don't want as much as a half-penny from you.'

'We enjoyed your music,' said the parish priest, 'and we'd like to reward your efforts.'

'Well, if you would,' said the piper, 'would you do this for me. When John is dying tonight ask him what will be my fate on the Day of Judgment.'

'I'll ask, alright,' said the priest, who was astonished, 'but who will I say was asking?'

'Oh, just say: "the piper".'

'Fair enough!' said the priest.

He went on ahead of them through Ráithe playing lovely music until they reached the gable-end of Seán's house. And though he was with them right up to the house, the moment they went inside they forgot all about him. They anointed Seán and he was very weak. The priests stayed a good while and in the end they came out to go home. The parish priest noticed a dark shape under an elder tree nearby and remembered the piper. He went back into the house and asked Seán the question. Seán wasn't a bit surprised at the question but turned over and said:

'If he finds enough blood in his body to write his name, he'll go to Heaven.'

The priests came out and the piper walked ahead of them to the bridge again and waited for them there.

'Well, what did he say?' said he.

'He said,' said the priest, 'that if you can find enough blood in your body to write your name you'll go to Heaven.'

The piper threw down his pipes, took a penknife from his pocket and drove it into his chest. But not one drop of blood came out. He stuck the knife in again and again but all that came out was a sort of foam like you'd get on the river.

'My poor man,' said the priest, 'who are you or where do you come from?'

'I'm a spirit that's been going round since the beginning of time who never did any harm to anyone, but since I'm not going to get to Heaven I'll do nothing but evil from now on!'

And he vanished from sight in a shower of sparks. The priests went home, very surprised but they never saw the piper from that night on and they didn't know how Seán knew what would happen to the spirit on the Last Day.

63. The Card-Player and the Big Man

There was a man in this part of the country once who lived for card-playing and drinking and bad company. One day he went to town and met up with this bad company. They went into a public house, as they usually did, and went into a small room there drinking whiskey and playing cards. They stayed there till very late in the night. When the man was going home he took a short cut. It was through an old burial-ground but he wasn't a bit afraid because he had plenty of whiskey drunk. As he approached the old burial-ground a voice called out:

'Come in over the ditch,' said he, 'and take a particle out of my tooth.'

'I'll not come in,' said he, 'but let you come out to me.'

'I can't come out,' said the voice, 'but let you come in to me.'

With that, the man put his two hands on the ditch and vaulted in over it. He put his hand in his pocket and found a horseshoe nail. He moved toward the place the voice was coming from and what did he see under a big tree but an enormous man wearing a red cloak or mantle.

'Open your mouth,' said he, 'till I take out that particle.'

The big man opened his mouth so wide that the other man thought he'd swallow him, body and soul. Every one of his teeth was six inches long and as sharp as a cobbler's awl. When he stuck the horseshoe nail under the tooth the big man let a roar out of him that wakened all the dead in the cemetery. The man thought that the Day of Judgement had come. All the dead were dressed in white shrouds. The big man asked him would he like to see where these people lived and, before he could answer, the man stamped on the ground three times with his foot. The ground opened and the two went down. When they went down they walked and walked and walked still more until they came to a huge lake. It wasn't a lake of water but a lake of fire, and the man saw hundreds of thousands of people in the fire, screaming and moaning.

'Do you see that crowd out there?' said the big man.

'I do,' said the man.

'Those people there are in Hell,' said the big man, 'and they'll never, ever get out of it. Now,' said he, 'come along with me and I'll show you another place.'

They walked on until they came to another lake, and there were thousands of people moaning in that lake, all tied with chains to beds of fire.

'Now,' said the big man, 'that's Purgatory. Those people expect that they'll escape from there some day. Come along and I'll show you another place.'

They went on and came to a huge meadow and there were hundreds of thousands of people in the meadow. They all had wings but one wing was broken on each person.

'Those are the cursed angels that rebelled against God in Heaven,' said the big man. 'They committed the sin of pride. Now,' said he, 'walk on and I'll show you another place.'

They came to a little, narrow, twisting boreen with a big wide road beyond it. There was an angel guarding the little boreen with a sword of light in his hand.

'Now,' said the big man, 'that's the road to Heaven and nobody can go there without dying first. Now,' said he to the other man, 'I'll be leaving you and I won't see you again for seven years. I'll give you some advice before parting with you. If you keep on with the card-playing and drinking and bad company you'll end up in one of the places I showed you earlier.'

With that he left the young man. It was bright daylight when the youth got home to his own house. He changed his ways after that and he was well-mannered and kind till the end of his days.

64. The Stream of Orthalán

When children were born long ago and died before they were baptised – apparently it wasn't as easy in those days as it is today to find a priest to baptise a child – people used to think that it wasn't right to bury such children, or those who were born dead and couldn't be baptised, in consecrated ground. The most suitable place to bury them was thought to be in a place between two estates, on the boundary between two estates where one side was owned by one landlord and the other was owned by a different landlord. And they used to think that those children weren't lost, for want of baptism, and wouldn't end up in a bad place but went to the Stream of Orthalán. And they used to say that when this world was over, those were the people who would re-populate the world in place of the present people when this world finished after two thousand years.

Saints

There are so many saints mentioned in Irish folklore and so many stories about them that it would take many, many volumes to tell them all. Since this book could only make room for a very few of them, I decided to confine myself to a few examples about the most famous saints: Patrick, Brigid, Colm Cille and Martin. These stories are only a small fraction of those told about those saints but I hope they give a representative flavour.

This collection is a mixture of truth, fiction and borrowings from the lives of other saints. But this is the usual pattern in every country. As was the case with Our Saviour and the Blessed Virgin, they are attempts by the laity to fill the gaps in their knowledge of the saints. Even written biographies of saints are often based on folklore. The stories were the people's homage to the saint, and his fame can be assessed by the degree otowhich he is remembered by the people.

Christians had a great interest in the lives of the saints during the Middle Ages and it was then that many of these stories originated. They prayed to them, they honoured them and sang songs about them. They borrowed from the classics and other writings to compose stories about their favourite saints. Certain places took great pride in their patron saint, as witnessed by the feast days and patterns that were so very common long ago and continue in many places down to the present day. Very often a saint is associated with a particular rock on which a footprint is discernible, or with an old church that has long since gone to ruin. And, of course, their memory is preserved in the practice of giving their names to infants at Baptism.

The reader need not be in the least surprised to hear that a certain saint lived when our Saviour was preaching, or that Saint Brigid, say, helped the Blessed Virgin. Neither should he complain that a certain episode (such as Saint Colm Cille's coffin floating across the sea from Scotland to Ireland) is also told about a different saint. He must remember that these stories simply are not history, but attempts to fill the gaps left in history.

65. Saint Patrick and Crom Dubh

There's a certain Sunday in the month of July, the last Sunday in the month, and in this part of the country it's called Crom Dubh's Sunday. And the reason it's called that is that, in Saint Patrick's time, Crom Dubh was a pagan and on that very Sunday he became a Christian. Crom Dubh lived somewhere in Connaught. It was probably in County Mayo, at the time Saint Patrick was in Connaught himself. And Saint Patrick was staying not far from where Crom Dubh lived. Crom Dubh knew about him and indeed they both knew about each other. Saint Patrick used to talk to him now and again but, if he did, Crom Dubh wasn't ready to become a Christian. But even so, himself and Saint Patrick were very great with one another, even if he wasn't one. They were so friendly with one another that Crom Dubh sent his servant to him with a present of the quarter hind of a beast he had killed. And the servant came with the hindquarter of beef to Saint Patrick's house and he told Saint Patrick that this was a present his master had sent him.

'*Deo gratias*!' said Saint Patrick.

The servant went back home to his master, Crom Dubh, and Crom Dubh asked him:

'Did Patrick thank me much,' said he, 'for the quarter of beef I sent him?'

'I couldn't say,' said the servant, 'that he thanked you at all, because I couldn't make out, for the life of me, what he said. I never in my life heard anybody use even one of the words he said. I don't know what he said.'

'I've another quarter here,' said Crom Dubh, 'and bring it over to him and say I sent it as a present to him, till we see will he thank me for the second quarter.'

The servant took the second quarter and took it to Saint Patrick's house and told Saint Patrick that this was another quarter that his master had sent to him as a present.

'*Deo gratias*!' said Saint Patrick.

The servant went back and his master asked him when he got back:

'Did Patrick thank you for the second quarter I sent him?'

'The same thanks he gave for the first one,' said the servant. 'I don't know, for the life of me, a single word he said!'

'I've another quarter here, as good as those two,' said Crom Dubh, 'and I'll send it to him till we see will he thank me for that. Take this with you, the third quarter, and bring it to him.'

The servant brought the third quarter to Saint Patrick's house and left it there.

'And here's a third quarter,' said he to Patrick, 'that my master sent to you.'

'*Deo gratias*!' said Saint Patrick.

The servant went back to his master.

'Well! What sort of thanks did you get for bringing the third quarter to him?' said Crom Dubh.

'The same thing he said always,' said the servant. 'For the life of me I don't know what he said but it was the same thing he said each of the three times.'

'Away with you now,' said Crom Dubh, 'and tell him to come over here to me, that I'm asking him and not to delay in coming.'

Crom Dubh's intention was to kill him for not thanking him enough and for not getting down on his knees giving thanks for the three quarters of a beast he had sent him.

'I'll be with you,' said Saint Patrick. 'There's no time to be lost so I'll be with you.'

Saint Patrick went over to him and he was only in the door when Crom Dubh asked him:

'What sort of thanks was that you gave me,' said he, 'for the three quarters of beef I sent you?'

'Oh, I gave you great thanks,' said Patrick.

'You didn't thank me at all,' said Crom Dubh.

'Oh, I did indeed, I gave you great thanks,' said Patrick. 'Have you a scales?'

'I have,' said Crom Dubh.

'Would you have another three quarters of beef as good and heavy as the three quarters you sent me as a gift?' said Patrick.

'I have,' said Crom Dubh.

'Put them on the scales,' said Patrick.

Then he wrote *Deo gratias* three times on a piece of paper. He put the three quarters of meat on one side of the scales and Saint Patrick put the piece of paper, with *Deo gratias* written on it three times, on the other side of the scales. The piece of paper with *Deo gratias* written on it three times lifted the three quarters of beef, and it was far heavier than the three fine quarters of beef that Crom Dubh had.

'Oh, Patrick,' said Crom Dubh, 'I'm the one in the wrong! For God's sake, baptise me and my household and all belonging to me! They must become Christians today.'

And that's why they call the last Sunday in July Crom Dubh's Sunday. That's the day there's a big crowd on the Reek in County Mayo. There's also a big pattern in a place called Mám Éan between the Twelve Bens in Conamara. And ever since that day Crom Dubh's Sunday is held on the Sunday that Crom Dubh, the pagan, became a Christian in Saint Patrick's time.

66. The Puck Goat

Saint Patrick went to Achadh Ghabhair and started to build a monastery there; and he had no idea how he'd gather stones or other materials for it. There was a heathen there, Crom Dubh, and he went to talk to him and he promised to lend him a horse and cart for drawing stones.

Saint Patrick began to build the monastery and when he sent a messenger to Crom Dubh asking him for the horse and cart he was told to go up on a nearby hill and catch the big puck goat that was there and harness him to a cart to draw the stones! The messenger went back and arrived home to Saint Patrick and told him that the response he got was to go and get the puck goat and use him to draw the stones. Saint Patrick told the boy to go and get the puck goat; so he went and caught the puck goat and harnessed him to a cart and began to draw stones with him. As he was drawing them everybody was amazed at the fine job he was doing.

All was well. But food for the workmen was getting short, and Crom Dubh had promised it to him, having said that he'd give him anything he wanted. He sent a man to Crom Dubh to ask for a bullock to kill for the men and, indeed, Crom Dubh told the messenger to go and take a bull that was out in the field to kill for the men. Nobody could ever come near that bull without being killed. The boy went for the bull and the bull went along with him until he was killed and eaten by the men. Saint Patrick told them to keep the bones and all the other leavings and leave them on the table and to throw nothing away. They kept the bones and saved them until all of the bull was eaten; and, when it was, Crom Dubh sent his servant to Saint Patrick to demand the cost of the bull. He had been promised that there would be no charge as the bull was a present; and so Saint Patrick told the servant to get up and spread out the skin on the ground and toss all the bones into it. The servant got up and did as he was told. The bull got up and began to graze on the grass. Crom Dubh's servant brought the bull home to Crom Dubh and, of course, they were all amazed at what had happened. Saint Patrick continued building the monastery; and the puck goat drew the stones.

Then Saint Patrick got a call to go to the Reek and he had to go to the Reek. And he found plenty to do there. The devils were there – we might as well say it – the devils were on the Reek, and he had a right job to get rid of them from the Reek. But then, when he had banished them to the devils' side of the Reek, their mother attacked him and he had an almighty job to get the better of her. And they are all on the devils' side of the Reek ever since.

Then he set off to visit Lough Derg of the Saints. There was an old road there that people used to go and nobody ever went that way that wasn't killed. Nobody ever knew why. There was a serpent in Lough Derg of the Saints, and the serpent used to rise up and kill passersby. Saint Patrick went there and spent two nights and two days in the water, fighting the serpent with his sword. In the end, he discovered that there was a mole on her side but he was unable to find it. In the end he came across the mole and stabbed it, drawing blood. One side of the lake is red ever since and the other side is clear water.

67. The Soul that Kissed the Corpse

In Saint Patrick's time in Ireland there was an old man dying in a very backward place. The poor man hadn't a relative or friend to send for a priest or brother to give him Extreme Unction in preparation for his last long journey. Our Saviour was coming to visit Saint Patrick and He saw the poor man's predicament. He whispered in Patrick's ear to hurry to visit the poor man. Patrick hurried to him and anointed him with the Holy Oils.

With that, his soul left him but it didn't do so unknown to Saint Patrick, because Patrick saw the soul go three times one after the other, from the body to the door and back again and the soul kissed the corpse each time. Patrick was very surprised at that – he never saw the likes before – and he asked Our Saviour the reason.

Our Saviour said to him:

'The soul was sad to leave the faithful, decent body which had kept it so clean, without sin in this life!'

68. The Blacksmith and the Tinker

Saint Patrick was brought to Ireland as a slave when he was a boy. He was sold to a farmer in Ulster, for five pounds, to work as a swineherd. However, part of the bargain was that the master would give Patrick his freedom if he could repay the five pounds to the farmer at any time. Patrick used to be out on the hill every day minding the pigs and used to pray to God every day asking for the money so that he could give it to the farmer and gain his freedom. In the end, there was a big sow rooting in the ground one day, and what did she root up but a big lump of gold! Patrick saw the yellow lump and took it in his hand but had no idea what it was. That evening he brought the lump to a tinker, to ask him what it was or what it was worth.

'Arrah,' said the tinker, 'that's a lump of solder that I lost yesterday! Leave it there after you!'

Patrick didn't leave it because he knew that it wasn't solder at all, and he took it to a blacksmith. The blacksmith told him the truth that the lump was gold and was worth a hundred pounds. The blacksmith bought the gold from Patrick for a hundred pounds, and Patrick blessed him and cursed the tinker who tried to trick him. That's why blacksmiths are lucky ever since and tinkers have nothing but misfortune. Patrick paid the five pounds to the farmer and he was given his freedom, and he had the rest to take home. He studied for the priesthood and went on to be a bishop so that he could come and teach God's religion in Ireland again.

69. The Water of Eternity

Saint Patrick was out for a walk one day and came to a forge on the side of the road. He went into the forge and the blacksmith was very busy at his work. After a while a cowherd came in to them; he was idle and lazy. The smith asked the herd to work the bellows, which he did, but in a slow and lazy fashion. After another while, who should come in but a tinker and the tinker was very loud and foul-mouthed. The blacksmith was working hard. After another while, who should come in but a druid. He had a vessel in his hand and the vessel was full of something.

'Take this from me,' said the druid to the blacksmith, 'and wash your skin with what's in this vessel and there's no danger that you'll ever grow old.'

'And what have you got in it?' asked the blacksmith.

'The Water of Eternity,' said the druid.

The blacksmith turned to take the vessel but the cowherd, who was blowing the bellows, shouted at him:

'Use the hot iron or I'll stop blowing the bellows.'

The blacksmith went to the fire to take out the iron and the tinker took the vessel from the druid and threw the contents over a heap of coal in a corner of the forge. Saint Patrick was annoyed with the tinker for spilling the Water of Eternal Life over the coal. I can't remember all he said but this is what he said to the tinker:

'You'll be travelling the world and nobody will want you, and the cow-herd will bear the weariness of the blacksmith.'

That's how it is ever since. No matter how old or ancient the coal is it always looks new, with the same shine on it always. No matter how hard the blacksmith works, he's never tired; and the cowherd is always tired. And, at the same time, tinkers are always travelling and walking the country.

70. The Miraculous Yield of Milk

At the time Saint Patrick was going round working miracles, he came in to an old woman on a fine spring day. The old woman was very good-hearted. He asked her for something to drink and she said she had very little, that the cow was nearly dry but whatever drop she had she'd give him, and welcome. She told the servant-girl to go out and milk the cow for whatever drop she might have; and she was taking a small vessel with her.

'Bring a fine big vessel with you,' said Saint Patrick.

She was very surprised at that, but she brought a can with her and the girl didn't leave the cowshed until she had filled the can from the cow. There were three or four men working there, sowing potatoes, and she called them in so that they could drink their fill of milk, more than they ever drank from a single cow in their lives before. And they were very pleased with the amount they got to drink.

Before that time, cows never gave more than the full of their horns of milk.

71. The Twelve Apostles

When Saint Patrick first came to Ireland people were making out that he was a saint. Himself and the twelve apostles were out walking one day and they came to the house of a Protestant. The Protestant had workmen cutting timber for firewood and when he saw them coming he said to the men that this was Saint Patrick coming.

'And we'll find out now if he can work any miracles,' said he.

Saint Patrick came over and began talking to the Protestant but the Protestant wasn't paying him much heed.

'Now,' said Saint Patrick, 'this pile of timber here is old and seasoned. You have it cut a year.'

'That's right,' said the farmer.

'The timber you're cutting now is not as dry as that.'

'It isn't,' said the Protestant.

'Now, which of them will make the hottest fire?'

'Oh, the seasoned timber,' said the Protestant.

'Alright,' said Saint Patrick. 'I'll put my twelve apostles here in that pile and let you put timber all round them and over their heads, any way you want. Let you put twelve of your men in the pile of fresh timber. It won't burn so quickly and it won't get as hot.'

'That's right,' said the Protestant.

So they put the twelve apostles together and the dry timber around them, and the Protestant put twelve of his men in his own pile and they set fire to the two piles. As they burned, the dry timber burned more quickly than the fresh timber. When it had burned out, the twelve apostles came out of the heap of ashes, each one wearing a green cap on his head. When the Protestant went to look for his own men, there wasn't a bone or a pick of them left that hadn't burned to ashes! When the Protestant saw that:

'Now,' said he, 'that's proof that Saint Patrick is a saint.'

And he was converted by Saint Patrick. He believed everything he told him. And I heard, whether I heard right or wrong, that that's the reason that every one in Ireland wears a green ribbon, from that day to this, on Saint Patrick's Day.

72. As God Wills, So Will the Weather Be

In the old days, long ago, when Saint Patrick was building the church of Saint Patrick in County Down, there were three or four masons working on it and they were lodging in a country house about a mile away and came to work each morning. This morning the woman of the house got up and got their breakfast and when she called them they got up and ate their breakfast. One of them said to the other that the morning didn't look too good and that it looked as if it might rain. And the woman told them that when she was getting up early that morning she saw the sun rising and it was very red and didn't look good and it was likely that the day would come wet, that she saw the crows flying through the air screeching, and saw the deer heading for the woods for shelter, and that she had always heard that those were sure signs that the day would be wet, that they would only be putting a journey on themselves going to work and coming back again and they'd have nothing to show for their day. They only got paid for the number of hours they worked each day.

Still and all, one man said to another that they had better go ahead, whatever the day turned out like, wet or dry, that Saint Patrick was in a hurry to get the church finished and, even if the day didn't turn out fine, the rain wouldn't melt them. They took up their tools and went off until they came to their place of work. They were a little late arriving on account of all the time they spent debating and wondering whether they'd come or not. And Saint Patrick was waiting there for them and he asked them:

'Tell me, men,' said he, 'why weren't you here earlier? You're later today than any other day.'

'We wondered should we come or not,' said one of the men. 'The morning looked so bad we thought it would turn wet and the woman of the house we're staying at told us that she was up very early this morning and saw the sun rising and it was terribly red, that she saw the crows flying through the air screeching and saw the deer going into the wood for shelter and that the day looked bad, and that she'd always heard that a morning like that would end up in a wet day.'

'Start off now,' said he, 'and work as fast as you can and you'll do good work yet. And never again,' said he, 'any day that you are working here, don't be a bit afraid that it will rain. And I'll give you another bit of advice:

'Do not heed a crow or a deer,
Never heed a woman's words;
Whether the sun rises early or late,
It's as God wills, the day will be.'

It turned out a fine day, the finest ever, and the men believed that Saint Patrick had worked a great miracle. And they got paid the same as they got the hardest day they had ever worked.

73. The Three Curses

'Listen carefully now,' said Saint Patrick to his servant-boy, 'I'm going to sleep and I'll be raving. I'm afraid of my life that what I say won't be good when I'm raving so be sure to listen to whatever I say.'

Saint Patrick went to sleep then and when he was a good while asleep he began to snore. He wasn't long snoring when he began to rave.

Then he spoke in his sleep:

'Bad luck to Ireland!' said he.

The boy was listening to him.

'If there is, may it be on the tops of the rushes!' said the boy.

Saint Patrick slept again for a while and began to rave:

'Bad luck to Ireland!' said he.

The boy answered:

'If there is, may it be on the highest part of the white cattle!' said he.

The highest part of white cattle is their roar. Saint Patrick fell asleep for another while and when he was raving he spoke again in his sleep:

'I've said it twice before and I'll say it again: Bad luck to Ireland!' said he.

The boy answered him:

'If there is, may it be at the root of the furze!' said he.

After a while, Saint Patrick woke up.

'Tell me, my boy,' said he, 'did I say anything in my sleep?'

'You did,' said the boy.

'And what did I say?'

'You said: "Bad luck to Ireland!" three times.'

'And what did you say?'

'The first time you said it,' I said "May it be on the tops of the rushes!" The second time, I said "May it be on top of the highest part of the white cattle!" And the third time you said it, I said "May it be at the root of the furze!"'

'Musha,' said Saint Patrick to him, 'you're the best boy that was ever in Ireland!'

And that's the reason that the priest should have a boy serving him at Mass.

74. The Marvel of Friday the First Of May

When Saint Patrick was going round Ireland, he came to the house of a heathen in the north of Ireland. His wife and family converted to the Catholic faith but he wouldn't convert. One day, they were out taking the air and they saw a bush that wasn't very big, growing from one stump, such as it was.

'Now,' said the heathen to Saint Patrick, 'if you can get that bush to talk, I'll convert to you.'

When Saint Patrick had prayed for a while, he asked the bush if it had been there for long and the bush said that it had.

'But how did you come to be there?' said he.

'There were herring-buyers who used to buy herrings in Galway and go selling them all over Ireland with their horses, and one of the horses got a thorn in her hoof when she was passing the little bush of Armagh and it stayed in her hoof till she came here; and it stuck in the mud and I'm here ever since putting roots in the ground and branches in the air.'

'You must have seen and heard a lot of marvels since then?' said Saint Patrick.

'I never saw nor heard anyone marvelling at any marvel like the Marvel of Friday the first of May.'

'And is that all you can tell me about the Marvel of Friday the first of May?' said he.

'That's all,' said the bush.

'Is there anyone around here that's older than you?' said the saint.

'There's an old man in such and such a place,' telling him the name of the place.

He went to the old man and asked him had he any marvel to relate or had he heard of the Marvel of Friday the first of May. He said he'd heard of it but could give him no account of it, except to say that he had heard of it.

'Have you any other news for me?' said the saint.

'I have, a marvel that everybody marvelled at, and I saw it with my own two eyes,' said he. 'There was a steward here once and, when he died the whole of the village, even if they all came to help, couldn't lift him into his coffin. An old man who lived here said that maybe if they got four other stewards they might be able to do it, some way or another. They came and lifted him and put him in his coffin and carried him off on their shoulders. A sudden mist came down and the people following couldn't keep sight of them and nobody ever saw the four stewards alive, any more than the dead steward, since then.'

'Hum! Hum!' said Saint Patrick. 'Is there anything in this place older than you that might be able to tell me something about the Marvel of Friday the first of May?' said he.

'There's a raven in such and such a place that is so old that it has an anvil worn out from rubbing its beak on it from the time it goes to sleep there at night till it wakes up in the morning.'

He went off till he met the raven, and put his stole round his neck and asked the raven was he there.

'I am,' said he.

'Are you long there?' said the saint.

'I'm here so long that I have this anvil worn down to the place of my two feet,' said he, 'and all I do is rub my beak on it every night when I come to sleep on it.'

'Did you ever hear talk of the Wonders of Friday the first of May?' said Saint Patrick.

'I can't give you any account of it, except to say that I heard talk of the Wonders of Friday the first of May, and that's all I know about it.'

'Is there anything round here that's older than you?' said he.

'There's a deer on such and such a hill,' said the raven, and he's a lot older than me.'

The saint went off to the place where the deer was, and Saint Patrick put his stole round his neck:

'Are you there, deer?' he said.

'I am indeed,' said the deer.

'Are you long there?' said the saint.

'I'm here since the times of the fathers. I think there are very few alive now that were alive when I was born.'

'Then tell me some marvellous stories,' said the saint.

'I neither saw nor heard of any marvel, that I'd marvel at, except that I heard tell of the Marvel of Friday the first of May. But I can't tell you anything more about it.'

'Is there anything at all in Ireland that's older than you?' said Saint Patrick.

'There's the Blind Salmon of Assaroe,' said the deer.

He went to the banks of the Pool of Assaroe and put the stole round his neck.

'Are you there, Blind Salmon of Assaroe?' said Saint Patrick.

'I am,' said he.

'Are you long there?' said he.

'You could say I'm a good while here,' said the Salmon.

'I'm sure you can tell me about the Marvel of Friday the first of May, then,' said Saint Patrick.

'My woe, my desolation, my eternal ruination! I'm the one that can tell you rightly about that! I was here on the morning of Friday the first of May. At sunrise I leaped out of this pool full of hope and courage and, between rising and falling, the water froze so hard that I couldn't break it; and I started pounding on it, trying to break the ice, until, in the end, I was so tired that I had to lie there on it and the crows came and picked the eye out of my head and so much of my blood flowed out on the ice that it melted it. I'm here, ever since, except for my trips out to sea,' said he.

Saint Patrick was satisfied then that he had found out about the marvel. He went home then with the son of the heathen to the heathen's house, hoping to convert him to the true religion. When they came in to the heathen, Saint Patrick asked him would he convert.

'I saw a dead man down there today, and I'll show him to you tomorrow, and if you can make him talk I'll convert,' said he.

Next morning he told one of his men to go and lie on a certain heap of stones and pretend that he was dead.

'And be very careful not to wake up,' said he, 'if Patrick pokes you!'

Saint Patrick and the heathen went to the place where the supposedly dead man was lying. When Saint Patrick came up to him, he put his foot on him and said:

'If you're asleep, may you sleep enough,
If you are not asleep, may you never rise up!'

The man was awake, but he never rose again.

'Now, will you be converted?' said the saint to the heathen.

'I wouldn't convert now if you buried me alive under seven feet of clay!' said he.

'If that's your decision, then suffer it!' said Saint Patrick.

Saint Patrick and the son of the heathen dug a hole, seven feet deep, for him and put him in it. When the son turned away from the grave, he burst out crying.

'I know you're sorry after your father,' said Saint Patrick to the son.

'I am,' said the son.

'Come on, so,' said Saint Patrick, 'and we'll dig him up.'

When the son came over to the grave there was nothing there but earwigs and beetles and he cried his heart out.

'Now,' said Saint Patrick, 'your father has been saved by your tears of repentance: his soul is with God and his body has been eaten by the beetles.'

'I believe that we've converted everyone around here,' said Saint Patrick.

'You have,' said the son of the heathen, 'except for two brothers and their mother, but you'll have no trouble converting them. They're good decent people.'

'We'll go to see them tomorrow,' said Saint Patrick.

They went to see them next day, and when they saw Saint Patrick coming they were delighted. When he came up to them they gave him a hundred thousand welcomes and said that they had been hoping for him to come for ages, ever since they heard of him, and that was a long time ago. He baptised the two of them then. When the two had been baptised, one of them asked:

'Why didn't you baptise me as well as you baptised my brother?'

'I did,' said Saint Patrick.

'You didn't,' said the brother again.

'I didn't baptise you,' said Saint Patrick, 'because I had a good reason for it,' said he.

'And what was the reason?' said the brother.

'One of his descendants will be a great saint,' said he, 'but none of your descendants will be a saint. But some of your descendants will be good men. And that's why I baptised him better than I baptised you.'

Then he baptised the mother and they kept Saint Patrick and the other man in their house for a week. And from those two brothers came the finest stock in Ireland.

75. The Woman in the Tavern

When Saint Patrick was in Uíbh Ráthach – he was never here in Corca Dhuibhne -–he was travelling around and he went into a tavern one day and asked for a pint. The woman went to the vessel and was filling the pint and went to hand it to him.

'Fill it up,' said Saint Patrick.

She put another drop in it, but it still wasn't full.

'Fill it up,' said Saint Patrick again.

She put another drop in it. It took her three attempts to get it full.

'Look over to your right,' said Saint Patrick.

She looked and saw a big, well-fed dog on top of the barrel.

After a year and a day had passed, Saint Patrick was going that way again and he called in again and asked for a pint. The woman filled the glass to the brim.

'Did you fill every pint to the brim like that for the past year?' Saint Patrick asked her.

'I did,' said the woman.

'Look over to your right,' said Saint Patrick to her.

She looked and saw a small dog, with his bones sticking out through his skin walking back and forth on top of the barrel!

76. 'It's a Long Monday, Patrick'

At the time Saint Patrick was preaching in Ireland, he used to walk from place to place with people coming to him in droves, listening to his teaching and being baptised by him. They say he never went west into Kerry at all, except for once, when he was on the borders between Cork, Kerry and Limerick, when people came to him with a most distressing story. They said that there was a monster in their neighbourhood which was very ferocious, and not a year went by that she didn't eat a few people; and they asked him to come with them and banish her from the place. He said he'd go, and he went.

When they got to the place they pointed out the spot where she usually was and Saint Patrick went to look for her. He took his book and began to read from it and when he saw the monster she had to stay still. He got her under control and banished her south before him to Mangerton Mountain. When they got to the foot of the mountain he drove her up ahead of him to the top of Mangerton. There's a lake on top of that mountain. The Demon's Hole they call that lake since, and its depth is unknown, it's so deep. When they got to the edge of the lake Patrick took the monster and threw her into it and said to her:

'There, now, stay there till the Doomsday Monday!'

Which she did. But, they say that on every Easter Monday since that time, she comes out in the morning and stretches out on a little grassy plot on the edge of the lake. In the evening, when she's tired of lying on the grassy plot, just as the sun is going down, she shakes herself, lets out a sigh and says:

'Musha, it's a long Monday, Patrick!'

77. The Salmon's Leap

They say that it was Saint Patrick that gave the salmon his leap and put the twisted head on the plaice, and this is how it came about. When Saint Patrick was travelling around Ireland, he had most of the people converted, but there were still a good few pagans and they wouldn't accept his teaching at all.

One day when Patrick was walking, he was going along the bank of a river and he met a group of men who were fishing. Now, these fishermen were pagans and they wanted to ridicule the saint. As Patrick was passing, one of the fishermen said:

'Wait, Patrick, and you'll get a fish!'

'I'll wait,' said Patrick.

So he sat down on the bank of the river. In a short time one man pulled in a very big fish but, if he did, he didn't give it to Patrick. He threw it into the basket they had for their fish. Patrick got up and made to go but another of the pagans said:

'Wait, Patrick, and you'll get the next fish we catch!'

'I'll wait, so,' said Patrick and sat down again.

It wasn't long before they caught another fish but they didn't give it to Patrick and threw it in the basket again. Patrick got up and was about to go when a third pagan said to him:

'Wait, Patrick, and you'll get the next fish we catch!'

'Musha, I'll wait,' said Patrick and sat down again.

This time he sat on a high knoll a bit back from the river. The next fish they caught was a plaice. Up till that time the head of the plaice was as straight as any other fish in the river; but when the plaice saw the pagans mocking the saint she wanted to join in the fun. She twisted her neck and turned her head and looked at him over her shoulder with derision. And when Patrick saw that she was sneering at him he said:

'May your head stay as it is!'

And it stayed that way. She couldn't straighten her neck or turn her head around and ever since that day the plaice has a crooked head. As Patrick was thinking of getting up from the knoll the salmon jumped clean out of the river and landed in his arms. And Patrick said:

'I grant you the gift of leaping!'

And ever since, the salmon can leap better than any other fish and always will.

78. Saint Patrick to Judge Ireland

When Saint Patrick first went to the Reek he was badly needed there. He cast the Thunderbolt into the lake and threw his bell at it. Then he built a house, to spend his life there, and built a chapel too. An angel came to him from God Almighty and told him that he was needed in such and such a county in Ulster much more than he was needed on the Reek.

'I've no wish to leave here till I die,' said Saint Patrick. 'I won't go to Ulster unless I'm well paid for it.'

The angel asked him what kind of payment he had in mind.

'Only this,' said he, 'to be the judge of Ireland on the Day of Judgment.'

The angel went back to Heaven with the story. The Saviour said that that was something he couldn't get. All the saints and apostles came begging Him to let him have it but He refused. When the Blessed Virgin saw what was going on she came to hear what they were saying and she got him the permission. The angel came back to Patrick and told him that his wish was granted. Off he went to Ulster. And that's where the top bishop must always be, because it was there that Patrick died. But if he had died in Mayo, then the top bishop would have been in Mayo.

79. The Hole of the House of Liabán

When Saint Patrick was going round Ireland, baptising and converting people, he came to Ceann na hAbhann, east of Gort. There he turned east towards Tobar Muire as night was falling. He went into this house and asked for a night's lodgings from the woman of the house.

Will you let me stop here for the night?' he asked her.

Musha, upon my soul, I can't,' said she

You can't? Where's the man of the house?'

He's out looking after the stock.'

Well, is there anywhere around that I could hang up my book?' said Saint Patrick.

There is,' she said, 'out in the stable there.'

He hung up his book on the rafter and spent the night in the stable. When Saint Patrick got up in the morning there was a swallow-hole where the house was and the pair of them had been swallowed down the hole. And that's the Hole of the House of Liabán, and it's still there.

80. Saint Brigid and the Blessed Virgin.

When the Blessed Virgin had Our Saviour she was ashamed to be churched in the chapel in front of the people; but she met Saint Brigid and told her that she was going to the chapel to be churched, but that she was ashamed that everybody would be looking at her. Don't let that bother you at all!' said Saint Brigid, 'I'll come along with you and I'll put on this fancy-dress.'

So she dressed herself up. She put on the fancy dress over her body and head and covered herself completely in such a way that nobody would look at anything else but her, because nobody ever saw such a rig-out in their lives. Saint Brigid told the Blessed Virgin to go ahead of her and she'd follow on, and there'd be no question that anybody would look at her, since they'd all be looking at Brigid. That's how it turned out. They went ahead and the Blessed Virgin was blessed. Nobody looked at her from then on.

The Blessed Virgin was very grateful to Saint Brigid and said to her:

'Brigid, I'm going to put your feast day ahead of my own from now on.

Saint Brigid has that day ever since — the first day of spring is her feast day and the next day is called the Feast of Mary of the Candles in the Temple.

81. Saint Brigid's Prayer

Saints used to come to Ireland long ago and indeed at other times too, and there was nowhere they liked better than Ireland to travel round in. But when Saint Brigid came to Ireland she didn't know much about it; and she came into a house to pass the night and was looking for lodgings there. She was well received. She got a little room that wasn't very big; so she went in there. It might have been a bed of straw on the ground or it might have been a four-poster bed, I just don't know. But when she went into the room to go to bed she said this prayer:

'There are four corners on my bed,
There are four angels on them spread,
Matthew, Mark, Luke and John,
To bless the bed that I lie on.
All night I will be lying here,
In care of Christ the Lord, so dear.
And if I die before I wake,
I pray to God my soul to take!'

A man came in to the room, intending to molest her, and saw four soldiers surrounding her and he wasn't long getting out.

'Why aren't you going in?' someone said to him.

'Oh,' said he, 'there are four soldiers minding this one. She must be an angel from God or some such. No one could get near her. He'd have no business there.'

82. The Protestant and the Ice

Before there was any bridge there, Saint Colm Cille made a causeway from one side of the lake to the other to get to Mín an Lábáin. When the water is low, you can see the causeway there, from that day to this.

Very many years afterwards there was a great frost in Gartan, one winter, and the lake froze over completely. A Protestant walked over on it until he was more than three-quarters of the way to Mín an Lábáin. He shouted out that he'd make a liar of Colm Cille, because Saint Colm Cille had said that nobody would ever cross by that causeway but himself.

'Colm Cille had to build a causeway but I'm able to walk on top of the water.'

The ice broke under him and he fell through and the ice cut his head off! And as the head floated off on the ice it shouted out three times:

'I'm damned! I'm damned! I'm damned!'

From that day till this, the Protestants in Gartan respect Saint Colm Cille.

83. The Half-Salmon

Saint Colm Cille was crossing one day at a place they call Bridge Isle, between two lakes in Gartan. There's only a little bit of land between the two lakes with a small stream connecting the two lakes. There was a Protestant fishing in the lower lake and he caught a salmon and Colm Cille asked him for a bit of it. He wouldn't give it to him.

'Well,' said Saint Colm Cille, said he, 'neither you nor anybody else will ever catch another salmon in that lake again!'

It is true, there is not a salmon in the lower lake and there won't be until the Day of Judgment. They come up to the mouth of the bridge but they have to turn back again before they go any further. Some time afterwards a Protestant caught a salmon in the lower lake, a sort of a half-salmon it was.

It wasn't really a salmon, more like a brown trout. Himself and another Protestant began arguing. He said that Saint Colm Cille was a liar, that here was a salmon.

'That's no salmon,' said the other Protestant, 'because if it was a salmon it wouldn't be down there after what Saint Colm Cille said.'

With that, the salmon leapt out of the Protestant's two hands and went into the lake that the salmon were in!

84. 'Colm Cille's a Liar!'

Once upon a time Saint Colm Cille was travelling round from place to place. Where did he end up but near a place where men were coming in from Maol Rua. As they were coming in, one of the men said:

'There's Colm Cille,' said he, 'and he'll be asking for some fish.

'Oh,' said the other man, 'we'll give him one.'

'We will not,' said he, 'we'll put the nets on top of them and tell him we caught nothing.'

When the boat came ashore:

'Did you catch anything?' said Colm Cille.

'We didn't,' said he.

'If you didn't, may you catch them and if you did, may you not!' said Saint Colm Cille three times.

Next day, when they went out fishing and threw out the nets, the salmon would rise on one side of the nets and land on the other and they couldn't catch as much as one.

Time passed at Maol Rua for three score years or maybe more. The servant-boys of a Protestant were collecting seaweed on the strand and what did they see in the seaweed but a salmon. They came to the door of the big house. A woman came out:

'Colm Cille is a liar, after all!'

With that the salmon took wings and flew off and from that day to this there hasn't been a salmon in Maol Rua.

85. Colm Cille in Toraigh

It's a long time since Saint Colm Cille and his apostles came around this way in a curragh made of cowhide. They went on round the shore till they cleared Cnoc Fola and made port in Port Uí Churraoin or, as the people up there would say, Bun an Inbheara. They walked on up till they were on top of Cnoc na Naomh at a place they call Corr na Leabhar. There was a nice flat patch of grass there and they camped on it.

When they were there a fair while, performing miracles and baptising and so on, one of the saints said, one day, that they should go to Toraigh. Colm Cille said that if any man of them could throw his staff to Toraigh he'd follow it. One of the saints threw his staff, saying that, with the help of God and his own effort, it would reach Toraigh. The staff didn't get past the high-water mark at Mín Lárach. There it fell. The second man came along and said the same thing: that, with the help of God and his own effort, he'd throw his staff as far as Toraigh, and the staff didn't reach farther than the high-water mark in Mín Lárach. Colm Cille said:

With the help of God and my own effort, I'll throw my staff to Toraigh.'

And the staff hit the high-water mark in Toraigh. Colm Cille and his apostles got into their leather currach and rowed till they landed in Toraigh. All of the people of Toraigh, all pagans, gathered together and said they would not allow them come ashore. He asked permission to spread out his cloak on the high-water mark in Toraigh. Mac Ruairí granted permission. When he spread out his cloak, Mac Ruairí jumped out on to it. The cloak kept spreading and every man and woman jumped in on to it except for three, Tadhg, Úna and Áine and a mad dog. Those three jumped into the sea at Gob an Deilín and when the dog jumped too he left the tracks of his four feet on the point. Tadhg, Úna and Áine went westwards, three or four miles west of Gabhla, and they're there from that day to this; and every seven years they'll hoist their sails and try to make it back to Toraigh. That is their fate and they'll keep sailing forever until a man of the Mac Ruairí Clan lays eyes on them. Then the commotion will start and they'll begin lamenting and their lament will be:

'My three sorrows, nine times over, Toraigh to the north and Árainn.'

Then they'll return and wait in the same place and the Mic-a-Gorra are there from that day till this and every seventh year they'll set sail again.

Then Colm Cille set to; he built a chapel and baptised all the people in Toraigh. There's a stone on the island and they call it the Stone of Toraigh. And everybody says that if the Stone of Toraigh is turned on you you're finished. I don't know if it was the daughter of Balor that left it there, or maybe the pagans, but it's been there from all eternity and nobody can remember how it got there. But Colm Cille built a church and he left a pillar stone in the old grave-yard and there's another pillar stone above that; and there's a hollow in the stone — it's not very big — and it was a human hand that put one stone on top of another. No matter how much water you take out of it, the stone is always full. But, this stone they call the Stone of Toraigh, if you took it with you to Dublin under your arm, it would be back in Toraigh the following morning if you went there to look for it. And it was ever said that, no matter what you did or what you didn't do, if the Stone of Toraigh was turned on you, no good would come of it. An awful lot of priests tried to get rid of the stone but every one of them failed, but they say that Sagart Beag Ó Dónaill hid it and that it has never been found since.

86. Colm Cille and the Crows

When Colm Cille was a young lad he was living with an uncle named Féardaí Rua. Féardaí had a little bit of land which he worked himself. One day he was sowing oats and, when he shook out the oats he was sowing, the crows were coming and taking the seed from the ground. Féardaí went in home for his dinner and asked Colm to go out and scare off the crows from the oats. Colm went out and it wasn't long before he was back. Féardaí spoke to him, very cross, and asked him why he didn't stay outside and mind the oats from the crows.

'Oh,' said Colm, 'there's no crow out there now!'

'There's no crow out there?' said Féardaí. 'Where are they?'

'They're inside in the barn,' said Colm.

Féardaí dashed out and when he looked round there wasn't a crow to be seen in the air or anywhere, and then he went to the door of the barn. He opened the door and as soon as he did, such a flock of crows flew out that they took Féardaí with them and he didn't land on the ground till he was half a mile away! Féardaí walked back to the house and said to Colm:

'I made a bad job of that! You'll have to put the crows back in again.'

'Oh,' said Colm, 'let you put them in now! When I had them in you let them out!'

87. Peril of the Sea

At the time Colm Cille went to Scotland, when he arrrived in Scotland he was very glad to leave the sea behind him because he met a very stormy day there. And, when he set foot in Scotland, or the island he landed in first, he told the monk that was with him that nobody would ever drown who invoked and placed himself under the protection of God and Our Lady and Colm Cille.

'Nobody will ever drown, so,' said the monk, answering him.

'When the time comes,' said Colm Cille, 'they won't remember the saying.'

And it is said ever since that there is nobody who places himself under the protection of God and Our Lady and Colm Cille, before going to sea, but will arrive safely ashore.

88. How Colm Cille Left Ireland

Long ago, in the time of the saints, Colm Cille was in Árainn and Saint Enda too was there. And Colm Cille began to transcribe a book belonging to Enda; and, when it was transcribed, Enda didn't want to leave him the book he had copied from his own. A bitter quarrel arose between the two on account of the book. And, since Colm Cille had written the book, from Enda's book, he wanted to keep it and that was the cause of the war between them. As the story goes, there was such a quarrel between them that, when all the saints came together, they imposed, as a penance on Colm Cille, that he wouldn't live anywhere that he could hear the sound of Enda's bell ringing.

Then he had to leave Árainn Mhór. He went down to the shore and stood on a stone there and the stone floated off, with himself on top of it, until it came to a place called Casla, the other side of Galway Bay, on the Conamara side. There's a holy well named after Colm Cille there since, and lots of people come from all over the county, and other counties too, on pilgrimage on the ninth of June each year.

Colm Cille couldn't stay there long because, every day that Enda rang his bell in Árainn, he could hear it in Casla; so he didn't stop until he went to Ulster, to County Down. He built a very big monastery there and did plenty of work for many years. When he had all the work done and suffered great hardship and trouble, he was walking round the monastery one fine day and what did he hear but Enda's bell ringing. He decided then that he'd have to leave Derry and go to Scotland and convert as many people there to Christianity as had been killed in the war. Fair enough. He began to get ready to go to Scotland. Now, the monk that was with him told him that he must not go by day, nor look behind him, after all the hardship and trouble he had suffered, so he must go by night.

'And you'll wake me when you hear a cock crowing?' said Colm Cille.

'I'll do that, said the monk, I'll give you a call.'

The night wore on. The monk didn't sleep a wink but Colm Cille slept soundly. The night passed till daybreak and no cock crowed. In fact, no cock crowed until it was well time for breakfast. And when the cock crowed, he wakened the monk and he called Colm Cille.

'Why didn't you call me,' said Colm Cille to the monk, 'when you heard the cock crow?'

'No cock crowed in Derry until now,' said the monk.

Colm Cille said:

'May Kilsallagh never have a cock,
May the cock have no head,
And may no cock ever crow in Derry
Until this time of day!'

They say that no cock ever crows in Derry, from that day till this, before ten o'clock in the day.

However, he said that he must go at once, and he got a horse and got it ready. He mounted the horse and the monk mounted another. They went off towards a port where there was a boat that would take them to Scotland. And Colm Cille told the monk to look behind them and tell him what he saw. He looked and:

'I see,' said the monk, 'a huge black crowd over all of Derry.'

'Oh, Derry will fall to the black faith yet!' said Colm Cille.

They travelled on. It seems that they had to go a good long way to get to the port where the boat was to take them to Scotland. And he told him to look behind again and tell him what he saw when he looked. The monk looked behind for the second time and saw a big strong dog and a little spaniel fighting over a bone. But the little spaniel took the bone from the big strong dog and made off with it.

'I saw,' said the monk, 'a big strong dog and a little spaniel fighting over a bone and the little spaniel took the bone from the big strong dog.'

'Oh, the Spaniards will have Ireland yet!' said Colm Cille.

Soon they came to the port where they were to sail from to Scotland in the boat, and they went to Scotland. And Colm Cille converted more than twice as many to Christianity in Scotland were killed in the battle in Ireland in the war about the book being copied.

He stayed in Scotland until he died. And he always wanted to die in Ireland. And when he died, and before he died at all, his heart was in Ireland, and he wanted his body to lie in Irish soil after his death. He told the monks attending him and those surrounding him when he died to put him in a stone coffin and leave it on the shore. They did as he asked. He was placed in a stone coffin and it was left on the shore at a place where the tide came in every day. But they say that the coffin came to Ireland with the body of Colm Cille inside and landed on the shore at Derry.

There was a farmer there who had a lot of cattle. And in summertime, when the weather is very hot, the cattle run down on the strand to the sea and go into the water to cool off. And one of the milch-cows began eating the seaweed that was growing on the stone coffin. At the time, nobody knew what kind of stone it was. When she had eaten all the seaweed she began to lick the stone and she had more milk every day than any of the cows that were eating grass. The steward noticed how much more milk she was producing than any other cow so he began to watch her. And he found her on the strand every day licking this stone. He decided that there was something miraculous about this stone, with the amount of milk the cow gave when she wasn't eating a blade of grass but licking the stones on the shore. A lot of people came along with him to look at this stone. They noticed that there was a sort of lid lying on top of the rest and they decided to lift the lid. It was as if the stone was in two halves with a sort of groove between them. They raised the stone that was on top and found the body of Colm Cille inside.

They took it away with them then and decided that the right place to bury it would be along with Saint Patrick and Saint Brigid. When they came to the graveyard where Saint Patrick and Saint Brigid were buried it is said that the two graves moved apart and made room between them for Colm Cille so that the three are buried side by side in the one graveyard.

89. Saint Martin's Night

Saint Martin's night falls nine nights after Halloween. Blood should be shed on that night or the night before or even a couple of days before. Martin will accept it before, but he won't accept it after. Any house that doesn't spill blood for him can't expect to have luck during the year. People kill geese, ducks, hens or anything else, just so that blood is spilled. The blood must be poured at the four corners of the house. If the fishermen are out on that night they have great luck; they bring home plenty of fish. It is a great virtue to draw blood for him and he then gives great luck to everybody in the house.

There was an old woman long ago and she had nothing under the sun. She was terribly poor, with nothing to her name. Saint Martin's night came and she was distracted when she had nothing to kill for him.

'May God and Christ help us and Our Lady save us!' said she to herself. 'What will I do at all?'

A neighbouring woman came in to her and told her that it wouldn't make a bit of difference and to forget about it, that Martin wouldn't hold it against her since she couldn't help it.

'Oh woe, for the love of Jesus Christ!' said she. 'Are you asking me to break the tradition of seven generations before me? Upon my soul I won't.'

On the spot, she took a knife and what did she do but cut off the little toe of her foot and went to the four corners of the house with the blood, without saying 'hoo' or 'haw'. Then off to bed with her, delighted with herself.

'This world is only a passing thing,' said she. 'The seed will live but the hand that sows it will die.'

They say that God never turns His back on his own children, and it's true, and the old woman could prove it. She got her reward. Riches came to her all at once. A relative of hers died, a man that never ate enough in his life, and he had to leave her the thousand pounds he had saved. God sent it to her.

They say that Saint Peter was the first person to shed blood for Martin and the custom remains since then.

90. Saint Martin and the Gambler

There was a man and woman long ago and they had a child. The man was always playing cards and he was very addicted to them. He won lots of money and other things too, playing.

One Saint Martin's night he was gone and the wife and child were at home. It was the custom in Ireland in those days, and indeed right up to the present, to shed blood for Martin. The old people say that he will accept it before but not after. The woman was upset that she had nothing to kill for that night and she knew that Martin wouldn't accept it after that night. She had the child in the cradle and she thought that she might draw a drop of blood from the child's finger; she took the knife and cut his finger and the blood began to flow. In the end she couldn't stop it and the child died.

Some time later, a travelling man came in to her and asked for lodgings for the night. She said that she had very little room but that she'd put him up, and she did. She was working about the house during the night and was very sad. Late in the night the man of the house came home with a fine piece of meat he had won at the cards. He gave the stranger a great welcome and told the wife to prepare supper, which she did. As they sat down to supper the man asked his wife where was the child and she said he was asleep.

'I don't care,' said he, 'I won't eat a bite until you take him up.'

The poor woman knew otherwise.

'Oh,' said the stranger, 'take him up for his supper.'

Over she went for the child and he was perspiring in his sleep! She threw herself down on her two knees and thanked God and the night that was in it. She told her husband what had happened with the child and they ate their supper more happily than she had expected; and when supper was over, the stranger told them that he was Saint Martin and he told them that it was he who had brought the child back from the dead. He asked the man of the house what kind of trade had he and he said that he played cards.

'Play fairly,' said Saint Martin, 'and no one will ever beat you in this life or in the next one, from this night on.'

And with that, the saint vanished. The man spent his life playing cards and nobody ever beat him at them. When the time came for him to die, he told them to put the cards in the coffin with him, which they did. The man went straight to Heaven and when he got to the gate Saint Peter wouldn't let him in unless he left the cards after him.

'Where will I go, so?' said he.

'Off with you to the place below,' said Saint Peter.

With that, down he went and the man below had a great welcome for him, and no wonder. The man below had two souls roasting on the fire and the devil asked him what he wanted. He said he'd been to Heaven but they wouldn't let him in on account of the cards. He said he'd wager his own soul against the two that were roasting on the fire and the devil agreed. They began to play and he beat the devil and took the two souls that were on the fire from him. Who were they but his father and mother and they went straight up to Heaven on the spot! He kept on playing until he had won a whole lot more and in the end the devil hunted him back up again. He went up to the man above again but he wouldn't let him in unless he left the cards after him.

He came back to this world and met a man who was stealing turf from the roadside. The poor man collapsed there and then – he thought that he was caught.

'Get up!' said the ghost, 'I'll do you no harm.'

And then he told him that he had been to Heaven and Hell and neither had any place for him on account of the cards.

'Here, take them,' said he 'and play them fairly and nobody will ever beat you as long as you live.'

He went off to heaven again and he had no delay in getting in this time; and he's in Heaven now. But he proved a match for the devil when he was in Hell!

91. The Little Black Sheep

There was a poor man living in Baile Móir once, and himself and his family were destitute. At this time of the year it was winter, and he was standing in an outhouse where they kept potatoes, with his two hands on the frame of the door, looking at the snow driving down hard from the northeast. He saw a sheep coming towards him, glistening with snow and he let her in the door. He felt sorry for her. He realised that she was hungry so he cut up six or seven potatoes for her and she ate them. When she had the potatoes eaten, she shook herself and wasn't she a fine strong little black sheep! There wasn't much flesh on her; she was fairly thin. He went to the stack and pulled a sheaf of oats and cut the oats off the sheaf and gave them to her, after the potatoes. Next morning, some of the snow melted and he told one of the children to drive her west to the field. The sheep stayed in the field. You'd think she was always there, she was so contented.

The poor man sent out word that he had found the sheep; he was an honest man apparently. When nobody near at hand claimed her, he spent some time travelling around looking for the owner. Now, wasn't he an honest man! He couldn't find any owner so the sheep stayed with him. But the following year the little black sheep had twin lambs and she stayed in the field without any spancel. Each lamb had a distinctive mark on its forehead, with four corners on it, like an ace of diamonds, and although he was poor – and the two lambs were ewes – he kept them. But the following year each of the two lambs had twins and so had the little black sheep and all of them had the distinctive mark on their foreheads. The next year all nine sheep had twins, making twenty-seven in all. From that year on, all the sheep had twins and he began to sell them and he made a pile of money out of them because he used to get five or six shillings more for each of them than the going rate for any other sheep. He went from strength to strength and he and his wife and family began to get a bit arrogant. They were full of arrogance and money and sheep!

There never came a Saint Martin's night, even on the poorest day ever he was, that he didn't kill something in honour of Martin.

'Now,' said he, 'it's no trouble to us to kill a fine sheep! Go out,' said he to his son, 'and find the best sheep we have and we'll kill it in honour of Martin's night.'

'Do not,' said his wife, 'and we'll kill the little black sheep instead. Bring the little black sheep,' she said to her son.

'Do not,' said the father to the son, 'but bring the finest sheep we have! The little black sheep is still serving us as well as any other sheep we have.'

The wife was so insistent that they had to do what she said. She persuaded them that the little black sheep was getting old and that it would be better to kill her instead of a young sheep. They had to do what she said. They killed the little black sheep and there wasn't much flesh on her. They put her on to stew for Saint Martin's night, and if they did they had no meat off her. She was stewing so long that they were testing her to see was she cooked and there was no sign of that at all!

They left her cooking that night and all the next day. She stayed the same. In the end they had to throw her out in the ditch in the haggard and even the dogs wouldn't go near her. The day after that again, the son was driving the sheep to the field. They used to keep them inside at night. But when he went to the field with the sheep, there was a fairy mound in the field with ferns and bushes and briars around it. The sheep never stopped till they came to the mound, and then they went into the mound, one after the other, with the boy watching them. He wondered where they were going so he followed the last one and there was a hole in the mound and they all went, one after the other, into the hole. The last one was entering when he caught up with it.

When the boy saw that the sheep had vanished, he started to cry because he was afraid of what his father would say. When he told his father where they went, the father and his brother took a spade and shovel with them so that they could make a bigger hole, so that they could follow the sheep because they thought it was just a hole. When they had been digging down for a while and throwing the clay above them to make room it suddenly brightened down below as good as it was above, with sun and warmth and fine weather. When they went down further there were roads and fields exactly like above ground.

They found the tracks of the sheep on the road and knew that it was their sheep that had gone that way. But they followed the road, finding the tracks ahead of them as they went. They followed the road all day. Around mid-day they saw the sheep some distance ahead. They were delighted that they'd found them. There was a big river crossing the road they were on and the sheep were on the far side of the river, while they were on the near side. The river was between them. There were men making hay on the far side of the river and they spoke with one another across the river. The haymakers asked them where they came from and what they wanted. They told them that they were looking for their sheep that had run away and that the sheep they could see ahead of them were like them.

'If they are,' said the other men, 'you can't have them now and you'll go home without them, because you had no regard for them when you had them and,' said they, 'it's all thanks to your wife! If she let them alone, and didn't have the little black sheep killed, you'd still have them but you'll never get them again so you may as well go home!'

They turned on their heels and travelled back the same road they came and came up through the same hole that they had gone down. It seems that there's another country down below us with people and animals living there just as there are here. They came home without a sheep or a lamb and it wasn't long until they were as poor again as the first day that the little black sheep came in the door to them!

92. The Cat and the Dog

There was a saint in Inis Gluaire long ago and one day he was going round the island to bless it. It wasn't long till he met a fine, good-looking woman and you'd think that she was the Beauty of the Sun. That was alright, the saint had a grain of soil in his hand to bless the island with and he was just about to shake it on the island, to bless the island, when the girl spoke to him and said:

'If you throw away what you have in your hand,' said she, 'I'll marry you.'

The saint thought long and hard about this. He looked all around him but when he saw her feet he noticed that they were cow's hooves and then he knew that she wasn't a mortal woman but an evil spirit. Instantly, the saint raised his hand and banished her out on the shore to a rock that they call Carraig na mBan now and she was never seen there again, because she was the devil's mother.

She went off then and kept going because she had failed to tempt the saint. She kept on going then until she came within three miles of Dublin. That was alright, she met a man there and asked him to marry her; and he thought that she was the finest woman anybody ever laid eyes on, so he did not notice anything different about her than he did about any other woman. He promised to marry her, and so he did. Time went by and they had a son and a daughter and they made their living at farming. One day the father and son were out cutting oats and that was the very time that Saint Patrick came to Ireland. On that day Saint Patrick came by and he began talking to them and telling them who he was.

After a while they were called to their dinner and the father told the son that he'd have to stay back minding the oats from the birds until he and the stranger returned.

'Oh,' said the saint, 'there's no need for any of you to stay back because they won't touch it. I can promise you that.'

They took the saint's word for it and all three went home for their dinner. When they got to the house there was a fish cooking for them and when it was ready it was served up to them. After a while, the saint noticed that the woman was surly and not a bit inclined to talk. When the fish was served up, the saint made the Sign of the Cross over it. They ate and drank their fill and when they were finished they went out again. The saint stayed with them the whole day and at the very end he said:

'Do you notice anything about that wife of yours that's different from any other woman?' said the saint to the father.

'I don't,' said the father.

'She's the devil's mother,' said he, 'wherever you met her.'

'Oh, God save us!' said he, 'is there any hope at all of getting rid of her?'

'Oh, there is indeed,' said the saint, 'if you're willing.'

'Oh, I'd do anything at all if only I could get rid of her.'

'Now,' said the saint, 'I'll be home with you again this evening, and I won't let on anything, but when she goes to bed I'll drive her out.'

Fair enough, in the evening the three of them went home again. They started talking and discussing things and never felt the night passing. When everything was done they got ready to go to bed and the saint stood up and put her out through the house; and she went up in the air like a lump of clay but, as she went out, she knocked down the side wall of the house.

'Now,' said the man of the house, 'what are you going to do with her two children?'

'I won't do the same with them,' said the saint, 'I'll leave them here to be useful to people.'

Then he turned the daughter into a cat and the son into a dog, and they say that that's why those two animals have such affection in them since that time, and always will.

I don't know if that's true or false, but it has been handed down on people's lips for as long as the present generation can remember and the generation before them too.

Return of the Dead from Purgatory

'Let us offer a Pater and Ave Maria in honour of God and the Virgin Mary and for the poor souls suffering the pains of Purgatory and especially for the souls of our own departed relatives and for every poor soul that has no one to pray for it and for the soul in direst need and for the soul most recently departed this life and for every poor soul who omitted a sin in confession, missed Mass or failed to complete a penance. We keep them in our prayers and may God pardon them this night! Amen.'

– an old prayer.

'If I were in heaven, wouldn't I be happy!'

– from a religious poem from Roscommon.

There is hardly any other type of story as plentiful in Irish folklore, or in that of many other countries too, as those that tell of people who had died and appeared afterwards in this world. Many people are firmly convinced that the dead, or at least some of them, have the power to return for particular reasons. Be that as it may, these stories are not as common nowadays as they once were. People view these matters differently now.

What makes the dead re-appear? There are very many reasons, if we are to believe the different stories. They say that they are allowed to leave Purgatory for a certain time every night, particularly at Halloween and Christmas. 'It is a time for the living to sleep and the dead to endure Purgatory' one soul told a man who was out late at night. The dead often re-visit, at night, the house they lived in before death and people used to prepare the house for their visits before going to bed themselves. Other stories tell of the dead arising at night in the graveyards to say prayers over the graves there. They often played a match with the fairies – indeed it's hard to distinguish clearly between the fairies and the dead in many stories. Very often the dead seek the aid of the living to shorten their term in Purgatory, for example, by clearing debts, completing a confession, hearing a Mass or making restitution for some offence. The dead sometimes give a sign to the one they meet, or they leave a physical mark on them. They don't necessarily appear near home; sometimes they appear thousands of miles away. The dead usually reappear as a result of an invitation or to fulfil a promise; but they can also appear of their own accord. They often appear to help their living relatives. On the other hand, they don't always reappear to be helpful or to do good; they are often malicious and vengeful. There are also stories about their attempts to abduct the living. According to the stories, they are mostly seen at night. The person seeing them must question them first or they won't speak at all. For every one who has spoken, there are stories of thousands of apparitions who gave no clue as to who they were.

Hell is a lake or room of fire, usually, although the person who is damned in this world has no sign of that. Likewise, Purgatory is a lake or slab of pain on which the dead suffer. And yet, we're told of people in Purgatory suffering in this world – these are the ones who speak to the living if questioned. Heaven is a broad meadow or a garden with sweet music to be heard in it; but the road into it is very narrow with an angel guarding the entrance. It is obvious from these accounts that these stories are major relics of our inheritance from the pre-Christian era with additions of Christian imagery. A student of the religious history of our people will find much to interest him in these stories.

93. The Hard, Greedy Woman

There was a couple long ago and they had no family. They only had a servant-girl in the house with them. One night a poor woman came to the door and asked the woman of the house for a night's shelter, as it was snowing outside, by the will of God. The woman of the house didn't want to let her in but the servant-girl asked her to let the woman in and said she'd work a week for no wages instead. The woman was hard and greedy and she let the poor woman stay in order to get a week's free work out of the servant-girl. Next day, it was snowing harder than ever and the woman of the house was saying that the poor woman must go, no matter how bad the day was, as she wasn't going to keep her any longer. The servant-girl had pity on the homeless woman, so she told the woman of the house that she'd work another week free if she allowed the woman to stay another night. She let her stay then till the following day and so the day and night passed and the poor woman was fairly comfortable

Next morning the woman of the house was up early and the snow of the previous two days was nothing to the snow that was falling that morning. In spite of that, the woman of the house said that the poor woman would have to go; that she wouldn't keep her another day for gold or for silver. The servant-girl had such pity for her when she saw the kind of weather that was in it and the sad state of the poor creature, that she offered to work a third week for no pay, if the poor woman was allowed to stay. The woman of the house would do anything to save three weeks pay, and she allowed her to stay another night. The next morning was the finest morning anybody ever saw and the poor woman went away, very grateful to the servant-girl.

Not long afterwards the woman of the house died suddenly. She was not long buried when the servant-girl began to notice that any time she fed the pigs, an eel came out of the stream that ran near the pig-sty and began to eat out of the trough with the pigs. The pigs moved to one side when the eel arrived, as if they were afraid of her and it wasn't long till the pigs started to get thinner instead of fatter. She told the man of the house what was happening and he went to see for himself the eel arriving when the food was put out for the pigs. He had an idea that it wasn't really an eel, so he went and told the story to the priest. He came and when the eel was eating out of the trough he began to read from his prayerbook. When the eel was leaving the sty the priest spoke to her and asked her who she was and what she was doing there. She answered in a human voice and said that she was the woman of the house who had died and had been given the penance of eating the pigs' food because, when she was in this world, she had been unjust to poor people and had often left her servants go hungry.

The priest asked her could anything help her or was there any way that something could be done for her. She said that if the servant-girl would give her one of the three beds reserved for her in Heaven, she'd be saved. The girl said that she would give her one of the beds and another one each to her father and mother and she hoped that she'd have earned another for herself before she died.

94. The Flannel Petticoat
There was a farmer's wife in a place called Baile na bPoc, and a poor woman called in to her looking for alms, and she had hardly a stitch of clothes.

'Have you no petticoat at all except that, my poor woman,' said the woman of the house.

'Musha, I have no petticoat, only like that,' said the poor woman.

The woman jumped up and she had a fine new flannel petticoat on her with her dark dress over it. She loosened the tape of her white petticoat and she dropped it down to her feet.

'Here, in the name of God,' said she. 'That is for you and put it on you.'

'Musha, may the blessings of God fall kindly on your soul!' said the poor woman.

The woman of the house had three daughters and each one was settled in a farm in the parish and doing well. After she died she was walking in the area and met the three daughters squabbling with one another.

'You got the shawl,' said one to the other, 'and I wouldn't get it.'

'You wouldn't get it,' said the other, 'because if she didn't think it worth her while to give it to me, I wouldn't have got it either.'

'There you are, squabbling together,' said the mother to them. 'I got more value out of the flannel coat I gave to the poor old woman than all I ever gave to the lot of you, because when I died,' said she, 'it was laid before me on the flags of pain when I was doing my purgatory.'

95. Between the Stirrup and the Ground

There was a man, long ago, and long ago it was. If I was there then, I wouldn't be here now; I'd have had a new story or an old story, or maybe I'd have no story at all! This man was the worst in the world, doing everything out of the way and robbing and stealing. One day he was riding his horse beside a river, and there was a sudden burst of sunshine and he heard someone laughing. He stopped his horse and he looked at this person.

'What are you laughing at?' said the man riding the horse.

'Well,' said the man in the waterfall, 'my son's son had a son last night and he's going to be a priest; and when he says his first Mass, I'll be released from here!'

'How long are you in there?' said the man on the horse.

'It'll be thirty years, come Easter Sunday,' said he.

'And what did you do out of the way?' said the man on the horse.

'What I did was,' said he, 'that when I was young I was always mocking and laughing at people and I had no pity on the afflicted.'

'Well,' said the man on the horse, 'I haven't a hope of being saved!'

And he got down off the horse to take the other man's place. And between the stirrup and the ground he was forgiven and sanctified, since he had examined himself in his heart and given himself up.

96. 'What Made Your Two Legs so Thin?'

There was this man going to the riverbank. He raised his head and looked around him. He saw the image of a man he knew when he was alive. He looked just like a ghostly image. He asked him what had made his two legs so thin.

Said the ghost:

'The grazing of two sheep made my two legs thin,

The sweat of workmen and overcharging the poor;
I trampled on the weak, and helped nobody
And I will not get to the right hand of God.
Doing my penance is all I care about,
Just as your fishing-basket is all you care about.'

97. The Poteen Debt

There was a man from these parts going to Galway long ago and the way he went
was around by the shore, the south road. He was going east until he reached a spot
called Cladhnach. There was a poteen house there and he went in and asked for a
drink; he asked for a pint of poteen and he drank it. And whoever was with him,
he took out his money to pay and the woman had no change to give him. He said
he'd pay her on the way back. Then he went off to Galway and did his business
there. He got a chance of a lift home in a boat and he thought it would be a pity
to miss it and have to walk all the way home. So he went on the boat. That was
the year the cholera was in Galway; and it seems he had caught the cholera and
he died on the way home near Black Head. He was brought home and buried.
Life went on for many years after and there was a man from the same part of the
country in America. And one day this man was walking down the street, in a place
they call Pittsburg, and he met the man. He told the living man not to be a bit
afraid, that he was in no danger.

'Take heart,' said he. 'The reason I've come to you here is because I owe
money to a woman in Cladhnach for some drink; when I went to pay her she
had no change. I told her I'd pay coming back. I got a boat home and I thought it
would be a pity to miss the chance for the price of a drink so I went on the boat.
There was cholera in Galway and I caught it and died on the way at Black Head.
I'm travelling ever since and I'll never get into God's Heaven until I've discharged
the debt. She never forgave me, and unless it's paid I can't get in.'

'Why didn't you tell one of your own people?' said the man. 'You'd be better
off telling them than me.'

'I often tried to tell them,' said the man, 'and the first thing they'd do was
to pull a knife to banish me so I wasn't able to tell them as a result. That same
woman that I took the drink from in Ireland is over here now and if I could only
manage to get the debt paid that's the only thing that's keeping me out of God's
Heaven.'

'If I paid it for you now,' said the man, 'would that be as good as if one of your
own paid it?'

'It doesn't matter who pays it,' said the ghost, 'as long as it's paid.'

'Will you come down with me now,' said the living man, 'to this woman's house to see can we settle it?'

'I will,' said he.

They went down and went in. The living man called for a drink and drank it. And he called for another and drank it. He drew down the name of the man from Ireland and asked her did she know him and she said she did.

'Do you ever remember him calling for a drink and not paying for it?' said he.

'I do remember,' said she. 'Once he was going to Galway and he ordered a pint of poteen and he never paid for it.'

'He didn't live to pay it,' said the living man, 'and I'd say he would have paid it if it wasn't for that.'

'Wouldn't you think that some of his people would pay it when he himself died?' said the woman.

'They probably didn't know about it,' said the man, 'and you might as well forgive him.'

'I'll not forgive him,' said she, 'and may God not forgive him either till they pay me!'

'If I paid you now on his behalf,' said the man, 'would you forgive him?'

'I'd forgive him,' said she. 'No matter who pays, it is all the one to me. I'll forgive him.'

'How much was it?' said the man.

She told him and he paid her.

'Forgive him now,' said the man.

'I forgive him,' said she, 'and may God forgive him!'

'Good-bye now,' said the ghost.

And off he went, out the door.

98. The Load of Straw

Long ago there were two old maids living up here in a place called Corr Mhín. They had an old bachelor, named Padaí, living with them. The women were very religious but Padaí wasn't, he had no regard for God or man. The women walked to Mass every Sunday and Padaí used to be raging at them when he saw them heading off. One Sunday at harvest-time the women were going to Mass and it seems Padaí was short of fodder, and as the day was fine, he wasn't a bit inclined to let them go. He threatened them that if they didn't stay at home he'd have their lives. One of the women was foolish enough to stay but the other said that even if he broke every stick in the house on her she wouldn't stay. Off she went and left Padaí and the other sister looking after the fodder.

That was alright. Time went by and so did the years and Padaí died. When he was on his deathbed the sisters did their best to get him to let them send word to the priest but Padaí wouldn't hear tell of it and he died without the priest. They waked him and buried him. The sisters took Padaí's death very badly and it wasn't long till one of them died. The other sister was left on her own then with no one to do a hand's turn for her.

They had a custom in those days that's gone now. Every village had a place where the straw mattress on which a person died was dumped after the funeral. There'd be a big hole or a cave or a swallow-hole or some such place to dump the mattress in. The custom was that the relatives of the dead person would go, maybe once a day, or as often as it suited them, to the place where the mattress was and say some prayers for them. One day, Padaí's sister and some other women went to say a prayer for her sister who had died. When she got to the place where all the straw mattresses were she couldn't tell rightly which one belonged to her sister and where did she get down on her knees but at the mattress of her brother! Very soon she noticed the other mattress shaking and a spirit spoke to her out of it. She asked her to come over to her, that there was no use praying for him as he was damned; but to pray for her; that she'd be damned too only for the day that she went to Mass in spite of Padaí. She said it was the only Mass she heard properly and that it was that Mass that saved her!

'But I'm not in Heaven yet,' said she, 'and that's what brought me here now, to let you know the cause of my troubles. When I was growing up as a little girl Padaí was very hard on me. He was too lazy to get up in the morning to feed the cattle and he used to make me do it, summer and winter, come hail, come shine. One morning he sent me for a load of straw for the cattle. I was in my bare feet and there was a good covering of snow on the ground. On my way down, our next-door neighbour had a stack of straw on and I thought to myself that there'd be no harm in taking a load of it on such a cold morning. So I took the load, and from that day till this I never let on to the man I took it from that I had done it. I never repaid him for it and I'll never make Heaven until I do, or until someone else does it for me!'

'Well, I'll pay him for you,' said the sister, 'as soon as I get home.'

She went home and brought a load of straw to the man and told him all about it.

'Oh well,' said he, 'if that has kept your sister out of Heaven, I'll never see the face of God, because I've stolen enough in my time to send half the parish to Hell!'

99. The Ghost and the Bishop

There was a place here in Ireland long ago and anyone who went by there, from sunset till sunrise, was dead by morning, and not a trace of him. Anyone who knew the place at all wouldn't go that way, only a stranger would. But there was a bishop living some distance away and he was dying. And it was much shorter to go for a priest through that place but no one had the courage to take it. It was much longer to go round by the road. There was a widow's son who said that he'd go by the short-cut because, if he went round by the road, the priest wouldn't find the bishop alive. He was a brave man and he hit the road and went by the short-cut. When he came towards this particular place, where there was a hawthorn bush by the side of the road, the spirit came out in front of him and he stopped.

'There you are,' said he.

'I am, indeed, and so are you,' said the widow's son.

'Where are you going?' said the ghost.

'I'm going for the priest,' said he, 'for the bishop who is on his death-bed.'

'Will you be coming back this way again tonight?' said he.

'I will,' said the widow's son, 'with the help of God and if I've an inch of foot left on me!'

'Fair enough,' said the ghost. 'You've saved your head this time.'

He went ahead and it was late in the night when he reached the parish priest and wakened him.

'Where are you going at this hour of the night?' said the parish priest.

'I'm coming for you,' said he, 'to attend the lord bishop who is on his death-bed.'

'Oh,' said the parish priest, 'go over to the curate and maybe he'll come with me.'

He went over and woke up the curate and the two went along with him. They began talking on the way and he told them about the ghost he had met. The parish priest said they'd be as well to go the long way round but the curate said they'd go by the short cut. So they went and the parish priest was walking boldly ahead until they got near the place and then he began to tremble with fear and began to stay back.

'Walk on,' said the young priest.

They walked on until they came to the place and there was the ghost ahead of them. The young priest spoke to him and they all spoke to one another.

'Well,' said the ghost to the priest, 'you'll go no further till you hear my confession.'

'Oh, I'm delighted,' said the priest, 'that you asked me. Kneel down here!'

The ghost got down on his knees on the side of the road and he heard his confession and gave him absolution.

'Get up now,' said the priest, 'on the farthest out branch of that thorn bush till I give you Holy Communion.'

The ghost got up and stood on the very farthest branch and the man took the Holy Communion in his hand and tossed it up in the air and the ghost caught it in his mouth. And then he fell down dead and there was no more about it.

Off they went then and were making for the bishop's house, with the parish priest striding out boldly. But the poor curate was in such a state that he took a handkerchief out of his pocket to dry the tears from his eyes. When they got to the bishop's house he was very bad indeed and the parish priest attended to him. And when he had finished attending to him he said:

'Musha, is it not a great pity,' said the old priest, 'that the ghost in the tree didn't make as good a way through life as you have! He'd have no fear then of facing his God tonight.'

'I have myself to thank,' said the bishop.

'I hope,' said the parish priest, 'if it doesn't put you out too much, that you'll come back to tell me, or give me some sign, of how you get on when you meet your God, and how the ghost that was in the tree tonight gets on.'

'I'll come,' said the bishop, 'if it is not too much trouble.'

The bishop died. Six months, or maybe a year, passed and the priest was walking beside his house one fine summer's day and he saw the bishop making for him. He spoke to him and they spoke to one another.

'Oh, musha,' said the parish priest, 'is that how you are?'

'It is,' said the bishop, 'I'm put out of God's Heaven until the Day of Judgement.'

'Oh, God save us all!' said the priest. 'Is it not a strange thing now, to see a man with such faith, who had lived a good life, in that condition. How did it go with the ghost that was in the tree?'

'The ghost that was in the tree went on the right side and I went on the left side. And the reason I was put out was the talk we had on the night you attended to me and I said, "I've myself to thank", and didn't thank the Lord God. And another thing,' said he, 'myself and the ghost were on the road to Heaven together and I took a dislike to him, thinking he wasn't fit to be seen with me in front of God, and that was the worst thing of all.'

'Is there anything in the world,' said the priest, 'that could do anything for you?'

'There is not,' said the bishop, 'except for one thing and you'd never do it!'

'If I could do anything for you,' said the priest, 'I'll do it.'

'Well, what it is,' said the bishop, 'is, that you should go out to a mountain glen or anywhere else where no one will see you, and where there'll be no one else present but myself and yourself and the God of Graces, and catch me by the two ankles; and you won't feel the slightest weight in me, no more than a bunch of feathers, and then drag me over stones and rocks and brambles and the roughest ground there is until you reduce me to rubble and make splinters of my bones!'

'I'd hate to do a thing like that,' said the priest. 'I wouldn't have the heart for it. Would you suffer as much as if you were alive?'

'Seventy-seven times as much!' said the bishop. 'And when you have that done you must say three Masses of the Holy Spirit for my soul and maybe that might save me!'

The priest did as he was ordered and when it was done and he had made bits of him, he offered Mass of the Holy Spirit for his soul three times. On the first day, when he said the first Mass, the bishop came on the altar in the form of a big huge bird, as black as coal, and when Mass was over he went away. When the priest said the second Mass he came on the altar with white spots on him here and there, speckled, and when Mass was over, he went away. But when he said the third Mass, he came on the altar in the form of a white dove and when the priest finished saying Mass the priest held out his hand and he came and landed on the palm of his hand and he kissed him from the top of his head to the soles of his feet.

'May Almighty God bless you!' said he. 'You have saved me!'

And off he went. Seventeen hundred and sixty blessings from Almighty God on the souls of the dead!

100.   A Child's Soul in a Tree

There was a man, long ago, who was a great thief. He was always stealing and robbing and making off with anything he could lay his hands on. Anything he put his eye on, he had to have it one way or another. He wasn't afraid of God or eternal damnation; he didn't care what happened his soul as long as he wasn't caught in the act of crime. He went on like that for a long time and as he got older he only got worse.

He went out, this night, and brought his axe with him and he didn't stop at all until he went in to the domain of a gentleman in the neighbourhood to cut down a big tree that was growing there and take it home with him. It was the dead of night when he got to the place where the tree was growing. He took off his coat and rolled up his sleeves and went to work, felling the tree. He was hacking away until he was nearly at the heart of the tree. He stopped to wipe the sweat from his face and while he was doing it a voice spoke from the middle of the tree and said:

'Shame on you! What are you doing to a poor soul that needs only another hour to complete its Purgatory?'

The robber began to shake with fear and the axe fell out of his hand from the fright he got.

'Who's that talking to me? Are you living or dead?' said he, when he came to himself.

'I'm a child,' said the voice, 'that was born at the first crow of the cock, was baptised at the second crow of the cock and died at the third crow of the cock. When I went to eternity, I was told that I wasn't yet fit to be in the presence of God, may he be ever praised, nor to go with the just into the City of Heaven; that I'd have to come back to this world again and spend twenty-one years in purgatory here to cleanse my soul of original sin. I was condemned to spend my purgatory in this tree that you are cutting down. I had to spend seven years between the bark and the wood on the cold, windward side of the tree, seven years more between the bark and the wood of the tree on the sunny side of the tree and the last seven years here in the heart of the tree. I've done the whole term except for one hour. When the cock crows my soul will go from this place and go into the presence of God and the just. Have patience for a while now and let me finish my purgatory!'

The man threw himself on the ground and beat his breast with remorse.

'Musha, God help the poor unfortunate sinner like me whose soul is covered with sins! What chance have I of going into the presence of God and the just when I leave this world, when an innocent little child, who never committed any sin, has to spend twenty one years in purgatory in this world before he can see the delights of Heaven?'

'You're not too late, yet,' said the voice back to him, 'better late than too late. It's for you and your likes that Our Saviour was crucified on the Cross. He'll forgive you if you repent. Go on your way now and give up your stealing and thieving forever, as long as you live, and God will reward you. You'll see His kingdom and His almighty power when you come into His presence.'

The man arose and put on his coat and took his axe off home. And from that day till the day he died, he did no more thieving or stealing but completely changed his ways. He gave back, as far as he was able, everything he ever stole, and he lived in the love of God and in peace with his neighbours from that day on.

101.　Cian of the Golden Horns

Cian of the Golden Horns lived to a fair old age and was a right robber. He let nothing past him that he didn't steal unless it was hot or heavy. When he got old he began to fear death and the world to come so he sent for the priest and made his confession to him. He told him everything he had done in his lifetime. He said that, unfortunately, he had spent his life badly, and had done a lot of stealing. And when he had told him everything, he said:

'Well, father,' said he, 'how do you rate my chances?'

'Oh, I've no idea in the world!' said the priest. 'I'm afraid you've spent your life badly and it looks like you'll go below! Now,' said he, 'if there's any way in the world you could do it, I'd love if you could let me know how you fare when you go to Eternity, and I'm afraid that's not far off!'

'Musha, since you ask me,' said Cian, 'if there's any way in the world I can, I'll let you know how I got on, but, if I don't, don't hold it against me!'

About two or three weeks later, the same priest was saying Mass in the chapel and there was a window facing the altar. It was a fine, sunny Sunday and there was a ray of sunshine coming in through the window and running across the chapel. By this time, most of the congregation had come in, except for a few stragglers, and this fine big strapping man came in with his overcoat over his arm and his hat in his hand and approached the altar. The ray of sunshine was coming from the window, and he looked round to see was there any seat vacant where he could sit down or put his hat and coat; and there wasn't a place handy, just people kneeling down. All he did was to take his coat and throw it over the ray of sunshine and, if he did, the ray of sunshine held up the coat! He took his hat and put it on top of the coat. He got down on his knees and blessed himself.

The priest was looking at every move he made, and he was filled with wonder at how he could get the ray of sunshine to hold up the coat and hat. He looked out at the congregation and called out to them, asking them did they notice anything unusual. Only three people answered him. They said they saw it all, indeed, and how it happened; and that it wasn't a living person that did it but some class of a saint, to say that a ray of sunshine would hold up his coat and hat.

'Oh, indeed, you're right,' said the priest, 'and you never spoke a truer word, that it can only be some class of a saint, for the ray of sunshine to hold up his coat and hat. I'd be very much obliged, kind stranger, if you'd tell me your name and where you come from.'

'Indeed,' said he, 'you knew Cian of the Golden Horns that you anointed on such and such a day. Sure you were talking to him three weeks ago, and you asked him, as a penance and a grave obligation, if there was any way in the world he could manage it, to come and tell you how he fared. That's who you have now:

'I'm Cian of the Golden Horns,' said he,
'My means outlasted my life;
I turned no one away from my door,

And God didn't turn me from His.
And, I'm afraid, the place you said I'd go,
Is where you'll go yourself!

I stole and I robbed all around me. If I met anyone in more need than myself I never put my own interests first but gave to people worse off than me. That's what stood to me. And all you're doing is collecting as much as you can from everyone you meet; you'd just as soon take from the poor as from the rich; or even the person that hadn't enough for his breakfast or that hadn't a shirt for his child's back, or his own either, you'd take the money off him as quick as you'd take it from one that had plenty!'

That's my story now, and the old people told me that it was true.

102.   Melting the Candlestick

Once upon a time there were two brothers and they were very good to one another. One of them was dying and he promised his brother that he would come back, on the night of the funeral, and tell him how he got on and where he was sent.

The brother was looking out for him and he couldn't wait till he'd see him and hear what he had to say. He went outside and he had to pass a dirty, wet place. While he was passing the mud he heard a moaning inside in it and he said:

'In the name of God,' said he, 'is it you who are there?'

'It's me alright,' said he.

'Oh! Oh!' said he. 'Is it not the cold spot you got?'

'Stick the top of your finger down here,' said he, 'till you see for yourself.'

He had a candlestick in his hand – it was a nice, quiet, calm night – and he didn't put down his hand but the candlestick instead. The bit of the candlestick that he stuck into the water melted and not a bit of the candlestick remained but what he had in his fist, the heat was so great.

'Am I long buried?' said he.

'Oh,' said the brother, 'you're only buried since yesterday.'

'Oh,' said he, 'I thought I was buried a hundred years!'

103.   A Visit to Lough Derg

There was a woman once and she was very poor and she thought she'd go to Lough Derg, which she did. She spent three days and three nights there, as usual, but when she was coming back she decided to return and make a visit for the soul suffering the most in Purgatory. She went back and did another three days and three nights in Lough Derg.

On her way home, what did she see but a lovely castle and a boy came out of it and invited her in; but she said she wouldn't go in as she wasn't good enough. Then he took a letter out of his pocket and gave it to her and asked her to go up to the house and deliver it to the man of the house in person. She went up and knocked at the door and a servant-girl came out and the woman told her to tell the man of the house to come out as she had business with him. He came out and she gave him the letter and he recognised at once that the writing was that of his son who was recently buried. What was in the letter was a request from the son to his father to keep this woman and make a lady of her because he was the soul suffering most in Purgatory and she made the visit to Lough Derg on behalf of his soul and got him into Heaven.

104.   The Man who Didn't Lament for his Children

Long ago there was a man who had three sons. Two of them died when they were young. Fair enough, the other lad grew up into a fine big man and he had the place for himself, working at home. In the end, his father and mother died and he had no one but himself. He was lonely enough for a good while. One night he was out walking and he hadn't gone far when he met his mother – she was dead for a while at this time.

'Musha, God help us!' said he to her, 'is this where you are, and I praying for you every day since you left this world?'

'Oh,' said she, 'my other two sons did more for me than all the prayers you ever said.'

'Well, if that's the way it is,' said he, 'I'll pray for you no more,' turning on his heel and going home.

Fair enough, when he got home he thought for a long time about what he should do. He got very frightened. He decided that he'd leave the place and go begging. Next morning, he was up good and early, got himself ready and hit the road.

He was very learned, because he had spent some time in college. He travelled on and on until he came to a house on the side of the road and in he went. The people of the house made him very welcome; there were only two sons, a daughter and the father and mother. They had a teacher for the daughter and when he left the lad began teaching her. The people in the house noticed that he was a much better teacher than the master so they kept him for the night. Next morning, he was about to leave the house, but they asked him to stay on with themselves always. Fair enough, he did that, and began teaching the girl again and kept at it for a long time. But, in the end, the girl fell in love with him, and she was so much in love that she fell ill of a broken heart. The lad was going to leave the house then but they were going to kill him and in the end he had to marry the girl. He stayed on living with the family. In the end they had a little boy and when he was baptised he died. The woman and her family were very sad after him, but the father didn't shed a tear.

Time went by and another child was born and the same thing happened. He died. After the burial, the sons asked their father:

'What sort of man is that you brought into this house?'

'Why?' said the father.

'We'll tell you why,' said they. 'Since the day his first child died he hasn't shed a tear for him.'

'There's no harm in that,' said the father. 'Let him go on his way!'

'We won't,' said they, 'but if it happens again he'll be shot!'

Fair enough, when the next child was born, the same thing happened. The child died and he didn't shed a tear. A few days afterwards, it was a Sunday, and the two sons got themselves ready quite early, and took their guns with them to be ahead of the man as he went to Mass, so that they could shoot him. After a while, the man went off to Mass, but as though he knew they were after him, he took a short cut to the chapel and so he was safe. When he came home after Mass, the other two, who had left home before him, were there ahead of him.

'Well,' said he, 'you two went off very early this morning but I didn't see you at Mass.'

'Of course you didn't see us,' said they, 'because we weren't going to Mass but chasing you, and you can be thankful you went the short-cut or you'd be dead!'

'Well, if that's the way it is,' said he, 'I won't stay another day here.'

He went back to his home again. The house was very lonely because no one had been in it for many a day but still he settled down there again. Fair enough, but his wife was very lonely without him and she took it so badly that she fell ill and had to stay in bed. She was like that for a good while and in the end the poor woman died of a broken heart. One night the man went to sleep in his own room. After a while, late in the night, he heard the sweetest music anyone ever heard and what was in it but his wife and three children coming for him! The poor man lay back in his bed and died. Next morning, fairly late, a neighbouring man went into the house and there was nobody there; but when he went into the room he found the man dead inside. And they say that the wife and three children came for him and took him up to Heaven with them.

Piety

'Give the first part of the day to the Eternal Father.'
– proverb from Farney in County Monaghan.

'What will come will go, and all that ever came has gone,
But the graces of God will never disappear.'
– Munster proverb.

'So it is that God alone
Is the object of our love;
Anything else under the bright sun
Should not be loved except for God's sake.'

Giolla Bríde Ó hEoghasa

There is no doubt that our forefathers, particularly the old people, were justly renowned for their piety. This is evident in the rich store of traditional prayers, religious poems and stories that they kept alive in their memory and passed down from generation to generation. These proved a rich source of spiritual support to them when the Penal Laws were in force, and, indeed, down to our own time.

Many of the stories in this section are so-called exempla. Priests used them in the course of their sermons to illustrate certain points of doctrine for their hearers. There are large collections of such stories in the literature of the Orient and of Europe and it would be well worthwhile to publish a book devoted to them, based on those in Irish folklore. Some of these stories have the appearance of having been composed by the laity in imitation of stories used by priests of religious orders.

In folklore, there was a special regard for the simpleton, or *duine le Dia*, who had received no knowledge of faith or religion from a priest but who lived a sinless life by the grace of God. The Creator preferred him to all others, according to some stories. For example, see how Our Saviour invited the simpleton to the feast because he took literally the priest's admonition to walk the straight road; how the sunbeam held up the coat of the herdsman from Sliabh Luachra; how the tree bowed down in the presence of the man without sin and how the minister's son saw the Holy Infant when the priest himself could not! God also loved the man with only one prayer who said it with fervour. All that was required from each of them was a clean heart and good intention, for want of better.

105.   The Straight Road

There once was a poor woman and she was always travelling. She had a little boy with her and he wasn't too strong. They were at Mass one day and the priest said in his sermon that anybody who kept to the straight road would never be in danger. There was a town nearby that had a short cut leading to it and the mother wanted to go the short way but the lad would only go on the straight road. While they were arguing about it who should come along but the priest, going home after saying Mass, I suppose.

'What's going on here?' said the priest to the old woman.

(She probably wasn't all that old, since she had the child.)

'This blackguard won't come along with me,' said she.

'Why don't you go along with your mother,' said the priest to the boy, 'and do what she tells you?'

'I'll go along with her, alright,' said the boy, 'but she must go the straight road.'

'Is it not all the one to you which way she goes,' said the priest.

'Then why did you say in your sermon today,' said the boy, 'that anybody who kept to the straight road would never be in danger?'

The priest said nothing for a while and then he asked the old woman would she leave the boy with him and that he'd rear him.

'Musha, Father,' said she, 'you'd need to have nothing else to do but keep an eye on him.'

'Don't you worry!' said the priest. 'Let him come with me and I'll rear him.'

'Musha, upon my word, I will, Father,' said she, 'and my blessing along with him.'

He took the boy away with him on his horse – whether he had a saddle horse or a coach I don't rightly know. He told his housekeeper then to give his food to the boy to bring to him at meal times. So it was the boy who used to bring his food to the priest always when the housekeeper had prepared it. There was a picture of Our Saviour, may He be ever praised, facing the boy as he went into the room, in a sort of hallway or some such. There was never a time that the boy passed it that he didn't leave a bit of food for the Child in the picture. On Christmas Eve the Child asked the boy who used bring the food for the priest would he like to celebrate Christmas with Him. The boy said he would if the priest would let him.

'Then you'll have to ask the priest,' said the Child, 'and if he lets you come with me, then we'll celebrate Christmas tonight.'

He went to the priest and asked would he let him celebrate Christmas with the Child outside.

'What child is that?' said the priest.

'The Child outside there,' said he, 'in the picture on the wall.'

'Was he talking to you?' said the priest.

'He was asking me would I go to celebrate Christmas with Him.'

'And how come you're so friendly with that child?' said the priest.

'We were never friendly with one another,' said the boy, 'but every time I brought food to you I always gave him a bit.'

'And did he eat it?' said the priest.

'I don't know whether he did or he didn't,' said the boy, 'because I never delayed except to leave it there and there was never a pick of it left when I returned.'

'Well, go out to him now,' said the priest, 'and tell him I'll let you go, if he'll let me go along with you.'

He went out and said that the priest would let him go if he could come too. He went back in to the priest and told him that he would let him come too.

'When you're going to bed tonight,' said the priest, 'call in to me.'

He called in and the priest told him to get inside himself in the bed and he did so. On Christmas morning the priest was late getting up for Mass and they went to call him. The priest and the boy were found dead in the bed, having received their Christmas invitation.

106.   The Overcoat and the Ray of Sunshine

There was a man living around here a long, long time ago who was a steward for a gentleman on Sliabh Luachra. He was in charge of cattle, sheep, horses, goats and kids and all sorts of other stock I can't remember just now. But one fine day, at the beginning of Autumn, he was in a glen and proudly going through his livestock; and he thought that he could hear the sweetest music that ever was, to the south of him, but there seemed to be a high hill between him and the place where the music was coming from. He threw off his overcoat, which was made of the skin of a bullock or an old cow or maybe a deer. He threw his coat over his shoulder and he ran to the top of the hill. He turned his ear towards the south and then he sat down. He could hear the music still and it was a golden bell ringing. (Gold was more plentiful in those days than it is now.) He felt and thought that he saw the odd person going to a house that had a green roof on it; and the reason that the roof was green was that the scraws on it had the clay side towards the rafters and the grass side facing up; the house was newly built.

'That's where the music is,' he said.

He went down to it and that's where the music came from. He went in. There was a ray of sunshine running from the south of the house to the north, as if there was a tiny little window in the wall; and the sun, glory be to God, was shining in a ray of sunshine over to the north wall. He threw his coat over it and it held it up – he thought it was there for that purpose. The overcoat hung there on the ray of sunshine and the people there paid far more attention to it than they did to the priest or the altar. And the priest himself saw it. The coat stayed there and the people were in no hurry to leave, and he realised that he was the cause of their delay, looking at him. He took the coat and walked out; and they walked out after him, and they kept looking at him.

'Musha,' said he to a person talking to him, 'when will ye be here again?'

'The seventh day from today,' they said.

'Musha, I'll come here too,' said he. 'This is a grand place to come. I didn't find out about it till today and my heart is glad. I thought I'd fly through the air coming to such fine holy music! I'll come,' said he, 'next Sunday again.'

He was as good as his word. When he got home his mother and father asked him:

'Oh, my poor little lad, what kept you since morning? We were afraid something had happened to you.'

'Oh, nothing happened, father and mother, I was at a place where there was lovely music!'

'Oh,' said the father, 'you were at Mass, my lad. I saw it once myself. I was there once too.'

'You're right, father,' said he, 'that's what it was. I'll go there again in a week's time, seven days from today.'

'Away with you, son.'

He made himself ready a bit better than the previous time, but it was the same cowhide coat that he had. He had nothing else to wear. He arrived there. Before he went in he saw a man and woman talking together a little distance from the house. He guessed that they were fond of one another or great with one another in some way. And when he went inside and threw his coat on the ray of sunshine, it wouldn't hold it up. Bad enough! He threw it on it again and it didn't stay. He threw it on it a third time. It didn't stay. He put it away somewhere instead. Everybody there was looking at it – the overcoat that the ray of sunshine wouldn't hold up for him on the second Sunday. They didn't know the reason and he didn't either, except that it was the will of God. The priest asked a boy that was serving Mass:

'Would you ever tell that stranger there in the congregation not to leave till I have a word with him.'

He went and told him.

'I won't go,' said the cowherd 'I won't go.'

He waited there till the priest came to him, after all the people had left. Then the priest came down to him.

'Where are you from?' said the priest to the cowherd.

'From Sliabh Luachra,' said the cowherd.

'From Sliabh Luachra?' said the priest.

'Yes,' said the cowherd.

'You walked a fair distance.'

'I did,' said he. 'But if I did, I thought nothing of it, coming to such lovely music!'

'Oh, that was there alright,' said the priest.

'It was,' said he.

'But, what did you do out of the way,' said the priest, 'since last week, when the ray of sunshine held up your coat, till today when it wouldn't hold it up?'

'I don't know, Father,' said he, 'what it was, or what I said that made it do that. But I saw a man and woman talking together some distance away, on my way here. If it wasn't that, I don't know what it was.'

'Oh, that's it now,' said the priest. 'That was plenty reason. More than enough. Enough to make the ray of sunshine refuse to hold up your coat for you. Now, let you stay at home and don't come here again. What company have you, my good man, at home?'

'My father and mother, but they're very old. I'm old enough myself but I'm strong and supple still.'

'What do you work at?'

'I'm in charge of sheep and cattle and horses and goats and deer and lots of other things like that.'

'Stay at home and look after them,' said the priest. 'Look after your work always and never come back here again!'

But the priest I heard telling this in a sermon said:

'That doesn't apply to us,' he said. 'We have to come here. We are obliged by the Church to come here to hear Mass.'

107.   How Sanctity Conquered Destiny

There was this farmer and on an evening like this, around dusk, a young man called in to him, dressed as a priest. He asked the man of the house for a night's shelter and the man of the house said he was welcome.

'But we have a certain problem tonight,' said he. 'The woman of the house is having a child. Stay if you like, I'm not putting you out, but you might not have too peaceful a night.'

'I'll stay here on the settle,' said the traveller.

And stay he did. Later on in the night, the midwife came down to them from the room and said that the child would soon be born.

'When the time comes,' said the traveller, getting up from the settle, 'let me know.'

She told him, and the traveller spoke to her, asking her to delay the birth a while.

'How long?' said she.

'Five minutes,' said he.

'I couldn't, not even a minute!' said she.

'He was born under a planet (destiny) that will hang him,' said the traveller.

He stayed till morning and in the morning, when he had eaten his breakfast, he took a book and a pen and he wrote out a little booklet.

'Here, now,' he said to the father, 'put that round this child's neck and don't let a living soul open it until he's able to read it for himself.'

The father did as he was told and the traveller went up to the room to the mother and said goodbye. Then he went off. The child, Seán, was well cared for and lacked for nothing and grew up and, when he was old enough to go to school, he went to school. One evening, when he came home from school, he asked his mother why he always had to have this thing taped round his neck.

'Musha,' said she, telling him, word for word, what had happened, 'if you're able to read it, there's nothing stopping you taking it from around your neck and reading it.'

He opened the booklet and read it, and what was written in it was that he was born under a planet that would hang him. He closed it up again and put it back around his neck.

When he grew up to be a man he took good care of himself and good care of his soul, and did nothing to darken his soul. The poor man went off and went to County Limerick. He took employment there with a farmer and was diligent and hard working. There was another lad sleeping in the same room, but they weren't in the same bed, and one night he heard Seán getting up out of the bed and putting on his trousers and going down the stairs and out the door. At the same time, the next night, he noticed the same thing and he told his master about it.

'Well, now,' said the master, 'if you hear him tonight, let me know.'

They went off to work, himself and the other lad and the master; later on in the day Seán yawned.

'It seems to me that you didn't get enough sleep last night,' said the master.

'I didn't sleep well at all, master,' said he, 'nor the night before either. I've had nightmares for the last two nights and the nightmare is that I think I'm on a scaffold and that I'm hanged.'

Things rested so until the third night and as soon as ever the lad heard him leaving the room he called the master.

'Well, now,' said the master, 'follow him and wherever he goes keep up with him, step by step, and I'll follow you.'

He followed him step for step and he never, ever stopped until he got to the chapel. He went into the chapel and the lad followed him in and so did the master. There was no corner of the chapel that wasn't brightly lit, so as soon as they went in they got down on their knees just inside the door. Seán went to the altar and two angels came down and erected a scaffold on the altar and hanged Seán. Seán then got down and went out the door and, as he did, the lights went out. They went home and the lad went to bed. Next morning when Seán and the lad got up and had their breakfast, the master came round.

Well, Seán,' said he, 'did you sleep last night?'

'Musha, no, master,' said Seán, 'not a wink; and it's the same story, I thought I was hanged again last night.'

'You were, truly,' said the master. 'You were hanged. And now I think that a saint like you shouldn't be working at all.'

The master told the story to the parish priest and the parish priest did his best. They took in Seán and gave him an education and it turned out in the end that Seán became a priest before he died.

That's my story, and if there's a word of a lie in it, so be it!

108.   The Tree that Bent Down

There was a man in this place and he was short of hay in the spring, and he went to a neighbour's and said to himself that he'd take a load of his hay and, when he had hay of his own later, he would return the load. He took the load and came home with it. When the priests came round the area to hear confessions he told them what he had done. He said he had taken a load of hay from such and such a man and, when his own hay grew, he'd return the load to the neighbour's haycock. Soon afterwards he went visiting in the house that he had taken the hay from. And the woman of the house said to him, laughing:

'Why didn't you come here and ask for a load of hay and you'd have got it, and two if you wanted them! You had no need to steal it.'

'Who told you I stole your hay?' said he. 'There wasn't a soul in Ireland knew what happened except myself and the priest and the Son of God; that's all that knew it!'

'The priest told me, and he said it was no sin for you and that you were a saintly man; and that was all he had to tell about you.'

'I'll never go and I'll never confess to a priest again as long as I live!' said the man. 'I thought that a priest wasn't allowed to tell a man's confession.'

He went home and was very upset that the priest told on him. When they came to hear confessions the next time, the priest sent for him but he wouldn't go. The priest said nothing that time until he came the next time and then he went to the field where he was digging potatoes and he asked him:

'Why aren't you going to confession?' said he.

'When you bring me the hat I lost thirty years ago I'll go to confession to you! You'll find it as easy as you found it to tell my confession to the man I took the hay from! Nobody knew that I took that hay but myself and yourself and the Son of God, and I'll never again go to confession to you!' said he.

The man went off and went to the parish priest and told him all about it.

'Away with you now,' said the priest, 'and tell your confession to a little tree outside in your garden. If you see the tree bending down, you'll know you are forgiven.'

He went off and it wasn't long till the tree was falling down. And the priest told him that, when it fell, he should take a sprig of the rottenest old branch that was on it and stick it in a hollow or in a bog hole and to leave it there a while before he looked at it again, and then see would it show a green shoot. He went and stuck it there and nine days later he went to look at it and there were blossoms on it! And he went to the priest and told him and the priest told him that he was forgiven, that there was no sin on his soul and that he was a good man.

109. The Minister's Son

There was a priest one time who used to say Mass every Sunday some distance from his house. The minister's house was near the chapel and the minister's son used to follow the priest, every Sunday, right into the chapel and up on to the altar. The priest told the minister that his son was following him to the chapel and not to put the blame on him as he had tried to stop him following him, but it was no use, he would still follow him.

'Oh, I'll keep him away from you!' said the minister.

He went home and took him into the room.

'What are you doing, following the priest?' said the father to him.

'I'm not following him,' said the son.

'You are,' said the minister. 'Didn't he tell me?'

'If I told you what I see him doing,' said he, 'you'd kill him, sooner than me.'

'And what do you see him doing?' said the father.

'There's no day that he doesn't eat a beautiful, bright, little child! And I truly pity that little child!' said he.

The minister went off to see the priest.

'Do you know what he said?' said the minister. 'That there's no day that you don't eat a bright little child?'

'That's true enough,' said the priest. 'He sees Him, but we don't see Him, but we know that that's what we're doing. He is without any stain of sin, as bright as an angel, and God loves him, and that's why he showed Himself to him.'

'If that's the case,' said the minister, 'baptise the boy and baptise myself and his mother as well, and my whole household and all belonging to his mother and me.'

The priest spent a whole week baptising them all.

110.   Trust in God

There was a man in County Clare long ago, and he was a good man. His name was Donncha Mór. He was always praying. He had a big field of corn cut this particular day. He got up in the morning and was saying his rosary   he used to pray every morning. On that day it looked like rain and his wife said to him:

'Get up off your knees at once, Donncha Mór! It looks very like rain. The sun is blazing on the window and the raven is screeching. The rain will come and drench your corn!'

When Donncha had finished his rosary he got up.

'It's about time you got up off your knees, Donncha! Can't you see? It's going to rain!'

Said Donncha:

'I believe in neither crows nor ravens.
Nor in women's cross words;
For no matter how the sun rises,
It's God will how the day will be.'

Donncha went out binding the corn and he was hardly at the field before the rain began. The wife was running in and out, and telling the other women:

'Donncha Mór is out of his mind today! He's out there binding corn, and he's doing more harm than good, because he's tying it wet and that's a bad thing.'

Donncha's wife was very worried about the corn; it was pouring rain at the house. And she was complaining to the women inside:

'There's no way I can stop him now but to put down the dinner and call him for it!'

At dinnertime she put on the dinner for Donncha and went to the field. When she came in over the fence to the place where Donncha was, there wasn't a drop of rain falling in the field. She looked at the corn and not a drop of rain had fallen on the corn. She went over to Donncha.

'It's been raining hard over at the house since you left it and it seems there wasn't a drop here.'

'If it's raining at the house, it is not raining here,' said Donncha. 'You are lacking in faith, and you were always that way. And I'm afraid that you'll always be that way! If you had enough faith you wouldn't be half as much afraid of rain and storms as you are. If you trusted in God to settle matters, God would look after them, and everything would be alright. But it's hard to advise a cross woman with little sense!'

III.   The Faith in Árainn Mhór

The best part of two hundred years ago, there was no chapel or priest on the island of Árainn Mhór. There was an old man ill on the island so the crew of a boat came to Ailt an Chorráin, walked over to Cionn Caslach and told the priest that this old man was dying and that they'd like him to come with them and anoint him. The priest said he'd come. So they walked back to Ailt an Chorráin and when the priest saw the look of the evening, and how rough it was out in the bay, he said he hadn't the courage to go to sea that day, as it was far too wild but that he hoped there wouldn't be a bit wrong with the old man until the next day and he'd try to go then.

The men got into their boat, hoisted their sails and set out for the island. When they got ashore the old man was much worse and and his people didn't want him to die without the priest, so they asked a double crew to take a big boat so that this would give the priest more courage to come to the island. The men consulted together and took the big boat and came to Ailt an Chorráin again. It was very late when they arrived the second time, but they walked on to Cionn Caslach again and they called to the priest at the upper window. The priest got up and opened the window and when he saw who was there he said they were mad to set out on such a night from an island out at sea, taking their lives in their hands.

'Bad as it was,' said he, 'when you were here before, it's much worse now and I won't go to the island with you tonight!'

They walked back the same way to Ailt an Chorráin. They headed off to sea, leaving the land behind them. They ploughed their way through huge squally seas and just as they were going through the Scealpaigh, at the spot where the nineteen souls were lost last November, a wave came on board and almost swamped the boat. Then a second wave came and sank her. Next morning, Árainn Mhór was a very sad island. The old man had died and ten young men were lost. The people in the island consulted together and decided never to ask the priest to the island again. The island of Árainn went for eight years as pagans. Not a child was baptised there. Not a couple was married. No one got Extreme Unction before dying and not a grave was blessed there. That was the way it remained until that priest left Cionn Caslach and a new, young priest came there. When the new priest heard what had happened he took a sidecar and driver and went to Letterkenny to see the bishop. He told the bishop he was going to Aranmore the next day to see how things stood. The bishop asked him would he have the courage to go there and he said he would.

'Well, stay here for the night and I'll be with you tomorrow morning!' said he.

The priest and the driver stayed with the bishop in Letterkenny that night. Next morning the driver took the pair of them to Ailt an Chorráin and they got a boat there that took them to Árainn Mhór. When they came ashore on the island the bishop invited everyone in the island to a meeting in one place in the centre of the island. When they had all gathered, the bishop gave them a big long sermon and when he had finished preaching:

'I believe,' said he, 'that you've lost all the faith!'

'We have not,' said an old man, 'we never get up in the morning and we never go to bed at night without offering ourselves to God, and we say the rosary every night.

'Blessed be the One who made man and woman,
Blessed be the One who made night and day,
Blessed be the One who made the black sheep and the white,
No more wonderful than the ebb and flow of the sea.'

'I see,' said the bishop, 'that your faith is still strong except that you do not accept the priest.'

They gave confession and communion to all those on the island who had reached the age of reason. They baptised those children who had not been baptised. They married the couples that had come together during the period and they blessed those graves that had not been blessed. They started a new chapel for them. When the chapel was finished they sent a priest to them and there's a chapel and a priest on Árainn Mhór from that day to this.

112.   The Spaniard's Request

There was this Spaniard, a long time ago. He was born in Spain. And one day, he told his mother that he was going aboard ship to be a sailor.

'Well, if you are, *a rún*,' said the mother, 'pray on your rosary every time you can, that you'll have a priest with you before you die.'

He said he would. But the Spaniard went aboard and while he was aboard ship he began to save money. He kept the money in a belt round his waist, inside in a leather belt. In the end, he felt death approaching and he asked his shipmates, the sailors, to put ashore up there behind the valleys of land at Forónach. They did that; they launched a small boat at once and put him into it and landed him out at Forónach.

He crept along the valley then until he came to a bank. He sat on the bank; he was very weak after crossing the valley, feeling very sick.

There was a priest in Gleann Cholm Cille in those days and the priest came to this village on a sick call. Then the priest was to go on from this village to Teileann to stations to hear confessions. And the priest and his servant-boy were walking up Sliabh Liag and when they got to the top of Sliabh Liag and the mouth of Fochair Aoidh they heard this moaning.

'That's someone that's very weak!' said the boy to the priest.

The boy went searching and he found the man sitting under a bank. The priest went down to him. The priest asked him how he came to be there or where he came from. Then he told the priest how he had come from Spain.

'My mother asked me,' said the Spaniard, 'to pray on my rosary every morning, that I'd have a priest before I die.'

'Well, you have one now!' said the priest.

The priest heard his Confession and anointed him; then he and the boy brought him to a milking-hut that the people of Málainn Bhig had on the mountain. They left him in the hut. He gave the belt to the priest and asked him to build chapels with the money in it.

We have seen two chapels that the priest built, the chapel at Bun na dTrí Sruthán and a small chapel over there in Fearann Mhic Giolla Bhríde.

113.   The Value of a Pater and Creed

Long ago, we used to have landlords here and they were very much down on the tenants. They charged them twice a year; and those that charged high rents were the worst, they were the very worst. They used to take the cow or the calf or the yearling with them if the money wasn't paid. But where was the money? There wasn't any. There was an old man there, himself and his family picked bare by this tyrant who hadn't a thing left in the end.

'Now,' said he, 'I haven't a thing to give you. I've not a cow or calf, sheep or lamb, that you haven't taken already. I've nothing left. But I'll say a Pater and Creed for you every day for a year, and my blessing, if you leave myself and my family here.'

'How do we know,' said the tyrant, 'what your Pater and Creed for a year is worth?'

'We'll ask the parish priest,' said the poor man.

'Alright!' said the big man. 'Then I'll know how much a Pater and Creed are worth.'

So he said the Pater and Creed, faithfully and piously, every day for a year so that he could stay in the place and that everything would be alright. When the year was up the poor man went to the priest. He told him his story.

'Oh,' said the priest, 'it's so valuable that I couldn't put a price on it. We'll have to ask the bishop!'

Which they did. The bishop gave a note to the messenger sent by the priest.

'It's so valuable,' said the bishop, 'that I couldn't put a price on it. But I'll ask the Pope in Rome!'

Which he did. The Pope sent back a reply, a fine generous paper, saying that a Pater and Creed, said with a good, pure heart, and in a pious manner, was worth a bar of gold that would stretch from the ground far up into the sky, that was what it was worth. The message came to the bishop and the bishop sent it to the parish priest. The priest came to the tyrant, bringing the poor man and the paper with him and read him the paper.

'Oh,' said the tyrant, 'how will I ever be able to repay you, Tadhg?'

'Oh,' said poor Tadhg, 'I'm not asking that of you, master.'

'All I possess wouldn't repay you,' said the tyrant, 'or even a thousand times that! But you will have your land and little house,' said he, 'and I'll build you a far better house. You can have it till the day you die and for as long as anyone belonging to you lives. And don't die for want of anything! As long as I have anything myself, I'll give it to you, and you well deserve it from me!'

And, as far as I know, and as far as I can guess, that man wasn't as hard afterwards on his poor tenants as he was before. He gradually became more holy and wise, so that he came to realise that he was very unjust before. But it was that poor man, saying his Pater and Creed for a year, that brought him down and it was on account of him that he repented. Glory be to God and to the saints and the apostles!

114.   The Rosary

There was a blind man going the road one day, saying his prayers. He had his beads in his hand, saying the rosary on them. A young lad was coming towards him and he whipped the beads from him.

'Come back,' said the blind man, 'and give me back my beads, whatever kind of person you are!'

He came back and gave him his beads.

'When you go to the priest to Confession,' said the blind man, 'tell him that you spoiled the blind man's rosary, and ask the priest how much a rosary is worth. And, whatever the priest says it is worth, you must pay me that.'

Away he went, and, however long it was before he went to the priest, and I'm sure it wasn't long, he told the priest in confession that he had spoiled the blind man's rosary. The priest asked him:

'What did you do that for?'

'Musha, Father, I don't know,' said he, 'but tell me how much it's worth so that I can pay the blind man whatever the rosary is worth so that I can get him to forgive me for spoiling it.'

'Did he tell you,' said the priest, 'that you'd have to pay him what it was worth?'

'Oh, he did,' said the lad.

'Well, go to the blind man and say it's worth a penny!'

Off he went and himself and the blind man saluted one another.

'How much did he say the rosary was worth?' said the blind man.

'He said it was worth a penny,' said the lad.

'Oh,' said the blind man, 'and why did he say a penny?'

'Oh, that's what he said!'

'Go back to the priest and ask him how big that penny would be,' said the blind man.

He went, and called in to the priest and asked him how big the blind man's penny would be.

'Oh,' said the priest, 'it'd be big enough, so big that it would cover the whole world!'

'Oh, God save my soul!' said the poor lad, 'what am I going to do now?'

'Go back to the blind man and tell him and let the two of you settle it between you. Nobody knows,' said the priest, 'the true worth of a rosary and it was all the more valuable because the poor man was blind, and travelling the roads when you whipped the beads from him. And until he forgives you, I cannot give you absolution!'

He went off to the blind man, very heavy-hearted. He told him what the priest had said about the size of the penny.

'Ah,' my boy, 'I knew well that the rosary was worth a lot more than a penny!'

He asked the blind man to forgive him and he'd do anything he asked him. The blind man said he was forgiven if he promised never to snatch the beads from a blind man again. Then he went back to the priest and the priest gave him absolution.

115.   The Servant-Girl's Prayer

Once upon a time, there was a poor girl working in a farmer's house. I need hardly say that she worked hard from Monday to Saturday and even at night she wasn't allowed rest, because she had to boil potatoes and turnips for the pigs after the household had gone to bed. That's how it was with her, night and day, with never a rest except while the potatoes were boiling when she'd fall asleep unknown to herself. She'd have the light lit while she slept and people who'd be out at night used to wonder what was going on. Some people thought that there must be someone sick in the house while others thought that it was the girl who had the light on and that she must be with the fairies at night.

Anyhow, the rumour spread about the servant-girl and she was complained to the priest on account of her dealings with the fairy folk. The priest came to see the girl and questioned her, and he couldn't find any reason to believe that she had dealings with the fairies. Then he asked her why she had the light on and she told him all about having to sit up at night boiling potatoes for the pigs after she had done her day's work. Then he asked her did she say her prayers.

'I don't, except for one little prayer and that's all I know!' said the poor girl.

'Recite the prayer for me,' said the priest.

'This is it,' she said:

'I place my trust and protection in the Holy Trinity, in Sweet Jesus, and in the Blessed Virgin, in the Golden Angels that are highest in the City of the Trinity, in the Court of Heaven and in the Saints of the World, and in my Guardian Angel, night and day, as long as I live.'

No sooner had she said the prayer than her soul departed and an angelic beauty came on her face, which amazed them. The priest said that it was wrong to cast aspersions on people, and that the poor girl was a living saint.

116.   The Old Woman's Prayer

There was this old woman going around seeking alms. All she had in the way of prayers was one short prayer, but she said it often:

'May the Father, Son and Holy Spirit protect me from today till a year from today!'

She went in to a house one night and asked for a night's shelter. She was given it and went to bed in a room there. The house was a robbers' den; there were three sons and their father. The father was constantly praying to God to send them some sign that would make them mend their ways.

Now, the three sons decided to kill the old woman when she was sleeping. One of them went over to the door and peeped in through the keyhole. What did he see but a guard, dressed in a white robe and carrying a gun, walking up and down beside the bed! He told the other two brothers. The second brother looked into the room and he saw two guards. And when the third brother looked, he saw three guards! They had received the sign from God, and they gave up the robbing from that day on.

117.   How the Hens were Freed

One Sunday morning, there was an old woman on her knees with her beads in her hand. She had nine hens in the kitchen, eating grains of meal in the middle of the floor while she said her prayers and watched them. The fox came and grabbed one of them and made off with her through the door.

'You've done that, my fine boy,' said she, 'and may it do you no good! And no matter what you've done, I'm not getting off my knees.'

Five minutes later he was back and grabbed a second one.

'Oh, musha,' said she, 'if you took all belonging to me, I won't get off my knees till I've finished my rosary!'

He came a third time and took a third one.

'May the day do you no good!' she said. 'You won't leave me one! Even if you take them all, I won't get up off my knees till I've finished my rosary!'

She got up when she was finished and went outside and all nine hens were outside, just as they were that morning!

118.   The Honesty of the Old People

Once upon a time there was this man and he had three cows. He had no horse. He had two farms but he was a very long way from one of them. It was so far away he was unable to do anything with it. He said to his wife:

'Here we are with three cows, and two would do us, so I'll take one of them and see can I swap it for some kind of a horse.'

'Fair enough,' said the wife.

Off went the poor man. When he had walked a good distance he met a man on the road.

'Where are you going with the cow?'

'I'm going to see could I find anyone that I could swap her with for any kind of a horse.'

'Well met,' said the other man, 'I have two horses and no cow at all. I've a big family and plenty of food. Even so they can't eat a bite, and they're collapsing with the hunger for the want of milk, so we'll do a swap. What sort of exchange-money are you looking for?'

'I'm not looking for any exchange-money, but what are you looking for?'

They started arguing the toss back and forth, each man trying to give the other something extra.

'Well,' said the man with the cow, 'this is what we'll do: let you take the cow home with you and we'll meet here on this spot in a year's time, and whoever profited most from the deal will give the other man the exchange-money.'

A year later, the pair met again at the same place. Said the man with the cow:

'How did you get on since with the horse?'

'Oh, what a horse! I made more this year than I made in five before! How did the cow work out for you?'

'Well, my children were weak with hunger before, but now they're full, warm and stocky from the milk and food, so what exchange-money are you looking for?'

'Oh, well, that's not the way of it at all,' said he, 'it's I must pay you.'

The two of them kept on like that for a long time. In the end, a man came by, I think he was an angel.

'If you give me something, be it big or small, I'll settle the question for you,' said he.

The man with the horse said he'd give him so much and the man with the cow said he'd give him so much, as long as he'd settle the question.

'You won't give me anything beyond reason,' said the man. 'Give me the slightest thing, as long as it's money, and I'll settle the matter for you.'

When they offered it to him, he wouldn't take it.

'I fear very much for the coming times,' said he, 'compared to the times that are gone! I'm afraid the day is coming when the son will try to take advantage of the father and the father will try to take advantage of the son and compare that with the present day when nobody wants to take advantage of anyone!'

God Deals Justly

'God is a slow judge,
He never did other than what was just.'

— half-quatrain from Armagh.

'God's mill grinds slowly but it grinds fine.'

Munster proverb.

God's vengeance many be slow, but it's sure.'

Ulster proverb.

A great source of subject matter for storytellers of old, and indeed of the present too, is the fate that befalls a person who breaks God's commandments and fails to make atonement for his sins. 'We'll leave you to God!' people would say to such a person. He might get along well for years but, in the end, his day would come. On the other hand, dreadful trials could befall a just man who didn't appear to deserve them and stories were told to account for them on the basis that God had his own wise ends. 'A fate worse than death for a person could well be the best thing that ever happened to him.'

119.   The Butcher and the Priest

There was this butcher long ago. He had a priest staying with him. The butcher got up and saw a man going the road and he called him in. He hit him a belt of the cleaver on the forehead and, splitting his head in two, killed him. The priest was in his room, looking out through the keyhole while the butcher was committing the murder, and he never spoke. Shortly afterwards another man was passing the butcher's house and the butcher called him in. When he came in:

'You devil,' said the butcher, 'you've killed this man! I'll call the guard and have you arrested!'

The priest was listening to everything that went on. And the butcher went to the guard and said that this man had killed another man in his house. The guards came and arrested him. They took him away and held him until the day of the sessions. When they took him off to be tried, the priest said he'd go to the trial to make sure that justice was done. He was just about to go out the door when he decided he'd leave justice in the hands of God.

'Because,' he said, 'God will always do the right thing.'

He left it like that. The next thing he heard from the sessions was that the innocent man had been hanged! The priest decided that he wouldn't spend another day in God's service ever again, since that man had been hanged in the wrong, as he had witnessed what happened at the murder. All he did was to take off his priest's clothing and close the door after him, saying that he'd walk the world over until he found out why it was that God hadn't done justice between the two men.

He went off down the road, like any other poor man, in worn-out clothes. He travelled on for three or four days, suffering from hunger and cold, but he didn't mind. In another three or four days he was going through a lonely bit of countryside, without a house in sight, when he met a man, who looked like a gentleman, at a cross-roads.

'God be with you!' said the man to the priest.

'God and Our Lady be with you!' said the priest.

'Would you mind me asking you,' said the man, 'where you're going?'

'I don't mind at all,' said the priest. 'If I could find a place that would keep me,' said he, 'to take me into service, or any other kind of job, I'd be delighted. I'll have to earn my living.'

'You're just the man I'm looking for,' said the gentleman, 'I haven't a man or a woman with me, only myself, and when I go out I have to close up the door after me. And you happened along looking to enter my service! Here's the key and go to the house and unlock the door. There's a table laid with plenty of food and drink. Sit down and eat your fill; and when you've that done, there's a spade and pick and shovel just outside the door. You can go to the south of the house to where there's a sand-pit and you can start digging it up.'

He went. The man went off and said he wouldn't be back at the house for a while. The priest went to the house. He unlocked the door. He went inside. There was the table in the middle of the floor, with plenty of food and drink on it and a chair beside it. He sat down and ate his fill. When he had eaten, he nodded off for a while, and then he woke again.

'God help us!' said he, 'I thought, one time, that I'd never end up like this, but it can't be helped!'

He got up, without much inclination, because he had never done much work in his life. He went out. He took up the pickaxe, the spade and the shovel and began to work. He wasn't long at it till his hand started to get sore from lack of practice, since he had never done that kind of work before. He sat down.

'Oh, musha, God help us!' said he. 'Wasn't it a sad fate God had in store for me! But it can't be helped!'

He took a rest and then he got up again and started working and it wasn't long till he dug up a human bone from the hole. Then he dug up another and he got very nervous.

'I suppose,' said he, 'that according to my master's orders I'll have to do this work.'

He started digging again and throwing up bones until he had a whole skeleton dug up. Then he stopped and got frightened and troubled for digging up the bones of this person out of the hole. And he stood there looking and brooding. He wasn't too long standing there when the master came up to where he was:

'You're working away,' said he.

'I am,' said he, 'and I don't much like it, digging up someone's bones out of the ground!'

'You're doing that,' said the gentleman, 'and you can see yourself that you are. The man that was hanged at the session, it was he who killed the man you are after digging up and buried him in that hole you're digging today; and he was never found out. God will give a sign to you and everybody else that he acts justly, sooner or later. The butcher will be killed too, just as he killed the other man. God will act justly. And I know,' said he, 'how it was with you, as well as you know yourself, and that you gave up your position until you'd find out why God didn't act justly. Go off home now to the place you left. There's a priest acting for you ever since you left, and nobody in the whole world would know him from you, and they all think it is you, ever since you left home. It was God himself that sent me to tell you the true story and that he wasn't acting unjustly.'

The priest went home. He went into his house, as before. The people of the place thought that it was he who had been there, and that he had never left the place, because a priest from God had done duty for him from the time he left till the time he returned. He stayed in the service of God thereafter as long as he lived.

The blessing of the Almighty God and of His Church on the souls of the dead and may God protect all here!

120.   The Farmer who Lost his Sons

Once upon a time there was a fine, rich, independent man. He had three sons and he was so rich that he had a priest employed in his own home, and at his own cost, teaching his children and imparting knowledge to them. He was a fine, devout, respectable man. There was no day that Mass wasn't said in the house and nothing out of the way ever happened in the house.

The family were growing up to be fine, nice youths, but there's no joy that hasn't a sorrow too. That was ever said. It came to pass that the eldest son caught something and died and the man was very upset and discontented for a while. But in the end they began to pick up again and put their sorrows and cares behind them. But, shortly afterwards, the second son had a seizure, and the poor man lost him very suddenly. They were distracted and distressed, particularly the father and mother, but the priest was constantly consoling them and telling them to have sense and to remember that nothing was happening that was not the will of God. The man himself realised that it was enough for him to be left the youngest son. But that's not the way it turned out; he, too, was taken in a very short time, and he was left without anyone.

The day after the third son was buried he became like a madman. He wouldn't respond to anyone. He told his wife that he wouldn't spend another night in the house. He took off and headed down the road, with no idea of where he was going. He had gone a good distance when he saw a man with his back to the ditch beside the road. The man came out from the ditch and stood in the road in front of him.

'God and Our Lady bless you, my good man!' said he.

'God and Our Lady and Patrick bless you!' said the rich man.

'Where might you be going?' said the stranger.

'Musha, I swear to God,' said he, 'that I don't know where I'm going! I'm going without sense or reason and I'm sure you must be a stranger in this place since you don't know the cause of my distress and my trouble.'

'I am indeed,' said the stranger, 'but tell me where you're going.'

'I'm going to throw myself down in some glen or hollow,' said he, 'and I'll never be seen going home to my house again. I'm demented and distracted and distressed.'

'Don't do that,' said the stranger, 'have sense! Come along with me and maybe I could be of some help to you.'

He went along with him and they never stopped until they went in to the corner of a wood that was nearby.

'Would you like to see your sons?' said the stranger.

'I would,' said the rich man.

'Go over there,' said he, 'to the foot of that tree.'

He brought him with him and they went over to the tree.

'Come over here and stand behind me,' said the stranger, 'and look over my shoulder towards the tree.'

He stood behind him and looked over his shoulder towards the tree. Didn't he see his eldest son hanging from the tree with a rope round his neck and a big crowd of people around him, mocking and laughing at him.

'That's enough!' said the stranger. 'Come over here a bit.'

They went on another bit, nine paces. They went to the tree in front of them.

'Now, look over my shoulder,' said the stranger.

He looked, and saw his second son, tied hand and foot with a hard hempen cord, and a dagger piercing his heart, and the blood flowing out of him.

'That's enough!' said the stranger. 'Come on.'

He brought him another nine paces and said to him:

'Stand there and look over my shoulder.'

He looked and saw his youngest son lying on the flat of his back at the foot of the tree with his throat cut and the blood flowing out of it.

'That's enough!' said the stranger. 'Turn around now, my boy,' said he, 'and listen to me carefully!'

The rich man turned on his heel and began to listen to the stranger.

'God was so pleased with you,' said the stranger to him, 'that He didn't let you endure the deaths that were in store for your sons. Do you see those three there?' said he. 'That was the death in store for each of them, but God did not want it to happen. So he swept them off clean and decent, in good repute and honoured and esteemed, rather than have your heart broken and tormented seeing them suffering those awful deaths at the end of your days. Go home now, my good man,' said the stranger, 'and take good care of your house and your place, and go on as you did in your early days and do the will of the God of Glory and he will give you great blessings for the rest of your life. Do you know who I am?'

'I don't,' said the rich man. 'Who are you?'

'I'm a messenger of the God of Glory, sent to you because he wanted to show you these things. Go off home now and take care of your house and your place and your family and you'll have an heir before you die!'

The farmer went home and took even greater care of his house and his place. And after two years his wife gave birth to a son who took tender care of his father and mother to the very end of their days.

121. The Blind Man's Cross

Near the old graveyard of Míobhaigh, below Clontallagh, where they are still burying people today, there's a cross at a turn in the road as you go down to the graveyard by the old road. They tell me that the reason for that cross is this: there was a holy old man going around at that called Bráthair Mác Pháidín. He was very holy and used to go from place to place. He had no place of his own but spent the night in one house or another. He erected a cross near the chapel down beside the turn. He went on then until he came to Cnoc Righin and he put a stone standing there. When he was gone a bit up Cnoc Righin, it seems that a dove flew by and hit him between the two eyes, blinding him.

He was very worried then on account of being blind and unable to see, so he began praying. A voice spoke to him when he had finished praying, and asked him would he prefer to be blind in this life or blind in the next life. He said he'd rather be blind in this life as long as he'd be able to see in the next life. Bráthair Mac Pháidín walked on down and he had no idea where he was going. There was no road in those days and where did he end up but down at the sea. He went out on the rock at the far end of the strand on this side of Más Leac. They found him drowned at the foot of the rock and they call that rock the Blind Man's Rock, because that's where they found Bráthair Mac Pháidín drowned.

That cross was standing at Clontallagh for a long time, with a little heap of stones around it. One time there was a Protestant living in Machaire Bheag. He drank a lot and was a very cross man and it seems there was no one around could stop him. He pulled down the cross and left it lying there and broke a load of bottles in its place. Not long after, he went off to America and he lost his sight and hearing on the way, going to America, and I never heard what happened to him after that.

122. The Wheel of God

(a) There was a poor scholar going the rounds, long ago. There were no schools in those days, only poor scholars going around teaching. He used call very often to a big, strong farmer who had only one daughter, and if he did, didn't himself and the daughter fall in love! The farmer knew it well. The poor scholar was a fine man. One night the farmer and the poor scholar were sitting round the fire, putting questions to one another.

'Well,' said the farmer, 'what do you think Our Lord God, may He be ever praised, is doing now?'

The poor scholar paused and thought to himself for a while.

'He's making a wheel that will be turning around,' said he. 'The man that's down today will be up tomorrow and the man that's up today will be down tomorrow.'

'Well said,' said the farmer.

Well, the poor scholar was constantly coming and going and the farmer's daughter wouldn't marry anybody but him.

'Well now,' said the farmer, 'my daughter has fallen in love with you! Will you marry her?'

'I will.'

'I'll give you a thousand pounds with her,' said the farmer.

'I won't take a half penny of your thousand pounds,' said the poor scholar, 'because none of it is honest! I wouldn't take one halfpenny of your thousand pounds because none of it was honestly got! I'd rather take sixpence that you earned by the sweat of your brow than the thousand pounds you're offering me!'

'And how would I get that sixpence?' said the farmer.

'Tomorrow is a harvest day,' said the poor scholar, 'for the farmer next door and he's looking for men to cut the oats. He's offering sixpence a day for each man. Away with you now and work for him and when you have your sixpence earned in the evening you can give it to me. That's all the dowry I'll ask of you!'

The farmer did that, and he had never done a day's work before, but he set to. It was a warm, close day and the sweat was running into his shoes. He couldn't see the sheaf he was tying, with the sweat. When the day's work was done, the farmer paid them off, sixpence to each man. The farmer came home and gave the sixpence to the poor scholar.

When the poor scholar had got his sixpence, and got married, himself and his wife set off, and they were walking by a quay, like the one in An Daingean. The trawlers had come in and the fish were on the quay. They passed by the pier-head and the wife of the poor scholar got a great longing for a fish; and she said that she wanted, more than anything else in the world, a fish to eat for her supper, that it was a very long time since she had seen a fresh fish. Well there was a fine plump fish there and she told him to buy it. He asked how much it was and was told sixpence. That was all the money he had in the world, the sixpence that his father-in-law had earned the previous day. They took away the trout, carrying it on their finger; and when they got lodgings for the night they went in there; and when they wanted to prepare the fish they opened it and what was inside in the belly of the fish but a carbuncle! That's a very expensive, valuable thing, that's very rare, and you'd only find it in the belly of a fish. The poor scholar knew, well enough, what he had found. He took it to a well-off man and asked him would he buy it. He said he would.

'How much do you want for it?' he said.

'Three hundred pounds. It's worth that,' said he.

He got the three hundred pounds and lacked for nothing. Next day he told his wife that he'd give up the teaching and not go on as they were; if he could get a little bit of land he'd prefer that, to be working and doing business instead of going from house to house and place to place. And, as luck would have it, wasn't there the grass of two or three cows going and he bought it. He still had money to spare and it wasn't long till he had five or six cows and a horse and cart and sheep and pigs. Himself and the wife took to the farming so well that he was prospering and putting a lot of money aside.

Yes, but on my word, the father-in-law, his money melted away right and left. His family died and the money went, here and there. He was left with nothing. He was thrown out of his farm. His family was scattered far and wide and he had nothing to do but to go begging for alms. Away he went, with his bag and his stick, one night here and another night there, and where did he end up but walking into the house of the poor scholar, one evening on his travels! The poor scholar and his wife were up in the loft, looking out through the window. The house was a bit back from the main road. They saw the poor man coming to the house.

'Devil take me,' said the poor scholar to his wife, 'but that's your father!'

'My father! That a man that had a big farm of land and a thousand pounds would end up begging for alms!'

'I'm telling you that it's him,' said the poor scholar.

He came in looking for alms and they came down to him and asked him to stay the night, that he wouldn't get much farther now and he might as well stay. They recognised him well. He didn't recognise them. He said he'd stay if they didn't mind. After that he got his supper and they were sitting round the fire for the night. The poor scholar asked him who he was and where he came from.

'Were you well off once?'

'I was,' said he.

'What happened to your money?'

'It melted away, here and there.'

'Had you any family?'

'I had. Some of them went to the bad and one of them married a poor scholar.'

'Would you know the poor scholar now?'

'I wouldn't,' said he.

'Well, I'm the very man,' said the poor scholar.

Oh, Lord above, fear and shame and terror came over him, to say that he was coming after him looking for a night's lodging after all the money he had one time!

'Well, now,' said the poor scholar, 'didn't I tell you that your money was ill-gotten, and that one sixpence you had earned by the sweat of your brow from the farmer, that day, would be better for me than the thousand pounds I could have got from you? And that's the very sixpence that set me up! As long as you live now,' said he, 'you won't have to go begging for alms. I'll look after you till the day you die.'

'Oh, you won't! I can't stay!' said the farmer.

'You will stay,' said the poor scholar.

He stayed there till the day he died. That's my story now.

(b) There was a gentleman long ago and there was no telling all the money and wealth he had. As he was sitting down by himself one fine day, taking life easy in his comfortable chair, and looking around him, he saw a middle-aged man approaching the mansion, very badly dressed. His clothes were threadbare, and he wasn't fit to be let out the door by rights; but he couldn't help being poor and, maybe, hungry. He went up to the gentleman and asked him for alms in the name of God and the Virgin Mary.

'I'll give you that,' said the gentleman, 'if you'll tell me what God is doing today.'

The poor man paused, thinking to himself, and pondered.

'He's making wheels,' said he.

'Making wheels!' said the gentleman, bursting out laughing, and jeering at the poor man. 'And tell me, my poor fool, what is He doing that for?'

'I'll tell you that,' said the poor man. 'So that the man who's up today will be down for the next year, and the man who's down today will be up for the next year.'

He understood him well then. He put his hand in his pocket and gave him three pence or maybe sixpence – he wouldn't go any higher than that. The poor man thanked the gentleman.

'Don't bother with your thanks!' said he. 'Be off with you now and don't let me see you again!'

The poor man went off. He spent the next six months begging for alms and help from everyone he met. After the six months, he was walking one day and saw a white bag on the road in front of him and he noticed it because it was a long way from any house or people. He went up to the bag and it was packed tight with yellow gold. He threw himself down on his two knees on the spot and thanked God and the Virgin Mary and all the saints for the good they had done to him and then he took hold of the bag. He put it on his back and turned for home. He met neither man, woman or child until he got home to his wife and two children. He put the bag on the floor and the wife asked him what he had in the bag. And he told her that that was alms that the Son of God and the Virgin Mary and the angels had given him, a bag of gold. And it was.

Of course, immediately he got the gold, he began buying land and building houses and giving work to every poor person that came to him, until he had built a whole town. Away with him throughout Ireland buying every sort of beast with four legs under it – there's no use in trying to name them, for I couldn't.

He wouldn't leave a fair without buying up everything and then he had servants driving them home and putting them on farms.

Around the same time as the poor man found the bag of gold, there wasn't a house or barn belonging to the landlord, the gentleman, that didn't go up in flames the same night; his gold and silver were all burned and he only barely escaped with his life. That's what he got for mocking, the poor man! And all he could do was to set out with his stick in his hand, begging for charity from anyone who would give it to him, to see could he keep himself alive. Exactly a year afterwards, he heard tell of this gentleman that was buying and clearing out every fair, and that he was very generous, and that he could expect a fine hand-out from him. Around dinnertime one day he was very near the house of the poor man – as I'll call him – and when he saw this person coming, he had great pity for him, remembering how he had been once. When he came in the man inside recognised the landlord. He got up and shook hands with him and made him very welcome. He told the women who were working there to get a dinner ready for him.

'You know me,' said the landlord, 'but I don't recognise you.'

'Sit down and take your ease,' said the man of the house, 'until you've had your dinner. Then we can talk.'

He ate. And when he had eaten:

'I don't remember,' said the landlord, 'ever seeing you before.'

'You saw me alright!' said the man of the house. 'Do you remember such and such a day that a poor man came to you asking for alms in the name of God and the Virgin Mary? You said you'd give him that, and he laughed, and you asked him what the Son of God was doing that day. He told you that He was making wheels and you asked him what use had He for the wheels, and he told you that they were for the man who was up today to be down next year and the man who was down today to be up next year. You put your hand in your pocket and gave him four pence, and you told him to go away at once and not to be seen again.'

'I remember,' said the landlord, 'that that happened.'

'And don't you recognise him now?' said the other man. 'I'm that man.'

'Ah, God save us! I was in the wrong.'

The man of the house put his hand in his pocket and gave him five pounds and told him to stay in the house till the next day so that he could have an early start. When he ate his breakfast next morning, he took his stick in his hand and went out. He wished them health and seven thousand blessings as he went.

May all here present be seven thousand times better off this time twelve months! That's my story and the tale of the poor man for you now!

123. Treachery Returns

In the old days there used to be pedlars going round with baskets selling small, light items. They sold stockings and reels of thread and sewing needles and knitting needles and other light things like that, that they could carry a lot of in their basket; and they were making a living like that. But there was one of these pedlars coming to the house of a man who had some sons who were fairly grown-up; and there was one boy in the house who was great with a girl who lived nearby and he was thinking of marrying her. But she wouldn't marry him because he wasn't well off; he had no money. One day he was talking to the girl and he asked her, if he had enough money, however he got it, would she marry him.

'I will,' said she. 'It doesn't matter how you get the money,' said she, 'as long as you have such and such an amount I'll marry you.'

The pedlar was staying in the house of the father of this man at the time and he had an idea that the pedlar had a fair bit of money. And the young man decided that he'd go ahead of the pedlar to a lonely place and he'd take the money off him and kill him. And that's what he did. He went by a short-cut ahead of the pedlar, after he had left his father's house, to a lonely place; he accosted him and told him to hand over all his money to him and that he'd have to kill him.

'Don't do that,' said the pedlar, 'and I'll give you all the money I've got. I have sixty pounds in cash and I'll give it to you and I'll never tell a soul about it, or say I gave it to you, or that you asked for it, but don't kill me!'

'There's no use in talking,' said the young man. 'I'll have to kill you!'

So he killed the pedlar. When he was killing him, or when he was almost dead a voice spoke near to him:

'Treachery returns!' said the voice.

And he asked when.

'On your son's son after you,' said the voice.

He went back and told the young woman what the voice had said the second time.

'If it's that far away,' said the young woman, 'so be it! It won't bother me or you.'

Time went by and they had a son and he grew up to be a young man and married himself. And the son and his wife had a young son and they lived in the one house with the father and mother, who were fairly old by now. There came a night with thunder and lightning and rain and neither himself nor his wife nor their son, nor his son's wife nor the young son escaped alive. And that's the end that befell the man who killed the pedlar, and his son and his son's son.

124.   The Testimony of the Eggs

There was a pedlar going round long ago selling stockings and towels and that sort of thing – carrying them in a basket, as you'd see them, even today. But one day a young man intercepted him on the road to rob him of his money and kill him.

'For the love of God,' said the poor pedlar, 'don't kill me! For if you do kill me, you'll be found out even if it is the birds of the air that tell on you!'

'I don't care,' said the young man, 'I'm going to kill you anyhow.'

He killed him on the spot and when the pedlar was dying:

'May the Son of God and the birds of the air be my witnesses for this,' said he.

It wasn't many years later when there were men working in the place where the young man had killed the pedlar. They were making a new road or some such. There was a young man in charge of them who went hunting in the bushes that were growing there, and what did he find but a bird's nest with eggs in it. He looked at the eggs and there was writing on them. Written on them was the name of the pedlar and the name of his killer and the date and place where he was killed. The young man who killed the pedlar was arrested and he was hanged.

125.   'God Put him to Sleep'

There was this widow and she had a godfather living nearby. She hadn't paid the rent. So she went to her godfather, because her children were all very young and it was too far for herself to go to pay the rent – she wouldn't be home at all that night, it was so far away. She heard that her godfather was going to pay his rent so she went to him and asked him would he pay hers, as it was too far away for her to go herself. He said he would. Then she gave him the money.

Some time afterwards the bailiffs came looking for the rent. She told them she had already paid the rent. They asked her for the rent receipt. She said she didn't have it but that the man she gave the money to would have it. They gave her a second chance and went away, telling her to have the receipt the next time they came. She went to the field to the man she gave the money to, to pay the rent, looking for the receipt so that she'd have it the next time they came. When she asked him for it, what he said was: where was her witness? She said she had no witness only the God of Glory.

'The God of Glory was asleep!' said he.

She left the field then and went home. One of the man's little girls went to the field to call him to his meal. The little girl was beside him shouting at her father to come home to his meal but he gave her no answer. Then his wife went to the field, after the little girl came home, calling him to come for his meal but he made no reply to his wife. She was shaking him and talking to him but he made no answer. He was standing there with the spade under his arm. They called for help and he was brought home. They sent for the priest then and he hadn't a word for the priest. Then the priest asked who was talking to him last. They said it was a woman from the village that was talking to him in the field. The priest told them to bring the woman to him. The woman came in to the priest and he asked her what she said to him in the field. She told the priest that she had given him the rent to pay for her; she went to him in the field looking for the receipt, because the bailiffs were looking for the rent, so she went to get the receipt from him.

"'Where's your witness?" said he to me.

"'I've no witness," said I, "but the God of Glory." Then he said that the God of Glory was asleep.'

'Oh,' said the priest, 'God put him to sleep. The God of Glory put him to sleep.'

Miscellaneous

'No better choice than the King of the World,
No greater help than mercy.
No everlasting life but Heaven,
No greater grace than hearing Mass.'

— *Dánfhocail* (Ó Raithile), p.54

'Give and God will reward you.
Give lavishly and you'll get still more.
He who gives grudgingly to God
Will get equal measure from God.'

— *Seanfhocla Uladh* (Ó Muirgheasa), p.203

This is the last section of this collection of religious tales, which I have selected from the manuscripts of the Irish Folklore Commission. These stories are on varied themes: the Mass, uncharitable people, miraculous abundance and the basis for certain natural phenomena. I would not describe them as the scrapings of the jar because there are many other admirable stories in the manuscripts, which have not yet found their way into print. It would take a whole series of books to give examples of all the different religious tales our forefathers used to tell. And this too will come in its own good time, with the help of God.

126. The Man who Stopped Going to Mass

There was a man around these parts long ago and himself and the priest fell out with one another. Each blamed the other and they exchanged bitter words. For that reason, the man said to himself that he'd never again go to the priest's Mass as long as he lived. He thought that it was a great ease to his mind to keep away from Mass for spite on the priest, even though it was his own loss. Anyhow, he made his vow and stayed away from Mass for two or three Sundays in a row. On the fourth Sunday, a man came in to him around the time Mass was beginning and saluted him.

They saluted each other and were talking for a while, I don't know was it long or short. The stranger asked him:

'Is it any harm to ask why you aren't at Mass like the rest of the household, or are you living on your own?'

'My wife and family are at Mass,' said the man.

'Then why aren't you at Mass too?'

'Well, myself and the priest had angry words with one another and I decided I wouldn't go to another Mass of his, ever.'

'I see,' said the stranger. 'I'd like,' said he, 'if you'd come with me to the hill for a while – I'm going for a bit of a walk up the hill and since you're not going to Mass nor busy, maybe you'd come with me.'

'Certainly!' said the man.

The two of them went out and climbed up very high on the hillside. It was a very fine, warm, close day and the local man got so thirsty that he thought he'd drink anything to ease his thirst. He bent down to a stream and drank a drop of the water. When he tasted the water, he thought he'd never tasted a drop of water that was half as sweet as it, and he drank his fill. He told the stranger that it was the sweetest water that any man ever drank.

'Stoop down,' said he to the stranger, 'and taste this water till you see for yourself that it tastes as sweet as honey. No man ever heard of, and no man ever saw, water as sweet as it!'

'I won't drink it,' said the stranger. 'I'm not thirsty just now, and if it's sweet, it would only make me thirsty. But if it's as sweet as you tell me it is, then we should go to the place it comes from, since it's all that sweet.'

'I agree,' said the other man.

They followed the stream, be it far or near. They went on till they came to the place the stream was coming from. The source that the stream with the lovely sweet water was coming from was a place where a drowned dog lay in a bog hole; and the water that was flowing into the stream was coming through the drowned dog.

'Now,' said the stranger, 'if you knew that that was the water you were drinking, would you drink a drop of it?'

'Oh, indeed I wouldn't,' said he, 'even if I died of the thirst!'

'I see,' said the stranger. 'Well, when you and the priest were exchanging bitter words with one another, even if the priest was as rotten as the old dog in the bog-hole and if his soul was as black as coal with sin, the words that come out of his mouth, the words of God, are as sweet as the water you drank from the stream.'

The man was filled with sorrow, and he threw himself on his two knees and begged pardon of God and the Virgin Mary for what he had done out of the way, because he thought that the man who had come to him was a messenger from God, and he probably was. And he promised God and Our Lady that as long as he lived he'd never miss Mass another day, if he was able. Himself and the stranger saluted each other and parted. He never saw him again after that. But a short time later he went to confession and repented. He lived like a good Christian from that time on.

You should never take offence at a priest's words, if they reproach you. But it seems that the temptation of the devil is strong and it was the temptation of the devil that kept him from Mass all that time. But even if it's true that it is strong, the power of God is much stronger than it. He overcame the temptation of the devil and, with the help of God, we'll overcome it too, if we seek God's help. May God give everyone a favourable judgement on the Last Day.

127.   Hearing Mass

There was a woman once and she had a son a priest. The priest came home to her. He gave his mother a little box with a hole in the top of it.

'Put a stone in there,' he said to her, 'every time you hear Mass until I come back again.'

The old woman did that for a long time. One day as she was going to Mass she saw a herd of cattle trampling a potato field.

'I won't bother with them!' she said to herself. 'It wouldn't be right to miss Mass on account of them.'

She went off to the chapel. She wasn't long gone when she began to be sorry. She went back to the field and drove the cattle out of it. She was late for Mass that day. Some time afterwards, her son, the priest, came home to her. He looked into the box. There was only one stone in it. He asked his mother how many Masses she had heard since he was last there. She told him that she hadn't missed Mass except one day, in all that time, and she told him about the day the cattle were in the potato field.

'Well,' said the son, 'the Mass you heard that day was the only Mass you heard properly since I was here last.'

128.   The Baptism

There was a curfew in Ireland, and anyone who was out after nine o'clock at night could be shot by the soldiers. One night a poor man went for the priest to anoint his mother. The priest and himself were a bit afraid to be out after hours, but they went out nevertheless. They weren't far from Tuam when some soldiers passed them by, riding on grey horses. And because they were Protestants, not one of them saw them except the officer, because he had been baptised in the Catholic

Church, even though he didn't know that. Since none of the others said anything, he didn't either.

The next day, or maybe the day after that, the priest met him and the officer said:

'What were you doing, out late on such and such a night?'

The priest said that he couldn't have seen him and he said that he did.

'You didn't see me,' said the priest, 'nor could any other soul who hadn't been baptised.'

'I'm a Protestant,' said the officer, 'as far as I know, but I'll find out for certain tomorrow.'

He went home the next day, down near Dunmore, and he asked his father had he been baptised in the Catholic Church. The father told him he didn't know, to go and ask his mother. He went and asked his mother and the mother said that they had a housekeeper looking after all the children and she had insisted on taking him to the chapel. She brought him and he was baptised.

After that, he said he'd see to it that every member of his family would be baptised. Every one of them had to go and be baptised in the chapel.

129.   The Poor Woman in the Cemetery

There was a poor woman once and she had two children, and they were travelling the roads begging their food. She was going along one day and night came on herself and her two children, and it was the kind of place where there was nothing but big houses and well-off people, living fairly far apart. She made for the first big house she met and she asked for shelter for the night for herself and her two children, but if she did, she got a refusal at that house. She went to a second house and it was the same story, she was refused again.

She tried a third house and they told her that they had no lodgings for the likes of them (it was the woman of the house that said it) and to clear off and follow the path and go into a certain house where there was all the room in the world but that no one could come out of it. The poor woman went off with her two children and followed the path and where did she find herself only in a cemetery! It was a very dark night and she was getting a terrible pounding, falling over graves and stones and she couldn't find her way out of the cemetery. Herself and her two children had to sit down beside thc wall. She wasn't long there when she heard a horse and rider coming along the road and she decided to accost the rider, whoever he was. She did that and who was it but the priest's servant-boy. She told him her story: that it was the woman in that house over beyond that had directed her to the cemetery and she wasn't able to find her way out.

'Ah,' said the boy to her, 'she'll regret that! She'll be coming here herself tomorrow!'

I think she took sick and died that night, and I'm not sure whether the priest was with her or not.

130.   The Woman with the Miserable Heart

Once upon a time there was a very poor woman. She wasn't short of worldly goods, but she was miserable in her heart. She was very tight in her heart and she tried every way in God's earth to find ways to make a profit out of everything in this world.

But poor people were going around in large numbers and one year she had a room full of potatoes, a fine room, full to the brim. What did she do, when a travelling man came, only give him his alms and put the same amount of potatoes to one side, so that she'd know how much alms she'd given over the year and how many potatoes she'd given out. As she was putting the potatoes to one side, after giving the alms, they looked fine and healthy. But at the latter end of the year the room was empty and one of those days the man of the house said to her:

'I suppose, my little woman,' said he, 'that it won't be long till we've finished all the potatoes?'

'It won't,' said she, 'and they'd have done us a very long time between what we've divided and what we've given away. Come down,' said she, 'to the room till you see the heap of potatoes I have here; and I've given the same amount to the poor people all year, and they'd have lasted us a long time.'

He went down with her and when they went into the room there was a fine heap of potatoes in the corner of the room with a cover over them and they were sprouting and coming on fine, and he saw that they were fine and yellow and shooting.

'There's a fine heap of them there,' said the man of the house.

'There is indeed,' said she, 'and I've given the same amount away. And look how far into the year we'd have potatoes,' said she, 'only for myself!'

He went over to the heap and put his big paw into it to stir them and see if the potatoes inside were sprouting as well as the ones on top. But when he moved the top ones there wasn't a bit of a potato underneath but earwigs and beetles and worms and clay!

'Now look, my good woman,' said he, 'what you have after your time! What you gave away won't do you any good, because you had your heart stuck in it, and you've nothing for yourself either. You have it neither one way nor the other. You have it neither here nor there.'

131.　Swearing and Charity

There was a poor monk long ago going about begging for alms. He went into a house one night and asked for lodging and got it. But he wasn't long there when he heard the man of the house swearing and the monk said that he couldn't stay in the one house with him. He went off down to the priest and told him that he was lodging in that house over there and couldn't stay there listening to the man of the house cursing. The priest sent for the man and asked him why he was swearing. The man said he was always at it and just couldn't stop.

'Well,' said the priest, 'I don't know what to say to ye! But let the two of you go up that hill over there and come back to me in the morning and tell me how you spent the night.'

The monk went off up the hill and there couldn't have been a worse night, with storms and rain and thunder. When the man was up on the hill, he looked all around him. As he was looking around he thought he saw a light. He went toward it, in order to light his pipe there. He saw a house there. He went into it. He saw nobody inside except two children lying on a bed. As soon as he went inside, one of them moved one way and the other moved the other way and they beckoned to him to get into the bed between them. He got in and never in his whole life did he sleep as comfortably as he did that night.

The monk was walking up and down on top of the hill and he couldn't find a thing to give him shelter but a stick that was stuck in the ground with an old hat on top of it. When the night was over they both came down. They went to the priest.

'Well,' said he to the monk, 'how did you spend the night?'

'Very troubled indeed,' said the monk, 'without any shelter or any protection in the world, except for a stick stuck in the ground with an old hat on top of it!'

'How did you spend the night?' said he to the man who was swearing.

'I was hardly at the top of the hill,' said he, 'when I looked all round me. I thought I saw a light and went towards it, to see could I get a light for my pipe. When I got as far as it, I found a bed there with nobody in it but two children asleep on the bed. When I went in, one moved this way and the other moved that way and they beckoned me to come in between them. I got in and I never slept a night in my own bed as comfortably as I slept last night!'

'Well,' said the priest, 'did you ever give any charity?'

'I never let a poor person from my door without giving him something, and I never refused anybody a night's lodging.'

'Did anybody belonging to you ever die?' said the priest.

'I lost two children of my own when they were very young,' said the man.

'Well, those were the children that were in that bed! God put them there to give you shelter that night to repay you for your kindness to the poor. Go on home! Spend the rest of your life as you are. There's no harm in your swearing!'

'Well,' said the priest to the monk, 'did you ever give alms?'

'I did,' said he. 'I gave my hat to a poor man, one day, who had no hat.'

'That's the hat that was on top of the hill giving you shelter, and I'm afraid that, unless you do a bit better for the rest of your life, I don't know what will become of you!'

132.   The Cow from the Sea

There was a man and a woman long ago and they had six children. They were very poor and they hadn't a thing that anyone could see. The mother was praying to God and the Virgin Mary to get milk for her. She had nothing to give the infant but oatmeal water. The neighbours weren't good to her and wouldn't give her a drop of milk to rear the child and he was crying from morning to night. The man used say to his wife, every evening:

'I don't know how we're going to rear the children when we've no chance of getting a drop of milk.'

'Let you be quiet!' she'd say. 'Maybe God will send us milk yet!'

'Maybe God and the Virgin Mary will send us milk to rear the child,' he said, 'and all our children.'

He looked out one morning and looked down towards the sea. He saw a cow. He came in and told her that there was a cow down on the grass.

'Well, go out,' said she, 'and see does it belong to the neighbours, and if it does belong to the neighbours, tell them about it.'

He went out so when she asked him and went down to the neighbours. The neighbour said it wasn't his at all. He came back again and told her that it wasn't theirs.

'My good man,' said she, 'go down and see what sort of shape the cow is in.'

He went down and then came back again and told her that the cow was down on the grass with a fine udder of milk on her.

'Well, go back down and bring up the cow,' she said. 'A thousand thanks to God and the Virgin Mary!' said she. 'God has sent milk for us and for my baby and for all my children and I can keep praying to Him.'

He brought up the cow and she milked her. She got the full of a can of milk from her. Then he asked her, when she had milked the cow, to put her out again to see would she stay on the grass. She did that. And he was in and out watching her to see would she go off somewhere else. She grazed away and never stirred out of it. The woman told him to go down in the evening and bring her up again. He did, and he kept her in for the night. He put her out again the next morning and she grazed away and never stirred. She was brought in again at dinner-time and she milked her and he drove her out again and he kept an eye on her. He brought her back up again in the evening and kept her in for the night. He went on like that till the cow went back and was in calf.

'A thousand thanks to God,' said she, 'that my baby is getting milk!'

When she came back with her calf, they reared the calf. Then she went back again and she was hardly dry till she came back with another calf. They reared that calf too and watched her too in case she'd go away. When those two calves were reared she went back again, and came back with the third calf and they reared that till it was a fine yearling. One night the man said to his wife that there was too much on the grass now and maybe they'd be as well to sell two of the calves.

'Well,' said she, 'maybe you'd be better off leaving them alone.'

'The grass is not there to feed them,' said he, 'and we had better sell two of them.'

The cow heard that two of the calves were to be sold. So the cow went off along with her three calves back to the sea.

'Now look what you've done,' said the wife.

'I did a poor thing!' said he. 'I shouldn't have opened my mouth! If I had my chance again, I wouldn't say a word!'

'You're too late now,' said she, 'but I can keep on praying to God and the Virgin Mary; even if she's gone, I've my children reared!'

133.   Honey from Heaven

They say that, in the famine times, people who hadn't a bite to eat for breakfast used to go out in the morning with a cup and, in a very short time, collect the full of the cup of honey from the flowers. There was a lot more honey around in those days than there has been ever since, and it was easily collected provided you went out fairly early in the morning. The old people used go out every morning, and they considered that it was a gift from God, since they hadn't anything else to eat. It was as strong as the honey you'd get in a honeycomb today.

134.   The Poor Mower

There was a poor mower in Ireland long ago and he had a very large family and no means of rearing them except to take a large meadow and mow it. He'd get so much money for mowing the field. It was a Saturday night that he got one and he was so poor that he set out on Sunday morning to mow the field, without letting on to anyone, because the field was at the back of a hill.

As he was going along he met a fine gentleman.

'Where are you going today?' said the gentleman.

He told him that he was going to mow because he needed the money.

'Is not today Sunday?' said the stranger.

'I know it is but I've no choice.'

'How much would you earn today?'

'Six shillings,' said he.

'Well, today is Sunday, and here's six shillings for you and go back home!'

He took the six shillings and went. He was gone a bit when he thought:

'If I had this six shillings and today's earnings, I'd be comfortable!'

He turned back, and in the same place he met another man who asked him where he was going. He told him he was badly in need of the money.

'How much would you have earned for today's work?'

'Six shillings,' said he.

'Well, today is Sunday, and here's six shillings for you, and go back home!'

He went back and as he was nearing his house he began to think again:

'If I had today's pay and the twelve shillings I'd be a rich man! I'll go back again!'

He went back and in the same place he met a third man.

'Where are you going today?' said he.

'Mowing.'

'Isn't today Sunday?'

'I know it is but poverty leaves me no choice.'

'How much would you earn today?'

'Six shillings.'

'Well, here's six shillings for you, and don't let me catch you coming over the hill again! And I leave it as a legacy to all mowers that they're always poor!'

It was the same man that was there each of the three times. That's what left mowers poor ever since.

135.   The Hour Of Our Death

In olden days, the old people say, everybody knew the hour when he would die. It happened once that there was a man like that who knew that he was going to die next autumn. And when spring came and he was sowing his crops, what did he do, instead of building a fine solid ditch around the field, he built a makeshift fence of bracken and rushes. While he was building it, it happened that God, may He be ever praised and blessed, sent a messenger down to earth to see how His people were behaving themselves. He came up to this man and asked him what he was doing. He told him.

'And why,' said the angel to him, 'don't you build a proper ditch round your field instead of that make-shift thing?'

'I don't care,' said he. 'That'll do me till I reap the harvest. Let everyone else look after himself from then on! I'll have left this world.'

The angel went back and told his story and, from that day we, the whole human race, were deprived of the knowledge of when we were going to die.

Bibliography (1952)

Books referred to in the Notes:

Aarne, Antti and Stith Thompson, *The Types of the Folk-Tale. A Classification and Bibliography*, (FFC 74), (Helsinki, 1928).

Babrius, *Babrii Fabulae Aesopeae* (ed. O. Crusius) (Lipsiae, 1897).

Bladè, J. F., *Contes Populaires de la Gascogne* (Paris, 1886).

Bolte, Johannes and Georg Polívka, *Anmerkungen zu den Kinder- und Hausmärchen der Brüder Grimm*, I–IV, (BP), (Berlin, 1913–1932).

Carmichael, Alexander: *Carmina Gadelica,* I–IV, (Edinburgh, 1928–1941).

Chauvin, Victor, *Bibliographie des ouvrages arabes*, I–XII, (Liège, 1892–1922).

Child, F.J.: *The English and Scottish Popular Ballads*, I–V, (Boston & New York, 1882–4).

Dähnhardt (Oskar): *Natursagen*, I–IV, (Leipzig & Berlin, 1907–1912).

Ryan, John (ed.), *Féilscríbhinn Eoin Mhic Néill*, (Baile Átha Cliath, 1940).

Folk-Lore. A quarterly review of myth, tradition, institution and custom, I–LXII, (London, 1890–1951).

Folklore Fellows Communications (FFC), (Helsinki, 1907–).

Handwörterbuch des deutschen Märchens (Hdwb. d. Märch.), (Berlin & Leipzig, 1930–1938).

Herbert, J. A., *Catalogue of Romances in the Department of Manuscripts in the British Museum*, III, (London, 1910).

Journal of the American Oriental Society (JAOS), (Boston, 1849–).

Journal of the Royal Society of the Antiquaries of Ireland (JRSAI), I–LXXXI (Dublin, 1853–1951).

Kittredge, G.L., *Witchcraft in Old and New England*, (Cambridge, Mass., 1929).

Köhler, Reinhold, *Kleinere Schriften zur Märchenforschung*, I–III (ed. Johannes Bolte), (Weimar, Berlin, 1898–1900).

Pauli, Johannes, *Schimpf und Ernst*, I–II (ed. Johannes Bolte), (Berlin, 1924).

Publications of the Modern Language Association of America (PMLA).

Saintyves, P., *Essais de folklore biblique*, (Paris, 1922).

Thompson, Stith, *Motif-Index of Folk-Literature*, I–VI, (FFC 106–9, 116–7], (Helsinki, 1932–1936).

Ward, H. L. D., [See above, Herbert, I–II].

Wells (J. E.): *A Manual of Writings in Middle English*, (New Haven, 1916).

Notes

Versions of some of the stories in this book, as well as references to other versions, may be found in *Béaloideas* (the journal of the Folklore of Ireland Society), I–XLX, and in *Leabhar Sheáin Í Chonaill*, which Séamus Ó Duilearga edited for the Society. Further information about the international stories and the motifs of the stories here may be found in the two books referred to at the beginning of the Bibliography.

The references are laid out in the following order: name of the collector of the story; name, age and address of the storyteller; the date on which the story was written down; number of the volume and page(s) in which the original is to be found in the archives of the National Folklore Collection.

All proper names are given in Irish, except for the names of counties. The address usually consists of townland name, name of parish or district, and name of county. See http://www.logainm.ie/.

1(a).   Liam Mac Coisdeala: Dáithí Mac Gothraidh (60), Cill Mhiáin, Co. Mhaigh Eo [Co. Mayo]. 21/8/1936. NFC 238: 298–300.
        This story and the beginning of the next story are versions of a poetic carol from the Middle Ages.
            See Child, II, 1–6. Cherries, not apples, were the fruit most commonly mentioned in the carol. The lines of verse here are clearly not a translation but a re-telling in Irish of the original carol, because none of them are the same as the lines recorded by Child. The lines recorded here in Irish are only a small portion of the full carol.

1(b).   Liam Mac Coisdeala: Sally, Bean Uí Choscair (70), Cill Mhiáin, Co. Mhaigh Eo [Co. Mayo]. 10/10/1936. NFC 257: 164–167.
        The second part of this story seems to have no connection with the first part; it is usually told on its own. There are other examples in this book also of cases where a household didn't recognise that visitors were holy people until they had left, having performed miracles.

2.   Áine Ní Ruáin: her mother, Dúntas, Cill Lasrach, Béal Átha na Muice, Co. Mhaigh Eo [Co. Mayo]. December 1935. NFC 117: 182–185.

       This is a very common story. It is often the case that the lazy cowherd refuses the request of Mary the Mother of God, and arising from that is the proverb: 'The cowherds bear the tiredness of the smiths'.

3.   Brian Mac Lochlainn: Bean Uí Allúráin (86), Cluain Idir Dhá Abhainn, Baile na Cille, Co. Galway [Co. Galway]. 7/5/1936. NFC 236: 202–203.

       This little story compares the great love a mother bears for her son with his love for her, and sets out the reasons.

4.   Aodh Ó Dónaill: Sorcha, Bean Mhic Ghrianna (62), Rann na Feirste, Co. Dhún na nGall [Co. Donegal]. 30/7/1937. NFC 391: 507–509.

       This is a common theme in folklore – comparing a surly individual with one who is kind and generous – and frequently has the same message. 'The thing one fears more than death is often for one's good.'

5(a). Liam Mac Coisdeala: Séamus Breathnach (83), Cúil Leic na Liath, Eadargúil, Co. na Gaillimhe [Co. Galway]. 24/9/1936. NFC 257: 27–28.

       Our Lady, Our Mother, and St. Brigid are often portrayed as being contemporaries in these stories. It is the same with Our Saviour and St. Patrick. This story and the next are attempts to explain why crosses are made for the feast of St. Brigid.

5(b). Seán Ó hEochaidh: Seán Mag Fhionnaile (90), Málainn, Gleann Cholm Cille, Co. Dhún na nGall [Co. Donegal. 4/1/1936. NFC 142: 1758b-1759.

6(a). Liam Mac Coisdeala: Dáithí Mac Gothraidh (60), Cill Mhiáin, Co. Mhaigh Eo [Co. Mayo]. 14/8/1936. NFC 238: 196–198.

       Certain deeds and words are often proscribed and among them are commenting on the affliction of a handicapped person or drawing attention to something that has nothing to do with you. This story and the following one are examples of that. As for the phrase 'eating the cold flesh' consider the origin of the term 'back-biting' in English and its meaning.

6(b). Seán Ó Súilleabháin: Mícheál Ó hÚrdail (82), Ros Mhic Eoghain, Béarra, Co. Chorcaí [Co. Cork]. 4/8/1933. NFC 31: 158–162.

       The part of this story about the man who fed the pair of old misfortunates with mutton to keep them alive is more usually told as part of a much longer story, that about a penance put on someone to find three people holier than himself; one of these three was the thief who was stealing sheep in order to keep his aged parents alive. Seán Bráthair Mhá gCrochúir, or some such name, was the name usually given to that story.

7. Liam Mac Coisdeala: Sally, Bean Uí Choscair (70), Cill Mhiáin, Co. Mhaigh Eo [Co. Mayo]. 10/10/1936. NFC 257: 162–163. See note 1(b).

8. Seán Ó hEochaidh: Pádraic Mag Fhionnaile (80), Mín an Chearrbhaigh, Gleann Cholm Cille, Co. Dhún na nGall [Co. Donegal]. 19/2/1936. NFC 143: 2306–2308.
This is a common theme in these stories – explaining the origins of certain characteristics in people. The women don't escape either, because the folklore of other countries contains stories explaining why they are so talkative, so restless and so deceitful (that is, if they are any worse than men in this respect!)

9. Seán Ó hEochaidh: Séamus Ó hIghne (61), Mín an Churraoin, Ard an Rátha, Co. Dhún na nGall [Co. Donegal]. 18/8/1936. NFC 233: 4066–4067.
This is an attempt to combine a story from the New Testament with a story explaining characteristic marks on certain fish. There are many stories in the folklore of other countries also, explaining the origins of certain habits or characteristics of various animals, birds, fish and insects, some of them refering to St. Peter, and many having no connection at all with the Bible.
The man who cast doubt on the powers of Our Saviour and who died shortly afterwards is typical of those stories where someone breaks a rule or prohibition and pays dearly for it.

10. Liam Mac Coisdeala: Seán de Búrc (80), Áth an Chloigín, Eanach Dhúin, Co. na Gaillimhe [Co. Galway]. 26/5/1936. NFC 182: 555–556.
This story is found in other countries in Europe as well as in Ireland. In the usual version in this country, there are three Jews and one of them hides under a barrel or under a box when they see Our Saviour coming towards them along the road. His companions ask the Saviour what's under the barrel. 'There's a man in there,' he says. 'No, it's a pig,' the other two say. 'If it's a man, let him be a pig, and if it's a pig let him be a man!' says the Saviour. That's how the Jew who was under the barrel became a pig.

11. Tadhg Ó Murchú: Pádraig Mac Gearailt (77), Cill an Ghoirtín, Dromad, Co. Chiarraí [Co. Kerry]. 1/3/1936. NFC 308: 13–16.

This story is based on one of Aesop's fables (see Babrius, No. 117).

12.   Séamus Ó Dúgáin: Donncha Ó Fearaigh (72), Caoldroim, Gort an Choirce, Co. Dhún na nGall [Co. Donegal]. December 1936. NFC 280: 350–353.
'Four cobblers who aren't liars,
Four Frenchmen who aren't sallow,
Four priests who aren't avaricious,
That's twelve people you won't find in the land'.

That is strong talk, but I'm not concerned with it on this occasion except for the third line. The clergy were often accused of avarice, whether they deserved it or not, and evidence for that is the fact that this story is very common in this country. The reason that the clergy in general got such a bad name was that they had no fixed income and had to depend on the generosity of their congregations. I'm not aware of such a story about the avarice of the clergy in the folklore of any other country, although other faults of the clergy were commonly the subject of stories in other countries.

There was never any regard for the miser who hoarded money and would never spend it. However bad the person was who drank whatever he got, he was better in the eyes of the public, as these stories show.

The dough which grew into a tree when it was put into the heart of the fire is often told about Saint Martin in Irish folklore. It is clear that in peoples' minds this saint was particularly associated with the shooting and the growth of plants and the fertility of the land.

12(b).   Aodh Ó Dónaill: Sorcha, Bean Mhic Ghrianna (62), Rann na Feirste, Co. Dhún na nGall [Donegal]. 30/7/1937. NFC 391: 511–513. See the previous note.

12(c).   Liam Mac Coisdeala: Peadar Ó Ceannabháin (65), Aill na Brón, Maíros, Co. na Gaillimhe [Co. Galway]. 9/10/1935. NFC 155: 148–150. See note 12(a).

13.   Brian Mac Lochlainn: Máirtín Seoighe (51), Doire Bhéal an Mháma, Maíros, Co. na Gaillimhe [Co. Galway]. 18/7/1936. NFC 236: 473–475.
There is a version of this story in Pauli's collection (657) edited by Johannes Bolte. In other versions of this story in Ireland, the Saviour takes the poor man with him to a valley where there is gold on every blade of grass growing there.

14.   Aodh Ó Dónaill: Sorcha, Bean Mhic Ghrianna (62), Rann na Feirste, Co. Dhún na nGall [Co. Donegal]. 30/7/1937. NFC 391: 510.

See the notes under 12(a).

15. Séamus Mag Uidhir: his father, Dumha Thuama, Gaoth Sáile, Iorras, Co. Mhaigh Eo [Co. Mayo.] 26/3/1930. NFC 79: 619–620.

This story is very common in Ireland and in other countries in Europe. See Dähnhardt, II, 5; FFC, VIII, 22 (125); Child, V, 491.

16. Seán Ó Dubhda: Méin, Bean Uí Mhaoileoin (75), An Clochán Dubh, Corca Dhuibhne, Co. Chiarraí [Co. Kerry]. 1930. NFC 4: 67.

A common theme in the folklore of many peoples is the punishment (or the opposite) put on people, on animals, on birds, on insects, on plants and so on, as a result of their surliness (or kindness) to the Saviour, His Mother, Our Lady, or some other holy person.

17. ditto. See the previous note.

18. An Bráthair Columban Mac Craith: someone in Béal Átha an Ghaorthaidh, Co. Chorcaí [Co. Cork]. 1925. NFC 96: 50–54.

See note no. 15. As to the gift the poor woman received, see BP, II, 215, 438; Hdwb. D. März. ('Erste' nn. 112–149).

19. Seán Ó Dubhda: someone in Corca Dhuibhne, Co. Chiarraí [Co. Kerry]. 1933. NFC 3: 543.

20. Seán Ó hEochaidh: Séamus Mac Grianna (45), Leac Chonaill, Ard an Rátha, Co. Dhún na nGall [Co. Donegal]. 30/12/1936. NFC 270: 684–686.

21. Seán Ó hEochaidh: Séamus Ó Colla (65), An Luinnigh, Gaoth Dobhair, Co. Dhún na nGall [Co. Donegal]. 14/6/1938. NFC 539: 99–101.

Wells (155) has a somewhat similar story about lepers who were cured when they became incensed on hearing that the Saviour had been crucified.

22. Bríd Ní Shúilleabháin: Seán Ó Súilleabháin, An Baile Uachtarach, Baile an Fheirtéaraigh, Co. Chiarraí [Co. Kerry]. 20/7/1932. NFC 6: 497–501.

The girl in this story had her sins forgiven, but it is far more often the case that the people in such situations have all their wealth taken away, according to folklore.

23. Seosamh Ó Dálaigh: Máire, Bean Uí Dhuinnshléibhe (61), Baile Ícín, Dún Chaoin, Co. Chiarraí [Co. Kerry]. 14/9/1936. NFC 243: 452–463.
     See nos. 18, 19.

24. Máire Ní Ghácháin: Caitlín Seoighe, Inis Gé Thuaidh, Co. Mhaigh Eo [Inishkea North, Co. Mayo]. 1936. NFC 277: 86–92.
     No. 45 is another version of this story. It is not usually as butterflies, but as doves, that souls leave the body to go to Heaven in stories on this subject in Ireland. However, butterflies are mentioned in this context in stories from Germany, Brittany, Finland, Siberia, Japan, etc.

25. Seosamh Ó Dálaigh: Breandán Ó Líthe [Laoithe] (23), Baile Uí Chorráin, Muiríoch, Co. Chiarraí [Co. Kerry]. 22/3/1937. NFC 316: 536–553.
     This is an unusual version in Ireland of an international story. The reader of the following stories will find that a very common motif is the one where a key or ring is thrown in the sea and afterwards found in the stomach of a fish. See Chauvin, V, 17; Köhler-Bolte, II, 209; Saintyves, 402.

26. Liam Mac Coisdeala: Seán Mac Giollarnáth (55), Cora Phiairín, Muine Mheá [Co. Galway]. 22/10/1936. NFC 257: 423–433.

27(a). Proinsias de Búrca: Liam de Búrca (83), Seanadh Farracháin, An Ros, Co. na Gaillimhe [Co. Galway]. 13/9/1935. NFC 162: 276–284.
     This is a common theme in stories: the weakest or least suitable person in the family succeeds better in the world than anybody else. This is not confined to religious stories, of course. Examples of this are Cinderella, 'Mac Rí an Deachaoin', 'Leadaí na Luaithe' and many more. Storytellers, and indeed the general public, always were fond of the weakling.

27(b). Pádhraic Bairéad: Antoine Ó Catháin (66), Dubhoileán, An Chill Mhór, Co. Mhaigh Eo [Co. Mayo]. 21/1/1937. NFC 277: 273–279.
     See the previous note. Reference to examples of this (a king or someone similar being chosen by miraculous means) are made by Egerton, JAOS, XXX, 158; Chauvin, VI, 75 (239).

27(c). Pádhraic Bairéad: Seán Ó Maoilábhail [Maolfhabhail] (68), Dubhoileán, An Chill Mhór, Co. Mhaigh Eo [Co. Mayo]. 8/5/1936. NFC 191: 462–466.
     See note 27(a).

28.   Seán Ó Dubhda: Tomás de hÓra (82), Baile an tSléibhe, Fionntrá, Co. Chiarraí
        [Co. Kerry]. July 1931. NFC 4: 261.
        There is a reference in FFC XXIII, 142, to the benefits arising from the recovery of a
        Sacred Host that was lost.

29.   Liam Mac Coisdeala: Éamonn de Búrca (71), Aill na Brón, Maíros, Co. na
        Gaillimhe [Co. Galway]. 9/10/1935. NFC 155: 146–147.
        At present, it is not the parish priest but the bishop who has the power to deprive
        a curate of permission to say Mass, as was the case in this story. The general public
        always had a great affection for any priest to whom that happened, for any reason,
        and there's hardly a parish in Ireland that hasn't stories about them. The principal
        theme of those stories, usually, is the divine, miraculous power that those defrocked
        priests had which no other priest would ever have.

30.   Liam Mac Coisdeala: Pádhraic Mac an Iomaire (64), An Coillín, Carna, Co. na
        Gaillimhe [Co. Galway]. 14/11/1935. NFC 158: 108–113.
        In this story the spirit, Petticoat Loose, is masculine. Normally such spirits are
        feminine. In the case of spirits who are banished, they are generally sent to the Red
        Sea; they are normally placed in a confined space (between the foam and the water,
        say), so that they couldn't return. Usually when they are banished they disappear in
        a shower of sparks.
            It was a strong superstition that nobody ever went alone at night to fetch a
        midwife or a priest to anoint a person. He must always have a companion in case
        he'd meet a spirit on the road.

31.   Liam Mac Coisdeala: Pádhraic Ó Briain (70), Gleann an Mhíl, Mainistir Chnoc
        Muaidhe, Co. na Gaillimhe [Co. Galway]. 19/11/1936. NFC 257: 766–776.
        There are many stories about the questions that priests asked a female evil spirit,
        to find out what caused her damnation. Sometimes she admits at first that she
        killed a child; but the priest answers that it wasn't that that caused her to become a
        devil. Then she says that the child was unbaptised, but the priest gives her the same
        answer. The third time, she admits that she killed the child for payment; then the
        priest says that that is what damned her and banishes her outright. To come and
        go with the tide forever is a common penance in Purgatory or in Hell in these tales
        about spirits.

32.   Seán Ó hEochaidh: Anna Ní Shiadhail (72), Ceathrú na Madadh, Cluain Dá
        Chorcach, Co. Dhún na nGall [Co. Donegal]. 21/6/1939. NFC 626: 488–495.

It is no surprise, in a Catholic country like Ireland, that priests and ministers should be compared with one another and be in contention together in some of these stories, and that the priest usually wins. On the other hand, it should be said that in Lutheran countries in Northern Europe there was an element of mockery and scorn in stories told about both priests and ministers. That wasn't how it was in Ireland, except that the priest was shown as having more power than the minister.

33(a).   Liam Mac Coisdeala: Pádhraic Ó hArgadáin (50), Mása, Eanach Dhúin, Co. na Gaillimhe [Co. Galway]. 26/3/1936. NFC 181: 278–297.
Different names are given to the priest or brother who has a special room reserved for him in hell, depending on where the story is told. Father Seán Ó Daibhín, is the name most commonly used in Connaught; Brian Bráthair, or Father Seán Ó Briain, or Seán Bráthair Mhá gConchúir and such like are the ones used in Munster and Donegal.

33(b)   Anna Ní Éigeartaigh: Mícheál Ó hEochaidh (68), Na Curra, Cill Chárthaigh, Co. Dhún na nGall [Co. Donegal]. 21/3/1936. NFC 224: 110–122.
As to the promise to the devil written in blood, see FFC LXIX, 64.
    Conversations between a devout person and a holy picture or statue are part of No. 105 also. See the note on that.

34.   Liam Mac Coisdeala: Pádhraic Conraoi (68), An Baile Nua, Mainistir Chnoc Muaidhe, Co. na Gaillimhe [Co. Galway]. 2/11/1936. NFC 257: 620–623.
A common theme in stories such as this is the manner in which the devil is beaten and the soul in his possession is released. I don't know of any other version of this story in Irish folklore.
    As for possession of something you bought yourself, there is another reference at the end of No. 53.

35(a).   Seosamh Ó Dálaigh: Mícheál Ó Guithín (69), Baile an Bhiocáire, Dún Chaoin, Co. Chiarraí [Co. Kerry]. 27/10/1936. NFC 256: 49–61.
Professor Séamus Ó Duilearga has made a study of this story in *Féilscríbhinn Eoin Mhic Néill* (pp 522–534) where he has compared the versions in folklore and the tale *Echtra Nerai* in the old literature.
See the reference to this story in the Foreword.

35(b).   Liam Mac Coisdeala: Seán Mac Giollarnáth (55), Cora Phiairín, Muine Mheá, Co. na Gaillimhe [Co. Galway]. NFC 257: 434–441. See the previous note.

36.   Seán Ó Dubhda: someone in Corca Dhuibhne [Co. Kerry]. 1930. NFC 4: 44–48.

37.   Liam Mac Coisdeala: Pádhraic Mac an Iomaire, 64, An Coillín, Carna, Co. na
        Gaillimhe [Co. Galway]. 8/11/1935. NFC 158: 12–18.
        There are many references to poor scholars in the old stories. It is thought that
        they were men with a certain amount of learning as a result of time spent studying
        for the priesthood. They didn't succeed in becoming priests and they made a
        living afterwards going from house to house teaching the children of farmers
        or gentlemen. It is clear from these stories about them that the ordinary people
        credited them with extraordinary powers (reading the future in the stars etc.) and
        they often surpassed the priest in that respect.
            This story about a man whom Fate had destined to kill when he reached a
        certain age is similar in ways to the international story (ATU 934) about a man who
        was to be killed by a bolt of lightning when he reached twenty one. See No. 107,
        and the accompanying note.

38.   Seosamh Ó Dálaigh: Dónall Ó Súilleabháin (60), Baile Ícín, Dún Chaoin, Co.
        Chiarraí [Co. Kerry]. 14/9/1936. NFC 243: 491–512.
        There is some similarity between this story and the international story (ATU 930).
        See FFC LXIX, 51, 60, 230.

39.   Aodh Ó Dónaill: Seán Mac Grianna (32), Rann na Feirste, Teampall Cróine, Co.
        Dhún na nGall [Co. Donegal]. 12/7/1936. NFC 261: 51–54.

40.   Seán Ó hEochaidh: Conall Mac Cormaic (75), Doire Leac Chonaill, Leitir Mhic an
        Bháird, Co. Dhún na nGall [Co. Donegal]. 28/1/1938. NFC 472: 53–60.
        The devil adopted many disguises to deceive people. He used to appear as a dog, a
        goat, a cat etc. See Kittredge, 37–44, 178.

41.   Seosamh Ó Dálaigh: Seán Ó Grífín (58), Cathair Boilg, Fionntrá, Co. Chiarraí
        [Co. Kerry]. 28/9/1936. NFC 244: 254–257.
        It is clear from this, and other stories, that the laity thought that lay-baptism was
        not as effective as baptism performed by a priest. There is also frequent reference to
        the fact that children who died unbaptised travelled about as ghosts after death.

42.   Seán Ó Dubhda: Pádraig Ó Loingsigh (87), Baile an tSléibhe, Fionntrá, Co.
        Chiarraí [Co. Kerry]. 1934. NFC 5: 174–175.

43. Seán Ó Dubhda: Johnny Dhónaill Uí Shé (86), An Baile Loiscthe, Cill Maoilchéadair, Corca Dhuibhne, Co. Chiarraí [Co. Kerry]. 25/12/1930. NFC 4: 42–43.
    This story is a sort of parable to make the point that the devil might take a person at his word.
    See BP, II, 329–, and No. 55 in this book.

44. Liam Mac Coisdeala: Pádhraic Ó Briain (70), Gleann an Mhíl, Mainistir Chnoc Muaidhe, Co. na Gaillimhe [Co. Galway]. 9/11/1936. NFC 257: 671–678.
    This story and the five following it are examples of penances imposed on people to make atonement for sins committed by them. In some of the international versions of this story the person commits another sin which proves of benefit to his soul and all his sins are forgiven.
    See FFC LIV. As to the pins which were thrown in the sea and found afterwards in the belly of a fish, see the note for No. 25.

45. Liam Mac Coisdeala: Seán Ó Nia (28), Aill na Brón, Maíros, Co. na Gaillimhe [Co. Galway]. Easter 1941. NFC 794: 63–70.
    See No. 24.

46. Seosamh Ó Dálaigh: Micheál Ó Cinnéide (66), Baile Uí Chorráin, An Mhuiríoch, Co. Chiarraí [Co. Kerry]. 15/2/1937. NFC 315: 194–226
    See BP III, 167; Köhler-Bolte, I, 473; Ward, II, 664; Herbert, do. III, 343; Pauli-Bolte, 437.
    There is another similar story in Irish folklore – about a man on whom a penance was imposed for a sin he had committed, that he must kiss the first thing he met on his way home; it turned out to be an earwig and it stuck to the man's mouth when he kissed it; the man died shortly afterwards.
    I think it is worth relating a similar story from the folklore of France (Bladé II 201–209). A young man committed sin with a girl and wouldn't marry her afterwards; she died later; the man had to go to Rome to confess to the Pope; every bell in Rome rang of its own accord when the man and his companion entered the city; the sinner made his confession and the Pope sent for his companion; the Pope told him that they would meet an animal on their way home, and he would jump up on the back of the sinner; that happened; that night, when the sinner had gone to his bedroom on his own, with the animal on his back, a lot of noise and knocking were heard for a period of three hours; when the door of the room was opened next morning there wasn't a trace of the sinner or the animal inside.

47. Seán Ó hEochaidh: Niall Mac Giolla Bhríde (79), Más an Easa, Cluain Dá Chorcach, Co. Dhún na nGall [Co. Donegal]. 22/5/1939. NFC 626: 191–197.

    Cluain Beag and Cluain Dá Chorcach are both in the barony of Cill Mhic Neanáin in Donegal, Cluain Mánach is in the barony of Inis Eoghain Thoir in the same county.

    It wasn't at all uncommon to have rows and dissension between the relations of a married couple about where the woman would be buried if she died fairly soon after getting married, either in childbirth or from some other cause. Her people would want her to be buried with her own people in their local cemetery and the husband might not agree to that.

    It is a common motif in the lives of saints that a sinner is forgiven when a bird hatches her eggs in his hand.

48. Seán Ó Dubhda: Pádraig Mhuiris Uí Ghrífín (76), Baile Reo, Cill Chuáin, Co. Chiarraí [Co. Kerry]. 1932. NFC 3: 304–309.

    This story is printed in *Béaloideas* XVIII, 77–79.

    It is quite common in stories like this that the Pope himself is unable to grant forgiveness for certain sins. He sends the sinner to find a newly ordained priest, or maybe a saint, as is the case in this story. I don't know of any other story where the saint is said to live at the South Pole; a desert or a secluded glen is the more usual place in stories like this.

    As for the penance of making a long journey on one's knees, see FFC LXIX, 127.

49. Dr. Robin Flower: Seán Ó Súilleabháin (76), An Blascaod Mór, Dún Chaoin, Co. Chiarraí [Co. Kerry]. NFC 984: 395–398.

    In other versions of this story it is more usual for the moss (or green bough) to grow first on the stick of the thief while his companion's stick stays bare; then the thief says that he will donate half the blessings he has earned in Heaven to the saint accompanying him, and when God hears that he gives them both a place in Heaven at once.

50. Seán Ó Dubhda: Seán Ó Criomhthain (55), Cill Maoilchéadair, Co. Chiarraí [Co. Kerry]. 1/1/1930. NFC 2: 122–139.

    See FFC XXIII, 17, 115–194; BP, I, 276.

    As for hounds hunting people in Hell or Purgatory, see No. 51 and No. 56 (and the accompanying notes).

51.   Liam Mac Coisdeala: Seán Ó Clochartaigh (40), An Aird Mhóir, Carna, Co. na Gaillimhe [Co. Galway]. January 1936. NFC 159: 266–273.

There is frequent reference in these stories to rivers and waterfalls in the other world. See PMLA XXIII, 621–623.

52.   Liam Mac Meanman: Séamus Ó Ceallaigh (60), Cró na Doinne, Cill Taobhóg, Co. Dhún na nGall [Co. Donegal]. 4/5/1936. NFC 186: 134–147.

See the previous note.

53.   Seosamh Ó Dálaigh: Tadhg Ó Guithín (42), Baile na hAbha, Dún Chaoin, Co. Chiarraí [Co. Kerry]. 13/8/1936. NFC 242: 75–96.

There is a study by Jan-Öjvind Swahn of Lund University, Sweden, of an international story (ATU 425b) to which this story is related, and he has used material from Ireland in his research.

    In some of the versions of this story in the National Folklore Collection, the woman who is carrying the souls away from Hell meets the King of Sunday, the King of Monday, the King of Tuesday etc. Each of them asks her for the souls but she will only give them to the King of Sunday (or the King of Friday) because that is the only day that the souls are not wailing and complaining in Hell.

54.   Colm Mac Gill Eathain: Maitiú Mór Ó Tuathail (88), Na Creagáin, An Cnoc, Co. na Gaillimhe [Co. Galway]. 5/1/1945. NFC 969: 356–362.

The beginning of this story is not the same as that in other versions. A person might well say that it would be very remiss of the father and mother of the young girl to let her go off with a stranger that they barely knew. Another version of the story from Conamara gives a better picture of what happened. In that version the father announced that he would give his daughter in marriage to whoever did the following work, all in the one day: to plough and sow an acre of ground, to have the crop sprout and ripen on that same day, to reap and thresh the corn and sell the grain and place the result of the sale in the father's hand – all on the same day! It wouldn't be a bad man that could do that! Whoever tried and failed would lose his head. A couple of people tried and failed and lost their heads and that discouraged the young men of the place from trying to win the girl for themselves.

    Time went by and one Sunday a fine well-dressed man came to the house and said that he'd undertake the work the following day - he didn't like Sunday, he said. He had hardly gone when a whiskered, bedraggled man, riding on an old nag, came to the house; when he heard about the man who was to do the work the next day, he said that, maybe, the man mightn't come back at all, and that he'd start on the work that same Sunday. He was as good as his word. And by the evening he put the value of the grain into the girl's father's hand! They gave him the daughter then and he went off.

After a year, the brother took to the road and in the end he found the house where his sister was living with the strange horseman. She said she was happy with her life, with nothing to do but to wash blood out of towels that the horseman brought back every evening and have them clean for the next day. Next day, the horseman set him to minding the cows and told him to follow them wherever they went. Away went the cows through the fields until they came to the edge of the sea, and they threw themselves into it (with the young man after them) and they swam away until they came to an island in the middle of the ocean; he followed them ashore; they went through a wall of fire that stretched from one side of the middle of the island to the other, and they were burnt to their bones (the same thing happened to the young man); there was a well on the far side of the wall and they were all healed when they tasted the water.

The young man followed the cows then, and saw things that amazed him: thin cows in a field where they were up to their eyes in grass, and not a sign of nourishment on them; fat cows in another field and the ground as bare as the floor in it; a man tied to a gate and his face disfigured by sores and blood (this man asked the young man to release him, and he did); then he heard a bell ringing, like you'd hear a bell before Mass; the cattle lay down on the ground and the young man followed people into a chapel that was by the side of the road. The priest began to say Mass and blood began to ooze out of every part of his body during the Mass so that the altar-boy had to wipe away the blood with towels until Mass was over. The congregation went out on to the road then and the young man lost sight of the chapel and the people as if the ground had opened and swallowed them. The cattle began to move on and he followed them to an orchard; each one ate a bite of an apple and he did the same. Then the cattle took to the sea again and swam home, and so did he.

The horseman explained all the wonders to him that evening: the sea was Death; the island was the other world; the fire was Purgatory; the well was the Well of Graces; the thin cows in the grassy field were people who were suffering in the other world because they were never satisfied with the wealth they had in this life – they were now on short rations, without the means to taste the good food around them; it was the exact opposite story with the fat cattle in the bare field; a man in Purgatory was the man tied to the gate – he needed the help of a living person to cut short his time of suffering; the Saviour was the priest who was shedding his blood on the altar during Mass, just as he had shed it on the Cross; St. Joseph was the horseman, and it was he who was serving the Mass and wiping the blood from the Saviour; and the apples were the food of Heaven.

'Take your sister home to your father now,' said the horseman. 'I brought her here, by the grace of God, to save her from the devil – he was the well-dressed man who was to have done the work on the Monday; he'd have had your sister, body and soul, if the God of Glory hadn't sent me to rescue her. Take her away home with you now. You will receive food for three from Heaven, for yourself, for your sister and for your father, and when you have eaten it you will all die and will all go to Heaven together.'

And that's what happened.

55.   Seosamh Ó Dálaigh: Tadhg Ó Guithín (42), Baile na hAbha, Dún Chaoin, Co. Chiarraí [Co. Kerry]. 13/8/1936. NFC 242: 106–116.
      Some of this story is a bit like Aa. Th. 801. There are many instances of unusual penances imposed on people in the next world in different versions of this story. See BP III, 297–303.

      In the folklore of other countries also it is unusual for the devil to take a wrong doer with him, body and soul. See No. 43 and accompanying note.

56.   Seosamh Ó Dálaigh: Seán Ó Críomhthain (75), Com Dhíneól, Dún Chaoin, Co. Chiarraí [Co. Kerry]. June 1936. NFC 241: 165–171.
      There are similarities between this story and a feature called Odinsjaeger that is common in Scandinavian stories. See the references in Thompson (Motif-Index, E501).

57.   Seosamh Ó Dálaigh: Pádraig Sayers (59), Baile an Bhiocáire, Dún Chaoin, Co. Chiarraí [Co. Kerry]. 2/2/1937. NFC 304: 502–516.
      Clearly, this story was not composed by a priest or a schoolmaster!

      A generous heart and charitable nature were very laudable, as far as folklore goes. There is no shortage of stories about people who were rewarded by entry into Heaven for having given a small charity to some poor person, even though they had committed many sins against God.

      There is mention in many religious stories of a bed being ready in Heaven for the soul of a person who had earned it; there is also mention of more than one bed being earned for themselves by people who had done good deeds. On the other hand, there is also reference to beds of fire awaiting the souls in Hell.

58. Seán Ó hEochaidh: Seán Ó Curraoin (65), Machaire Gáthlán, Gaoth Dobhair, Co. Dhún na nGall [Co. Donegal]. 21/2/1938. NFC 472: 205–212.
See FFC XXIII,130.

59. Colm Mac Gill Eathain: Maitiú Mór Ó Tuathail (88), Na Creagáin, An Cnoc, Co. na Gaillimhe [Co. Galway]. 11/1/1945. NFC 969: 384–386.
In other stories about the transgression of Lucifer in Heaven, it is related that he sat on the Chair of Glory reserved for God Himself, thinking that he would be as powerful as the Creator as a result.

A common theme in the folklore of many countries is what happens as a result of the rebellion of the bad angels in Heaven. This is often given as the origin of the movements of the moon and the tides and for the existence of the fairies. These are all apocryphal stories.

60. Seán Ó Dubhda: someone in Corca Dhuibhne, Co. Chiarraí [Co. Kerry]. 1930. NFC 4: 119.

61. Proinsias de Búrca: Liam Ó Duithche [Dufaigh] (46), Baile an Tobair, An Ros, Co. na Gaillimhe [Co. Galway]. 20/2/1936. NFC 167: 357–361.
With regard to the classes of people who will never see Heaven, two other sorts are often mentioned also: people who give short measures (those who do not give the right measure or weight to those who buy things from them), and women who kill unbaptised children for payment.

In some stories, it is not when the missal is being moved from one side of the altar to the other that the man puts the question to the priest, but when the priest is consecrating the Host or the Chalice.

Very often, in this story too, it is mentioned that the fallen angels (the fairy-folk) will be admitted to Heaven if they have enough blood in their veins to write their names with it. It seems that they don't have even that much. This is an example of their similarity to the dead.

62. Áine Nic an Leagha: Cáit, Bean Uí Ghallchóir (90), An Ráith Íochtarach, Cloich Chionnaola, Co. Dhún na nGall [Co. Donegal]. 27/7/1937. NFC 409: 47–50.
See note 61.

63. Áine Ní Chonaill: Séamus Miller (50), Tuar Mhic Éadaigh, Co. Mhaigh Eo [Co. Mayo]. July 1931. NFC 76: 321–326.

A common subject in the folklore and old literature of many countries is an account of a visit that someone made to the other world and the sights he saw there.

64.   Liam Mac Coisdeala: Pádhraic Mac an Iomaire (64), An Coillín, Carna, Co. na Gaillimhe [Co. Galway]. 24/2/1936. NFC 160: 180–181.
      See the essay on 'The Burial of Children' by Seán Ó Súilleabháin, (JRSAI LXIX, 3.) See also note 41.

65.   ditto. 15/11/1935. NFC 158: 129–134.
      This is a very common story in both folklore and literature. See also Pauli-Bolte, 465.

66.   Proinsias de Búrca: Liam de Búrca (83), Seanadh Farracháin, An Ros, Co. na Gaillimhe [Co. Galway]. 23/9/1935. NFC 163: 104–108.
      To revive an animal by re-assembling its bones is a common theme in stories in many countries in Europe and further afield. See Thompson (Motif-Index, E32).

67.   Labhrás Ó Cadhla: Siobhán, Bean Uí Chadhla (70), Scairt, Cill Ghobnait, Co. Phort Láirge [Co. Waterford]. 1901. NFC 289: 50–52.
      This story seems to be an exemplum.

68.   ditto. 1918. NFC 289: 112–114.
      See No. 2.

69.   Áine Ní Chróinín: Diarmuid Mac Coitir, Doire na Sagart, Baile Bhuirne, Co. Chorcaí [Co. Cork]. 17/8/1932. NFC 42: 352–354.
      See Nos. 2 and 68.

70.   Liam Mac Coisdeala: Pádhraic Ó hUiginn (76), Cill Mhiáin, Co. Mhaigh Eo [Co. Mayo]. 14/8/1936. NFC 238: 186–187.
      A common theme in folktales is an abundance of food being given to a poor household after a visit from a saintly person. See No. 23.

71.   Liam Mac Coisdeala: Seán de Búrca (80), Áth an Chloigín, Eanach Dhúin, Co. na Gaillimhe [Co. Galway]. 6/5/1936. NFC 182: 307–309.

In these stories 'Scotsman' [*Albanach*] i.e. 'Protestant' is often used for 'Pagan'. This story tries to set out the reason for the wearing of the green on St. Patrick's day, like the story about St. Patrick and the shamrock.

72. Liam Mac Coisdeala: Mícheál Ó Coincheanainn (50), Rinn na hAirne, Eanach Dhúin, Co. na Gaillimhe [Co. Galway]. 31/3/1936. NFC 181: 348–352.
    A similar story is often told about Donncha Mór Ó Dálaigh. See No. 110.

73. Seán Ó Flannagáin: Séamus Ó Riagáin (83), Tóin Raithní, An Bheitheach, Co. na Gaillimhe [Co. Galway]. May 1937. NFC 354: 294–296.
    There are many instances in folklore of saints putting a curse on people, or things, or places, for one reason or another. See Nos. 77, 83, 84, 88. The purpose of those stories is to give an explanation of particular traits of the people, things, or places involved.

74. Peadar Ó Coincheanainn: Mícheál Mac Donncha (67), Roisín na Mainiach, Carna, Co. na Gaillimhe [Co. Galway]. Spring, 1931. NFC 59: 177–186.
    'The Night of May Day' is often mentioned in this story instead of 'The Friday of May Day'. Part of this story relates to items in early Irish literature. See Folk-Lore, XLIII, 376–409.
    To have a person buried alive seven feet under the ground, at his own wish, is a theme that often occurs in stories about King David and his son, Solomon.

75. Seán Ó Dubhda: Pádraig Ó Conchúir (14), Cill Chúile, Cill Maoilchéadair, Co. Chiarraí [Co. Kerry]. 1931. NFC 2: 40–41.
    This story would seem to be a parable, to warn people to avoid the sin of false measure.

76. Áine Ní Chróinín: Diarmuid Mac Coitir, Doire na Sagart, Baile Bhuirne, Co. Chorcaí [Co. Cork]. 15/8/1932. NFC 42: 341–343.
    The lake at Mangerton is not the only one in Ireland that is supposed to be so deep that it cannot be measured. There is another lake in the parish of Tuosist, in South Kerry, called Loch na Péiste because there is a long narrow ridge of mountain land above it; they say that some saint put a curse on an evil serpent that was laying waste the countryside and turned it into that form for evermore. It is a common theme in the lives of the saints that they banish serpents to lakes.

77. ditto. NFC 42: 297–300.

Regarding the crooked mouth of the plaice, see Dähnhardt, III, 24, IV, 192–7; BP III, 284; FFC VIII, 21, XXXVII, 89, LXVI, 91.

Regarding the salmon's swimming, see Dähnhardt, III, 222.

78.   Eoghan Ó Súilleabháin: Mícheál Ó Máille (86), Dumha Locha, Cill Chomáin, Co. Mhaigh Eo [Doolough, Kilcommon, Co. Mayo]. April 1936. NFC 191: 268–269.

79.   Seán Ó Flannagáin: Séamus Ó Riagáin (83), Tóin Raithní, An Bheitheach, Co. na Gaillimhe [Co. Galway]. 12/5/1937. NFC 354: 252–253.
See the book *Leaba na Caillighe agus Scéalta Eile* (Connradh na Gaeilge, 1910); there's a version of a story about this famous hole on pages 13–19, and an interesting note by Seosamh Laoide on page 78.

80.   Séamus Ó Duilearga: Seán Ó Conaill (73), Cill Rialaigh, Baile an Sceilg, Co. Chiarraí [Co. Kerry]. NFC 302: 25.
See No. 5 and the accompanying note.

81.   Liam Mac Coisdeala: Máirtín Ó Cualáin (73), Loch Conaortha, Carna, Co. na Gaillimhe [Co. Galway]. 25/1/1937. NFC 305: 566–568.
See No. 115. See also, Herbert, III, 356. This prayer is still quite common in the Gaeltacht; people recite it when going to bed.

82.   Seán Ó hEochaidh: Pádraig Mac Dáid (68), Duibhlinn, Gartán, Co. Dhún na nGall [Co. Donegal]. 31/5/1939. NFC 626: 254–255.
In stories of this type, a Protestant is referrred to as a 'Scotsman'. See Note 71.

83.   ditto. NFC 626: 252–254.
See No. 77, and the accompanying note.

84.   Seán Ó hEochaidh: Conall Mac Cormaic (75), Doire Leac Chonaill, Teampall Chróin, [Co. Donegal]. 28/1/1938. NFC 472: 48–50. See Nos. 77 and 83.

85.   Seán Ó hEochaidh: Seán Ó Curraoin (65), Machaire Gathlán, Gaoth Dobhair, Co. Dhún na nGall [Co. Donegal]. 1/4/1938. NFC 472: 461–466.
With regard to spreading out a saint's cloak this story is very like the one about St. Brigid, when she asked for as much ground as her cloak would cover. There is a similar explanation given for the rocks around the coasts of many countries, that they are actually people under a spell. There are many references in the folklore of

Donegal to the Stone of Toraigh, just as there are to Leac Chuimín in Connaught and to other stones to which a curse is attached.

86. Seán Ó hEochaidh: Séamus Mac Grianna (45), Leac Chonaill, Ard an Rátha, Co. Dhún na nGall [Co. Donegal]. 30/12/1936. NFC 270: 681–683.
This story is told about St. Colman, also.

87. Liam Mac Coisdeala: Pádhraic Mac an Iomaire (64), An Coillín, Carna, Co. na Gaillimhe [Co. Galway]. 16/11/1935. NFC 158: 144.
It was the custom for fishermen and sailors to say special prayers, imploring God to bring them safe from harm. Among these was the *Sciathláireach Bheannaithe*. There is an interesting description of the same custom in the west of Scotland in Carmichael, I, 326–339, and examples of the prayers that were said there.

88. ditto. 15/11/1935. NFC 158: 121–8.
There are many saints who are accused of having put a curse on something or other for some reason, but I think there are more about Colm Cille than any other saint. We learn from these stories that he was a man of great personality, as shown by the way the stories about him have lived on in folklore down to the present day. See Note 73.

89. A schoolchild in Inis Gé Thuaidh, Co. Mhaigh Eo [Co. Mayo]. 1936. NFC 277: 175–177.
See the reference to St. Martin in Note 12, (a) (b) (c). Many accounts have been collected by the Irish Folklore Commission, by questionnaire, about the manner in which our ancestors celebrated the Feast of St. Martin by the shedding of blood.

90. Pádhraic Bairéad: Seán Ó Maolábhail (60), An Mullach Rua, An Chill Mhór, Co. Mhaigh Eo [Co. Mayo]. NFC 134: 62–66.
See the previous story and the relevant notes.

91. Seán Ó Dubhda: someone in Corca Dhuibhne, Co. Chiarraí [Co. Kerry]. 1933. NFC 3: 467–474.
Regarding the wonders of the other world, see Note 51.

92. Pádhraic Bairéad: Seán Ó Maolábhail [Maolfhabhail] (69), Dubhoileán, An Chill Mhór, Co. Mhaigh Eo [Co. Mayo]. 16/1/1937. NFC 277: 261–264.

Inis Gluaire [Inishglora] is an island off the coast of Mayo which was frequently mentioned in former times, particularly in the folklore of Connaught.

In many of the stories, St. Martin is credited with creating cats and mice.

93.   Mícheál Ó Flannagáin: Máirtín Ó Flaitheartaigh, Bun Gabhla, Árainn, Co. na Gaillimhe [Co. Galway]. 1932. NFC 73: 358–362.

In the folklore of various countries, people are often said to return from the dead to this world, in the form of animals or birds or other creatures. They are said to be suffering their Purgatory. See Note 57.

94.   Seosamh Ó Dálaigh: Mícheál Ó Sé (91), Cathair Scoilbín, Cill Maoilchéadair, Co. Chiarraí [Co. Kerry]. February, 1947. NFC 982: 166–168.

The case where the woman gave a white coat to a poor woman and found that the same coat was spread before her on the flagstone of torments in Purgatory is an exemplum that is common in stories of this type. Say, if a man put a stone in a hole in a poor man's bed, in order to make it more comfortable for him, that same stone would be used, to his advantage, when weighing his good deeds against his sins in the next world.

95.   Brian Mac Lochlainn: Máirtín Seoighe (51), Doire Bhéal an Mháma, Maíros, Co. na Gaillimhe [Co. Galway]. 18/7/1936. NFC 236: 480–481.

This soul was spending his Purgatory in a waterfall in a river. In other versions of this very common story, two souls would be found suffering their Purgatory on either side of a rock or on the two sides of an ivy-leaf; neither would know that the other was there until he heard him laughing; one would ask the other who he was and what he was laughing at; the first would answer that a baby was about to be born that night, and that the child's son's son would become a priest eventually and would say a Mass for the speaker – it would be a long term in Purgatory! The second soul would then complain that he had no hope of that kind of relief; the other would immediately offer him half the benefits he hoped to derive from the Mass, and when God heard of the charity being shared he pardoned both on the spot. See Note 49.

96.   Liam Mac Coisdeala: Pádhraic Mac an Iomaire (64), An Coillín, Carna, Co. na Gaillimhe [Co. Galway]. 29/9/1935. NFC 155: 73.

The human form is the one usually adopted by the dead who return to this world, even though there are plenty of references in stories to spirits or ghosts who had other appearances (mostly as animals). The narrow legs that this ghost had are similar to the chicken legs referred to in similar stories from other countries.

97.   Liam Mac Coisdeala: Mícheál Mór Mac Donncha (60), An Más, Carna, Co. na Gaillimhe [Co. Galway]. January 1936. NFC 159: 241–245.
A frequent subject for stories in the folklore of this country is the man who dies in Ireland and appeares to a friend in the United States afterwards. I have, personally, heard a story in Baile an Fheirtéaraigh, Co. Kerry, about a man from that area who was working in San Francisco; on the night before the earthquake there (1906), the voice of a (dead) friend spoke to him, as he lay asleep, telling him to get up quickly and leave the city; he did as he was told and was spared at a time when thousands perished. It seems that there was a very strong bond between the Irish at home and their relatives abroad, both living and dead.

98.   Seán Ó hEochaidh: Anna Nic Dhuibhir (55), An Luinnigh, Gaoth Dobhair, Co. Dhún na nGall [Co. Donegal]. 10/10/1938. NFC 540: 374–378.
The penalty imposed on someone who violates the rule of rest on a Sunday was a frequent basis for stories in many countries. Likewise, in the case of a person returning from the dead complaining that he had to suffer in Purgatory for having stolen something – he would be released from pain if someone else made restitution for him.

99.   Liam Mac Coisdeala: Bhal Ó Donnchú (36), Banrach Ard, Maíros, Co. na Gaillmhe [Co. Galway. 21/9/1938. NFC 529: 188–193.
See No. 30 and the relevant note.
This is another example of the additional powers attributed in folklore to a young priest as against an old priest. See the preface to the section about priests in this book.
      A dead person who returns, by arrangement, to tell how he got on after his Judgement is a very frequent subject for stories in the folklore of Ireland.
As for saving a person's soul by cutting his body in pieces, see No. 33 (a) and (b) and BP II, 162.

100. Tadhg Ó Murchú: his father, An Sceachachán, Cathair Dónall, Uíbh Ráthach, Co. Chiarraí [Co. Kerry]. 1911. NFC 26: 147–150.
That a baptised child, who died soon after birth, should have to spend some time in Purgatory is contrary to current thinking, which is, that no penance is necessary. Maybe this is a parable to teach people to avoid stealing and plundering.

101.   Tadhg Ó Murchú: Pádraig Mac Gearailt (77), Cill an Ghoirtín, Dromad, Co. Chiarraí [Co. Kerry]. 1/3/1936. NFC 308: 58–63.

This is another story of a dead person returning to this world by arrangement. See No. 99 and the relevant note. Other references to versions of the story about the man who hung his coat on a sunbeam may be found in Thompson (Motif-Index, F1011.1). See also No. 106 in this book.

102.   Seán Ó hEochaidh: Anna Ní Shiadhail (73), Ceathrú na Madaí, Cluain Dá Chorcach, Co. Dhún na nGall [Co. Donegal]. 16/9/1939. NFC 640: 398–400.

See No. 99 and the relevant note. There is a reference to a story like this from Switzerland in Thompson (Motif-Index, E487).

103.   Pádhraic Ó Braonáin: Máire Ní Bhraonáin (67), An Clochán Liath, Cill Taobhóg, Co. Dhún na nGall [Co. Donegal]. 1935. NFC 212: 308–309.

The old people often did rounds at holy wells for the souls of their deceased relatives. This story is an example of the benefit of such prayers for a soul in Purgatory.

104.   Pádhraic Bairéad: Seán Ó Maolábhail [Maolfhabhail](68), Dubhoileán, An Chill Mhór, Co. Mhaigh Eo [Co. Mayo]. 8/5/1936. NFC 191: 476–480.

I myself took down a story like this from a woman in Tuosist in South Kerry. However, it was a priest who was involved in that story. His father, who had died a short time previously, told him that his own soul got more benefit from the three children who had died before him than all the prayers of his son, the priest. The son married subsequently and, when the three children that were born to him died, he left his wife and returned to the priesthood.

105.   Seosamh Ó Dálaigh: Muiris Ó Conchúir (77), Baile Uí Bhaoithín, Márthain, Co. Chiarraí [Co. Kerry]. Christmas 1947. NFC 1035: 152–156.

Comical stories often take as their theme what happens to a simple person like this little boy who followed 'the straight road' on the advice of the priest. Examples may be found in the versions of ATU 1696, in this country and abroad. This story is not a comical one, however.

As for simple people who left food for holy pictures or statues, see BP III 474–; PMLA XL, 93; FFC XC, 90.

A holy picture talking to someone – there is a reference to that in No. 33 (a).

106. Liam Mac Coisdeala: Máirtín Ó Cualáin (73), Loch Conaortha, Carna, Co. na Gaillimhe [Co. Galway]. 25/1/1937. NFC 305: 558–565.
     This is a parable. See No. 101 and the relevant note.

107. Tadhg Ó Murchú: Seán Ó Súilleabháin (45), An tImleach Mór, An Phrióireacht, Co. Chiarraí [Co. Kerry]. 15/9/1935. NFC 146: 191–195.
     There are plenty of examples in the folklore of Ireland of stories based on this type of subject: destiny overcome by bravery or piety. See ATU 934. See also No. 37 in this book and the relevant note.

108. Liam Mac Coisdeala: Sally, Bean Uí Choscair (70), Cill Mhiáin, Co. Mhaigh Eo [Co. Mayo]. 7/10/1936. NFC 257: 85–8.
     As for the tree that bent down to a saintly person, see Dähnhardt II, 30. References to the withered branch that sprouted may be found in BP III, 463, 465, 471; Dähnhardt II, 265; FFC LIV, 34, LXIX, 126, 129, 241; Saintyves 61.

109. Peadar Ó Coincheanainn: Mícheál Mac Donncha (67), Roisín na Mainiach, Carna, Co. Chiarraí [Co. Galway]. Spring 1931. NFC 61: 543–545.
     See the references to this story in Thompson (Motif-Index, v39.4).

110. Brian Mac Lochlainn: Seán Mac Conraoi (84), Cloch na Rón, Maíros, Co. na Gaillimhe [Co. Galway]. 15/9/1936. NFC 237: 129–131.
     See No. 72.

111. Aodh Ó Dónaill: Mícheál Ó Baoill (34), Rann na Feirste, Teampall Cróine, Co Donegal. 9/9/1936. NFC 261: 82–85.
     This island is on the west coast of Donegal.

112. Seán Ó hEochaidh: Seán Mag Fhionnaile (90), Málainn, Gleann Cholm Cille, Co. Dhún na nGall [Co. Donegal]. 4/1/1936. NFC 143: 1762–1765.
     A 'station' is sometimes called a 'confession place' or 'confession house'. It seems to be a custom in Ireland since the time of the penal laws.

113. Liam Mac Coisdeala: Máirtín Mac Fhualáin (73), Loch Conaortha, Carna, Co. na Gaillimhe [Co. Galway]. 25/1/1937. NFC 305: 569–573.
     Concerning the value of a prayer, see Nos. 65 and 114.

114. Nioclás Breathnach: Tomás Ó Cathail (80), Loiscreán, Seanphobal, Co. Phort Láirge [Co. Waterford. 1933. NFC 86: 93–99.
      See the previous note.

115. Labhrás Ó Cadhla: Pádraig Bearáin (68), An Cnoc Buí, Seisceannán, Co. Phort Láirge [Co. Waterford]. 1920. NFC 289: 108–110.
      See No. 81 and the relevant note. There are many stories in Irish folklore about people who were suspected of going about with the fairies.

116. Liam Mac Coisdeala: Máirtín Mac Toirealaigh (74), An Mhainistir, Mainistir Chnoc Muaidhe, Co. na Gaillimhe [Co. Galway]. 21/11/1936. NFC 305: 57–58.
      See No. 81 and No 115.

117. An Bráthair P.T. Ó Riain: Mícheál Ó Cinnéide, Cuas an Bhodaigh, Baile an Mhúraigh, Co. Chiarraí [Co Kerry]. 26/6/1933. NFC 11: 266.
      It was customary for people who were unable to attend Mass on Sunday to say the Rosary at home while Mass was being said in the chapel.

118. Seán Ó hEochaidh: Conall Mac Cormaic (75), Doire Leac Chonaill, Teampall Cróine, Co. Dhún na nGall [Co. Donegal]. 2/2/1938. NFC 472: 75–78.
      This story is probably a parable.

119. Liam Mac Coisdeala: Éamonn de Búrca (71), Aill na Brón, Maíros, Co. na Gaillimhe [Co. Galway]. 3/10/1935. NFC 157: 91–96.
      This story and the following one are parables.

120. Dr. Robin Flower: Peig Sayers, An Blascaod Mór, Dún Chaoin, Co. Chiarraí [Co. Kerry]. NFC 984: 469–474.
      See Nos. 50 and 107.
      It is often mentioned in folklore that a person could see invisible objects if he put his hand or his foot on the person beside him. See the references to this in Thompson (Motif-Index, D1821.1)

121. Seán Ó hEochaidh: Seán Ó Siadhail (68), An tArd Bán, Ros Goill, Co. Dhún na nGall [Co. Donegal]. 4/3/1940. NFC 694: 435–438.
      This is a motif in many stories, people having to make a choice between comfort in this life and eternal rest in Heaven. See No. 4.

122.   (a) Seosamh Ó Dálaigh: Seán Ó Grífín (58), Cathair Boilg, Fionntrá, Co. Chiarraí [Co. Kerry]. 25/1/1937. NFC 304: 234–246.

Concerning the wheel mentioned in this story and the next, see Köhler-Bolte II, 66.

122.   (b). Liam Mac Coisdeala: Éamonn de Búrca (78), Aill na Brón, Maíros, Co. na Gaillimhe [Co. Galway]. 25/7/1942. NFC 850: 365–369.

See the previous note.

123.   Liam Mac Coisdeala: Pádhraic Mac an Iomaire, 64, An Coillín, Carna, Co. na Gaillimhe [Galway]. 12/11/1935. NFC 158: 54–57.

See Pauli-Bolte 458.

124.   Liam Mac Coisdeala: Máire, Bean Pheadair Uí Cheannabháin (62), Aill na Brón, Maíros, Co. na Gaillimhe [Co. Galway]. 9/10/1935. NFC 155: 151–152.

This crime is revealed in many different ways, in international versions of this story. Sometimes a whistle or harp is made of the bones of the deceased or from a tree that grew on his grave and the music reveals the secret. This also occurs in the literature of Ireland in the story of 'Labhraidh Loingseach'.

125.   Seán Ó Dubhda: Máire, Bean Uí Shé, An Baile Loiscthe, Cill Maoilchéadair, Co. Chiarraí [Co. Kerry]. 29/3/1938. NFC 1115: 381–383.

This seems to be a parable.

126.   Proinsias de Búrca: Liam Ó Duithche [Dufaigh] (46), Baile an Tobair, An Ros, Co. na Gaillimhe [Co. Galway]. 12/3/1936. NFC 188: 67–71.

A parable. See the reference to it in Thompson (Motif-Index, V39.3)

127.   An Bráthair P.T. Ó Riain: Tadhg Ó Guithín (42), Baile na hAbha, Dún Chaoin, Co. Chiarrraí [Co. Kerry]. 1933. NFC 13: 154–155.

This seems to be a parable too, to teach people that it is not sufficient to attend Mass unless they hear it with attention.

128.   Liam Mac Coisdeala: Pádhraic Ó hUiginn (76), Cill Mhiáin, Co. Mhaigh Eo [Co. Mayo]. 14/8/1936. NFC 238: 190–192.

These stories were very common, telling the benefits of baptism. They were usually told in connection with events involved in the hunting of priests in penal times.

129. Tadhg Ó Murchú: Cáit, Bean Phádraig Uí Charáin (60), An Chathair Bhearnach, Dromad, Uíbh Ráthach, Co. Chiarraí [Co. Kerry]. 10/2/1937. NFC 308: 282–284.
There are other examples of hard-hearted people coming to a bad end in Nos. 4, 22, 50–52, 55–57, 79, 93, 101, 130, 131.

130. Dr. Robin Flower: Peig Sayers, An Blascaod Mór, Dún Chaoin, Co. Chiarraí [Co. Kerry]. NFC 984: 8–10.
This parable teaches that charity should be given with a generous heart.

131. Pádhraic Ó Maolomhnaigh: Mícheal Ó Maolomhnaigh (73), Tulach Mhic Aodháin, Maigh Cuilinn, Co. na Gaillimhe [Co. Galway]. 17/4/1935. NFC 266: 289–295.
See No. 57.

132. Seán Ó hEochaidh: Gráinne Ní Ghríofa (76), Mín an Chladaigh, Gaoth Dobhair, Co. Dhún na nGall [Co. Donegal]. 19/9/1938. NFC 540: 98–102.
This story is like the stories that are told about the 'Glas Ghaibhneach', another cow from the sea with a large milk yield. See No. 91 end note.

133. Áine Nic an Liagha: Sorcha, Bean Mhic Pháidín (67), Baile na Bó, Cloich Chionnaola, Co. Dhún na nGall [Co. Donegal]. 2/8/1937. NFC 409: 16.
This story has echoes of the story of Manna in the Bible.

134. Anraí Ó Corrduibh: Seán Ó Rothláin (70), Ros Dumhach, Na hEachú, Iorras, Co. Mhaigh Eo [Co. Mayo]. 1936. NFC 195: 375–378.
See Note 98. There is also mention in folklore that mowers have bad luck because they destroy herbs, which have curative properties.

135. Seán Ó Súilleabháin: Muircheartach Ó Sé (51), Eadargóil, Cill Cháscáin, Béarra, Co. Chorcaí [Co. Cork]. 4/8/1933. NFC 31: 136–138.
See FFC XXV, 142; LXVI, 84.

Index of Tale Types[*]

Tales Of Magic

*   From Hans-Jörg Uther, *The Types of International Folktales: A Classification and Bibliography*. 3 vols. FF Communications 284-286. Helsinki: Suomalainen Tiedeakatemia (Academia Scientiarum Fennica). First published in 2004. Reprinted in 2011.

Index of International Motifs[*]

[*] From Stith Thompson, *Motif-Index of Folk Literature*, I–VI [=FFC 106–9, 116–7], (Helsinki, 1932–1936). For further references, see T. P. Cross, *Motif-Index of Early Irish Literature* (Bloomington, Indiana, n.d.).

F. Marvels

F57.1	Narrow road to heaven.	63
F81	Descent to lower world of dead (Hell, Hades).	53, 63
F91	Door (gate) entrance to lower world.	33a, 58
F92	Pit entrance to lower world.	33b, 63, 91
F134	Otherworld on island.	55
F160	Nature of the other world.	91
F162.2	Rivers in the other world.	54
F162.2.6	Rivers of oil, milk, wine and honey in other world.	53
F167.1	Animals in the other world.	55
F171.0.1	Enigmatic happenings in other world which are later explained.	54, 57
F171.1	Fat and lean kine in the other world.	52
F171.2	Broad and narrow road in the other world.	63
F171.6.1	Man in other world loaded down with wood.	55
F232	Body of fairy.	62
F251.3	Unbaptised children as fairies.	61
F300	Marriage or liaison with fairy.	115
F360	Malevolent or destructive fairies (=pixies).	62
F384	Magic objects powerful against fairies.	61
F402.1.2	Spirit blocks person's road.	99
F412.2	Spirit made visible by standing on another's foot.	120
F571	Extremely old person.	28
F571.2	Sending to the older.	74
F771	Extraordinary castle (house, palace).	57
F773	Remarkable church (chapel, temple).	27a
F790	Extraordinary sky or weather phenomena.	74
F810	Extraordinary trees, plants, fruit etc.	57
F813.1.4	Brass apple.	50
F840	Other extraordinary objects and places.	57
F841.1.1	Stone boat (ship).	88
F942.1	Ground opens and swallows up person.	79
F955	Miraculous cure for leprosy.	21 (cf.)
F960	Extraordinary nature phenomena – elements and weather.	74
F962	Extraordinary precipitation.	18, 110
F966	Voices from heaven (or from the air).	38, 49
F970	Extraordinary behaviour of trees and plants.	27a
F971.1	Dry rod blossoms.	49, 108
F1011.1	Clothes hung on sunbeam.	106

H1132.1.2	Task: recovering key from the sea.	25, 35a
H1220	Quests voluntarily undertaken.	50, 54
H1235	Succession of helpers on quest.	74
H1270	Quest to lower world.	58
H1273.1	Quest to devil in hell for return of contract.	33a, 33b
H1291	Questions asked on way to other world.	50, 51, 52
H1292.4.1	Question (propounded on quest): How can the princess be cured?	27a, 28
H1292.5	Question (on quest): How can girl thus far avoided by suitors marry?	50
H1388	Quest: answer to certain question.	119, 120
H1411	Fear test: staying in haunted house.	53
H1533	Hanging test.	44, 50
H1553	Tests of patience.	37

J. The Wise and The Foolish

J21.17	'Stay at church till Mass is finished': counsel proved wise by experience. Delay saves youth from death.	38
J23	Merchants try honesty for a year and find it pays.	25
J172	Account of punishments prepared in hell brings about repentance.	63, 95, 100, 101
J225.0.1	Angel and hermit.	119
J320	Present values preferred to future.	4
J350	Choices: small inconvenience, large gain.	121
J556	Intemperance in honesty.	118
J1182	Punishment escaped by discomfiting condemner.	26, 44
J1261.7	Judgement Day a long way off.	76
J2477	Christ has too many debts.	13
J2495	Religious words or exercises interpreted with absurd literalness.	105

K. Deceptions

K210	Devil cheated of his promised soul.	34, 36
K212	Devil cheated by being frightened.	33b
K218.1	Devil cheated by having priest draw sacred circle about the intended victim.	30
K443.8	Priest induced to reveal secrets of the confessional.	108 (cf.)
K551.9	Let me live as long as this candle lasts.	36
K978	Uriah letter.	38
K1811	Gods (saints) in disguise visit mortals.	22
K1817.1	Disguise as beggar (pauper).	24, 42, 45

Q. Rewards and Punishments

Q1	Hospitality rewarded – opposite punished.	4
Q20	Piety rewarded.	120
Q40	Kindness rewarded.	
Q42.3	Generosity to saint (God) in disguise rewarded.	2 (cf.), 68
Q45.1	Angels entertained unawares.	90
Q147	Supernatural manifestations at death of pious person.	46
Q171.1	Forgiveness of sin for acts of charity.	101
Q172.1	Child taken to heaven: offers food to crucifix.	105
Q172.2	Man admitted to heaven for single act of charity.	94
Q211	Murder punished.	124
Q211.4	Murder of children.	31
Q220	Impiety punished.	47, 98, 114
Q221.1	Discourtesy to God punished.	125
Q224	Punishment for betraying confessional.	108
Q227	Punishment for opposition to holy person.	82, 83
Q280	Unkindness punished.	53
Q281	Ingratitude punished.	99
Q281.1	Ungrateful children punished.	46
Q286	Uncharitableness punished.	93, 129, 131
Q286.1	Uncharitableness to holy person punished.	22
Q291	Hard-heartedness punished.	61, 130
Q413	Punishment: hanging.	107
Q415	Punishment: being eaten by animals.	46
Q431	Punishment: banishment (exile).	88
Q457.2	Devil flays impious man.	43
Q482	Punishment: noble person must do menial service.	53
Q491.4	Toads and snakes devour corpse of rich man in his grave.	74
Q500	Tedious punishments.	55
Q512	Punishment: performing impossible task.	49
Q520	Penances.	43
Q521.6	Penance: holding midnight Mass until someone will make responses.	27a
Q522.3	Penance: creeping naked through thorns.	44
Q523.1	Penance: crawling to Rome on knees.	48
Q523.3	Penance: eating food offered to dogs.	93
Q541.2	Penance: standing in water for forty days.	49
Q551.1	Undutiful son punished by toad clinging to face.	46 (cf.)
Q552.1	Death by thunderbolt as punishment.	123

Index of Tale Types and Motifs

Tale no.	Motif
1a	D1648.2.1
1b	T551.1
2	cf. A1611.2, Q42.3
4	Q1, J320
5a,b	Q40
6a	C491
8	A1372
9	C50, A2217.3
10	A1681.2
11	U21.3
12a,b,c	cf. V222
13	J2477
14	N172
15	D2157.2, A2221.5, A2231.7.1
16	A2231.7.1, A2221.5
17	A2721.4, A2711.3
18	D2157.2, D2172.2, F962
21	cf. F955, E720
22	K1811, Q286.1, V410
23	D1652.1, V250
24	K1817.1, M121, E734.1, E754.2
25	*ATU 756a*: H1132.1.2, J23, D1031.1.1, B548.2.2
26	G303.3.1, K2155, J1182, H1132, B548.2
27a	F970, D2064.1, H1292.4.1, D1176, F773, Q521.6, E754.2, B548.2.2, L160
27b	H171
27c	L160
28	F571, H1292.4.1
29	H210, D1176
30	*ATU 810*: E261, D1385.3.1, K218.1
31	D1766.7.1, E121.5, E423.1.5, Q211.4

32	B121, E380, D1766.7.1
33a	*ATU 756b*: E281, G303.3, M201.1.2, E345, F91, H1273.1, Q561.3, E14, D1610.11
33b	*ATU 756b*: D1472.1.5, n4, m201.1.2, d1266.1, f92, h1273.1, k212, m218, e14, d1268
34	m201.1.2, g303.6.1.2, k210
35a	g303.3.1.4, g303.11.2, g303.3.1.8, d1601.18.1, c650, d1960, h1132.1.2, b548.2.2
35b	g303.3.1, cf. g303.16.17, g303.11.2, g303.16.7
36	*ATU 1187**: g303.3.1.6, n4, e340, k551.9, k210
37	m302.4, m341.1, n110, v52.2, h1553
38	s227, k978, j21.17, d1602.11, cf. g303.4.8.2, g303.9.3.1, d1030.1, g303.16.7, f966, c230, b172, g303.16.2.3.3, v250
39	g303.16.14
40	g303.3.3.3, g303.16.7
41	cf. e412.2, m91, e742, e324, g303.3.2, g303.16.1
42	n252, g303.3.1, k1817.1, d1454.6
43	*ATU 810*: q520, q457.2, d1381.11, c12.2
44	*ATU 756c*: k2155, h215, h1533, j1182, h1132, cf. q522.3, b548.2
45	z71.5, k1817.1, m121, e732.1
46	*ATU 756c*: v29.1, q281.1, h220, q147, q554.5, q415, cf. q551.1
47	cf. *ATU 756a*: q220, b256.1
48	cf. *ATU 756c*: v29.1, d1031.1.1, q523.1
49	*ATU 756*: d1031.1.1, q541.2, q512, f971.1, f966
50	*ATU 461*: h1220, h1292.5, h1291, h221.4, h1533, a463.1, f813.1.4, e501.4.1
51	*ATU 461*: h1291, e501.4.1, q560, a165.1
52	*ATU 461*: h1291, f171.1, f162.2.6
53	cf. *ATU 425b*: q482, h1411, v52.2, e351, e755.2, f81, q560, d1472, c211.2.2, q482, g303.8.3, a673, b325.1, a671, q280, E732.1, H94.4
54	*ATU 471*: H1220, D1275.1, C413, F162.2, F171.0.1, C413, F171.0.1, G303.3.3.1
55	F134, F167.1, F171.6.1, Q500, G303.7.1, R11.2.1
56	E423, E501, D323 (no. **55**), G303.16.7, G303.6.1.3
57	F810, F840, F771, D1030, D1154.1, F171.0.1, V511.1, D42
58	H1270, F91, D859.2, Q560
59	C320, V250, D1323.1, A106.2, A720, A755, A913, G303.8.1.2, V236, G303.6.1.2
61	V236, F251.3, Q291, D285, F384, A1500
62	E400, E751, F232, F360,
63	E401, E422.4, F81, F92, E487, A670, F57.1, F171.2, D1081, Z111, J172
65	V4.1, V331
66	B413, B256, E32, D1766.7.1, D2176.3

104	E222, E322
105	J2495, Q172.1
106	F1011.1, C50
107	M341, F1068, V230, Q413
108	cf. K443.8, Q224, D1648.2, F971.1
109	V39.4, D1820.1
110	D2140.1, F962, D1812.5, M300, A280
112	V52, V111
113	V4
114	Q220, V254
115	F300, D1860, V222
117	V254
118	J556, M92, M300
119	*ATU 759*: H1388, N270, A165.1, J225.0.1
120	*ATU 759*: H1388, F412.2, A463.1, N121.2, A165.1, Q20
121	J350, C51.1, Q559.2
122a,b	N111.3, L143, L412
123	M348, Q552.1
124	*ATU 780*: B131.1, Q211
125	Q221.1, Q582
126	V39.3
127	V46
128	V81, D1820
129	Q286
130	C776, Q291, V400
131	V410.1, Q286, V91
132	C935
133	D1037
134	C58
135	A1593